"In *Out of the Fields*, Ramon Resa has written a vivid and moving story of one man's journey. As a tale of one individual's strength, it is deeply touching and inspiring. But it is much more than a story about one person. Its true power is in the message it conveys to all readers about the immigrant experience in the United States and the extraordinary qualities and achievements that immigrants contribute to our society. Most Americans need only to go back a few generations to remind themselves that they, too, are immigrants to a young country. In that sense, Ramon Resa's experience symbolizes the struggles and strength of countless families. Whether Italian or Polish, Chinese or Irish, African, Mexican, Vietnamese or Sri Lankan—whether they came willingly or in shackles—waves of immigrants have built this country. *Out of the Fields* reminds us that we are fortunate that these waves continue to land on our shores."—David Wofsy, MD, Professor of Medicine and Associate Dean for Admissions, UC San Francisco School of Medicine

"Ramon Resa's telling of his life story was one of the most inspirational experiences I have had in my life. After I heard him tell his story, including how much it meant for one person to say, 'You are smart enough to go to college,' I decided I had no excuses for putting off mentoring. I'm just starting to mentor my second student, and when I meet with him, Ramon's experience comes to mind." —Philip Rose, City Manager, Los Altos (CA)

"After Ramon spoke to our University Rotary Club, everyone was in tears. He was easily one of our most motivational and inspirational speakers."—Noe Lozano, PhD, Associate Dean for Student Affairs and Director of Engineering Diversity Programs, Stanford University

"As teachers, we should try to be attuned to the silent cries and needs of our students. My students were amazed by Ramon, a man with the courage to share some very tragic experiences. They were even more amazed that, with such perseverance, one can be very successful in life."—Amparo Q. Alvarez, Watsonville (CA) High School

"Ramon's presentation of his life story was the highlight of our Freshman Conference. The style and substance of his speech were a perfect combination of an engaging and witty delivery together with a motivational message that called students to turn challenges into opportunities and commit their lives to community service. It is no easy task to maintain the interest of 160-plus freshmen college students during lectures, but he easily held their attention the entire fifty minutes of his presentation. And the way he tells stories, he's an amazing storyteller. They were really into it. Our program director was touched emotionally and was trying to hold back tears. Students said it was very powerful and inspiring, and after his talk, a long line of maybe thirty students waited to talk with him."—Miriam Attenoukon, Hudson and Holland Scholars Program, Indiana University (Bloomington)

"Ramon exemplifies a person who has successfully faced adversity and attained the impossible."—Linda Waud, Partners for New Generations

OUT OF THE FIELDS

to

The Friends of
Tulare County Library

Ramon Perez MD
9/10/11

Out of the Fields

*My Journey from
Farmworker Boy to Pediatrician*

Ramon Resa, MD

Foreword by **Jim Cathcart**, author of *The Acorn Principle*
and past president of the National Speakers Association

THE CARLSBAD PRESS
Porterville, California

TULARE COUNTY LIBRARY

Production Manager and Editor: Monica Faulkner, Faulkner Editorial Services
Interior Design and Layout: Robert S. Tinnon, Sam Kuo (Kuo Design), Kirk Thomas (Kirk's Graphics)
Proofreading: Rena Copperman, Veronica Spencer, Cynthia Cuza
Cover Design: Robert S. Tinnon, Sam Kuo, Kirk Thomas
Cover and title page art: Debbie Resa
Photographs on pages 355 and 393 and back cover by Jordan Ancel
Photographs on pages 386 and 388 by Eisha Zaid

"A Tale of Two Cousins," © 2010 The Regents of the University of California. All rights reserved. Reprinted with permission.

Second printing, printed and bound in the United States of America by Bang Printing, Valencia CA

9 8 7 6 5 4 3 2

ISBN-978-0-9841643-0-1
ISBN-0-9841643-0-8

Dedication

Writing this book has been much harder than I anticipated. It made me look back and reflect on the most important people in my life, and so I want to dedicate it to . . .

- Debbie, my wife of more than thirty years, who didn't laugh at my clumsy attempt to speak to her on that fateful day in 1976.
- My children, Marina and Joshua. They were my inspiration.
- My mother, Frances. Of course, without her I wouldn't be here.
- My brothers and sisters: Elsie, Matilda, Anita, Helen, Lucinda, Rosa, Olivia, Elia, Delma, Merced, Bill, Al, Esmael, Domingo, and Joe.
- Betty and Bobby, my long-lost full sister and brother.
- My half-brothers and sisters: Candy, Joe, Velma, Danny, Annette, Angel, and Terry.
- Ama and Apa, my grandparents, Sofia and Bonifacio Gonzales, who are now gone and who took me in when they didn't have to.
- And finally, all the teachers who made a difference in my life, but especially Mrs. Lambers and Mrs. Tobin.

Contents

Part Three: High-School Boy
(1968–1972)

Part Four: College Boy
(1972–1976)

Part Five: Medical Student
(1976–1981)

Part Six: Intern and Resident
(1981–1985)

Part Seven: Doctor

Foreword

Y GREAT-GRANDUNCLE WAS ONE OF THE EARLY settlers in Visalia, California. I've visited his gravesite there and heard stories about him from my mother. But I never knew him, nor do I have any idea what kind of a man he was. I simply know that he is my relative and he lived in Visalia.

Recently I met another man from California's Central Valley—Ramon Resa, MD, a truly rags-to-riches example of what is possible in America today.

Horatio Alger inspired a generation with rags-to-riches stories of poor boys who made their own way despite adversity and a lack of support or encouragement. There is even a Horatio Alger Association of Distinguished Americans (www.horatioalger.org), whose membership is made up of distinguished recipients of its annual Horatio Alger Awards, given to those who started with nothing but achieved great things.

Each year, the association also bestows its Norman Vincent Peale Award, named in honor of the legendary writer and speaker, who for 40 years was one of its most exceptional members, upon a member who has shown generosity, courage, tenacity, and integrity in the face of adversity. I had the privilege of knowing and sharing the speaking platform with Dr. Peale on more than one occasion, and he would have loved Ramon.

In fact, in my opinion, Ramon Resa is as much the embodiment of those traits as anyone upon whom the association has bestowed its honors to date.

Now that's a bold and potentially outrageous claim I'm making, so let's see if we can back it up with actual facts from Ramon's life. Age three: picking cotton, abandoned by his parents. Age eight: picking oranges, and still no prospects of a good life. Speech impediment, depression, poverty, abuse, neglect, discouraged from seeking his dreams...what were the odds that Ramon would even survive, much less become a success?

Yet, despite everyone in Ramon's world telling him "No!," something inside him caused his dream to survive and persist. He went on to remake himself into the person he dreamed of being, rather than the person he had been imprinted to be.

Ramon's story is truly "The American Dream." Deep within himself, he found the courage to pursue his vision of becoming a doctor, a healer who could save others from much of the misery that he had experienced. There were no outside forces working to fuel his confidence. In fact, just the opposite was true. Everywhere he looked, he encountered discouragement.

Ramon's story is the story of human potential, the unique personal potential that exists within us independently from any external source. It is also a story of hope and how we can keep it alive inside, even when there is no visible evidence that our dreams can come true.

I hope you read this book slowly and aloud with others. Share it, savor it, cry with it, let your heart glow with joy from it. Make this a book that stimulates deep reflection within you. Reflect upon your own dreams, especially the ones you've long neglected or nearly forgotten. You are not limited by your age, your health, your relationships, or your finances nearly as much as by your own unwillingness to dream and persist.

So, set yourself free to become the person God designed you to be. Let Ramon's book be the encouraging hand on your shoulder and the resonant voice in your ear that says, "You can do it!...I believe in you!...You are special and important to this world!...We need you!"

Ramon, you are a unique and gifted individual with an important place in history. Your legacy will be felt for many generations—maybe even forever. I am proud to know you.

In the spirit of growth,
Jim Cathcart
Thousand Oaks CA
2011

Prologue

STRUGGLE TO FIND A BEGINNING FOR MY STORY. Do I start with my first memories of picking cotton when I was three, or say something about the only picture I have of me as a baby, sitting in a dirt field looking abandoned? My son, Joshua, tells me, "Start with your father," but I never knew my father, so what am I supposed to say about him? What am I supposed to feel? When people ask me about him, I simply say, "I don't have a father."

All I know is that he got my mother pregnant five times before she turned twenty. I used to hold out a faint hope that someday I would find out he'd left me an inheritance. More than likely, though, he was a migrant laborer who worked wherever the crops led him. Maybe he was an alcoholic or a drug addict. I do know that he had to have been a person of no account. For all I know, he could be rotting in jail. I don't want to know. Why take on that baggage when I have plenty of my own?

They say that the sins of the father will be visited on the son. I'm afraid that this will come to pass or already has. Is my father's character part of mine?

I do know who my mother is, but all she did was give birth to me and my siblings, two of whom I didn't meet until I was almost an adult. She turned me and two of my brothers, Al and Domingo,

Me at 18 months in the backyard of Ama's and Apa's house

over to her mother, our "Ama," and to Ama's husband, "Apa." They raised us.

I've always called my mother "Frances"—never "mother"—and treated her like a distant aunt. She still lives in Goshen, the small Central California town where I grew up. But I've never made any effort to have our children, Marina and Josh, meet or visit her. In my world, she doesn't exist either as my mother or as their grandmother.

I first learned that I had siblings I had never known about when I was a senior in college and my girlfriend, Debbie, and I (we met during the first week of our freshman year at the University of California at Santa Cruz and got married four years later) went back to Goshen one weekend. While we were visiting with the family, a car drove up. Frances got out, along with a young man and woman. The guy looked a lot like me, but was taller.

"This is Bobby and Betty," Frances said. "Your brother and sister."

It turned out that Betty and Bobby were her first and fourth children, and that she had given them away, too. They grew up in the tough neighborhoods of East Los Angeles. Not only did Al, Domingo, and I know nothing about our father—we never knew about Bobby and Betty. Do I have more siblings or half-siblings out there somewhere? I have no way of knowing.

I do know that I'm the youngest of the five of us. Betty, the oldest, is five years older than I am, Al is four years older, Domingo is three years older, and Bobby is two years older. Before we found out about Betty and Bobby, Al, Domingo, and I used to joke that Frances had taken a year off between Domingo and me. But apparently not.

As Debbie and I were driving back to Santa Cruz after the weekend, she asked me, "How do you feel about meeting a brother and sister you never knew about?"

"I don't feel anything. . . . I've never seen them before, and I know nothing about them. As far I'm concerned, they're strangers."

"What about your mom? What do you think about her not telling you all this time? How do you feel about that?"

"I don't feel anything," I told her. "That kind of stuff is what I expect of my 'mother.'"

After I was born, Frances married a man named Cruz and had seven more kids. I guess she never considered taking us in because she was too busy having more babies. We used to visit her and our half-brothers and half-sisters when we were growing up. I knew she was my mother, but I never expected her to treat me like a son. And she didn't. I often wonder if she regrets what she did to us. She's never said anything about being sorry or wishing she had done something different.

Sometimes I ask myself why I've never tried to get her to tell me who my father was. Also, I know that some of my relatives, and even

Betty, have tried to ask her, but she's always refused to answer any questions. And at some level I don't really want to know.

Like everything having to do with my father, even my name is a mystery. On my baptismal certificate, the only official identification I had for many years, my last name is spelled "Reza" but with the "z" crossed out and an "s" in its place. Because of the "z," I used to fantasize that my father was a rich Iranian who'd had a romance with my mother. I imagined him making annual trips through the Southwest, meeting her year after year and each time fathering a child, and then disappearing, only to show up again the following year. I've never been able to find out anything about this spelling.

Some years ago, when Debbie, Marina, Josh, and I were all on a family trip to Carlsbad, New Mexico, we stopped at the hospital where I was born. I had never had a copy of my birth certificate, and Debbie felt we should get one. For some reason, I was reluctant, but Debbie said we should get it so I could apply for a passport. My baptismal certificate was so worn and tattered that I was having trouble using it for identification. We were told that the old records were no longer available and that we'd have to order a duplicate.

After we got home, I started filling out the application but never mailed it and forgot about it. One afternoon several months later, I walked down to our mailbox and found a letter from the State of New Mexico. Inside was a copy of my birth certificate.

I handed it to Debbie and said, "I never sent for this."

"I did," she replied. "I found the application in the trash, filled it out, and mailed it in. . . . What are you staring at? What's the matter?"

The certificate stated that my name was "Ramon Gonzales," not "Ramon Reza." There it was in black and white. "Gonzales." Ama's and Apa's name.

How can I describe what I felt when I learned that the name I had grown up with and passed on to my children wasn't really mine? I felt anger but also sadness and a sense of hopelessness. The whole time I was growing up, somebody knew my real last name but never said anything to me.

I later found out that Al only learned years later that he was "Gonzales," too. But Domingo was always "Gonzales" when we were growing up. Why was he given our grandparents' name, while Al and I got a fictional one? Who was this person named "Reza" or "Resa"? Did he ever exist? It's a total mystery.

I guess that not knowing who my father was has affected me more than I want to admit, especially now that I'm a father myself. I don't know what I missed. The only legacy he left me is the lack of memories. I can't even imagine visualizing any memories.

I know that by not learning about my history, I'm neglecting my duty to my own children and depriving them of a vital piece of their past. But, like me, Marina and Josh have learned not to ask questions or expect answers. All they know is that they have no grandfather from my side. If they ask about him, I say, "I don't know him or anything about him." And the matter is dropped.

PART ONE

Farmworker Boy

Back row (left to right): My sister Rosa, me, my brother
Mily (Esmael); standing: my brother Domingo
(left), my sister Delma (right), mid-1950s

CHAPTER ONE

Picking Cotton

Surrounded by a sea of white
White cotton
And dense fog to the horizon.
Where is everyone?

Abandoned again
On the dirt of a cotton field
There is no time for play
I have to earn my keep

I make my little mound of cotton
Piling it as high as it will go

And wait for someone
Anyone
To come and want me
I'm just a little boy of three

I'm standing in the middle of a cotton field. It's autumn, and the plants are taller than I am.

It feels as if I'm all alone in this sea of white, white cotton under the dreary white sky with moist white fog settling all around. The fog envelops the cotton field, and for a minute I feel panicky. I glance back to make sure that my grandfather's behind me somewhere.

This is my job at age three, to pile up the mounds of cotton. Every once in a while, I spook a cottontail. When he scampers away, I run after him as fast as my legs will take me. One time, I found a baby cottontail that was too scared to run. He just lay there motionless, trying to be invisible. As I picked him up and cuddled him, I felt his heart beating so fast that I was afraid he would die of fright. I couldn't reassure this small creature that I meant him no harm, so I gently placed him on the ground and watched him hop off.

I go back to piling the cotton as high as I can so Apa will be proud of me. He comes up behind me and pats me on the head. Then he shoves me forward to go make another pile. I'm too young to carry a sack. Apa's sack is long and sausage-shaped, and he carries it slung over his shoulder by a leather strap. As he stuffs the cotton into it, the sack starts bulging like a snake that's eaten a rodent. I watch fascinated as he shakes the sack up and down and the lump moves down to the sewn-up end. Unable to contain myself, I leap onto the sack, but Apa is shaking it so hard that I fall off into the dust of the field.

"Get back to work!" Apa yells.

I often try to get onto his sack and rest. He'll let me for a little while, but I'm extra weight and he's not that young any more—he's almost sixty.

I do anything I can to have a little fun. After all, I'm just a kid. I have lots of scratches on my arm and hands from the sharp tips on the cotton bolls. The cuts sting a lot, but there's no sense crying. Nobody pays attention. They all have cuts and scratches, too.

I also itch a lot due to the weeds that grow among the plants when owners don't bother to pay for weeding. Weeding is done in late spring when the plants are small and the ground is soft. We use a hoe and walk up and down the rows chopping the weeds. It's one of the easiest types of farmwork, but also the most monotonous. I do hoeing, too, with a hoe that Apa cut down to my size. The short-handled hoe is just the right size for kids like me. But for many years, until California banned the short-handled hoe (*el cortito*) in 1975, growers made farm-workers use them. This was torture because having to stoop all day often left the workers crippled with lifelong back pain.

Three or four years later, when I'm working in the rows close to the road, I can see all the cars going by. Early in the morning, the backseats are full of kids with their faces plastered against the windows. Most wave at us as they go by, but some stick out their tongues. I always won-der where they're going. On Sundays in the late afternoons, I some-times see the same cars and kids coming back the other way. Whatever they did on their weekend was probably more fun than chopping weeds.

Right now, I'm itchy, hurting, and cold. I've been cold all day. We get up before dawn. After our breakfast of eggs and tortillas, all of us kids and adults cram ourselves into our beat-up Chevy and set off in a caravan of cars filled with other relatives.

The older kids—Merced (Mercy), Bill, Rosa, Olivia (Lily), Elia, Esmael, and Al—squeeze into the front and backseats. We younger ones—Delma, me, and Joe—end up in the trunk with the lid partly tied down. If Domingo's along, he'll be in the trunk with us, but he stays at home with Ama most of the time because he's sick so much.

The trunk is freezing cold because the warmth from the car heater doesn't reach us. We bring our blankets with us and huddle together. I hope the drive is long so I can sleep a little more, but we're con-stantly getting bounced around as we go over potholes and around turns. We arrive in no time at all.

Climbing out of the car into the gloomy, overcast day is miserable. The sun still isn't out, but it's nice to breathe the clear air after all the exhaust fumes. However, the cotton's still wet from the moisture in the air, so the contractor won't let us go into the fields until the sun dries the cotton. We're paid by the pound, and once the cotton's dry it'll weigh less, so he won't have to pay us as much.

The grownups send us out to look for firewood. Soon we have a nice bonfire going. Puffs of air come out of the adults' mouths as they complain about having to wait. They want to get in early, while the cotton's still wet, so they can make more money.

I don't care one way or another. What I don't realize is that the delay will cost me later when I ask for a soda at lunch. The less we make in the morning, the fewer extras we get at lunch. I'll have to be satisfied with my egg-and-bean burrito. At least by lunch time the weather will have warmed up.

In the meantime, what I really want is some hot coffee to fend off the chill. I've been allowed to drink coffee for as long as I can remember. Each morning when I wake up, I take Apa's and Ama's coffee to them in bed, sipping at it as I walk so it doesn't spill over. I've learned to like it, especially with lots of sugar, the way Ama takes it. When I get to their bedroom, I have to be careful not to trip on the coffee can next to the bed that Apa uses to pee in during the night. Sometimes I think I've taken on this chore so they'll let me watch cartoons on TV. But the real reason is so they'll see me as useful and productive and essential— because I'm not really part of the family.

Ama took me and Al and Domingo in when our mother didn't want to keep us, and she's always telling me, "I took you in when no one else wanted you. I did it out of the goodness of my heart" and "I don't ask much from you except to be grateful." If I'm slow to sweep the floor or weed her flowers, she says, "This is how you reward me?"

I hate hearing her tell me how I wasn't wanted, so I try not to be worthless. I try to anticipate her wishes. And I outwork everyone in the fields, too, even the guys who are a lot older than I am. I don't want to feel like a burden. I want to make it so they won't say I'm nothing but trouble.

I'm young, but I know that something is amiss. I have a sense of being different from the family. I don't know why, but that feeling's always there. I wonder if Al and Domingo feel the same way, but we never discuss it. We only listen and do as we're told.

Ama is hard on Domingo, too, because he has a number of problems, including wetting the bed every night. She yells at him so much that he's afraid and ashamed to look at people and goes around with his head down looking forlorn and guilty. Every morning, before he goes to school, he has to wash the blankets. We don't have sheets, so the mattress smells of urine all the time. When I get older, I sleep in the same bed with him, and I constantly get soaked, but I can't get mad at him. We never discuss his problem or how he feels about it, and there's nothing we can do to help him anyway. No matter how hard he tries, he can't stop, so he deals with it on his own and withdraws more and more into himself.

Compared to Domingo's life, mine isn't bad. I feel worse for him than anything I feel for myself, and I try to make up for Ama's bad treatment. Although I'm two years younger, I feel like the older brother. If my blanket is wet and I get cold, I remind myself of the shame he feels every day and that he has to take Ama's complaints about how much extra work he creates for her—even though he's the one who has to take care of his own messes, and she leaves most of the chores for the girls to do anyway.

What's worse, something's wrong with his food pipe and he can't keep food down. He's very skinny and too weak to be able to work much, but Ama acts as if it's his fault, just as she seems to think he wets the bed on purpose. When he's about twelve, Ama finally takes him to a doctor, who says he has a narrowing of his esophagus. The only treatment is for Domingo to stretch it, so every morning after he washes his blankets, he has to dilate his food pipe. He starts with a small-diameter tube and progresses to wider ones over time, but this makes him gag, and when I hear him, I feel like gagging too. I don't like to watch him because it looks so uncomfortable that I usually throw up.

This treatment doesn't help. Year after year, he keeps losing weight and getting worse until Ama takes him to Valley Children's Hospital (VCH) in Fresno. His condition is so bad that he ends up there for months. We kids are too young to be allowed into his room, so we go outside to his window and try to talk to him. My last glimpse of him is seeing him in his hospital robe looking lonely and sad, and crying and begging to go home. I don't want to see him crying, so I turn away. Our house is full of people, but it seems strange without him.

Eventually, Domingo has surgery and we don't see him for a while because he can't come to the window. His stay in the hospital lasts for months, and when he's finally discharged he's still very thin. He shows us his scar. It's about ten inches long and runs in a raised fire-red line from his chest to his abdomen. It's the only time he lets us see it. But after surgery and months in the hospital, he still isn't able to eat well and he still has to use the dilator. And he still wets his bed. Now he has an ugly scar on top of it all.

(Years later, when I was doing my residency at VCH, I looked up his chart. I found out that Domingo had been in the hospital for much longer and had undergone many more procedures than I remembered. For years afterward, he continued dilating his esophagus to little effect, but in his late thirties he found a doctor who fixed the problem. From then on, ironically enough, he actually had to be careful so he didn't put on too much weight. I felt so relieved for him when the doctor helped him because he wasn't suffering any longer. And during all those years, Domingo never complained. Never.)

When I'm seven or eight, I graduate to my own sack. I'm still too young to pull a full-sized ten-foot sack, so Apa makes me one out of a flour sack. I strut around enjoying feeling it wrapped around me, and I pick with more purpose now that I'm no longer a child.

Sometimes I forget how heavy the sack gets when it's full and I have to carry it all the way to the cotton wagon.

"Here," Al tells me. "You can empty your sack into mine. It's bigger. You can add yours to mine anytime."

I'm glad because now I can go and can pick some more. I fill up my sack again and am proud when I see how much it weighs. More than thirty pounds! I'm making three cents a pound, so I'll make almost a dollar. Then Al gets his sack weighed. It's close to a hundred pounds. So he makes three dollars. It doesn't dawn on me until later that he got the money for the cotton I had picked.

After the weighing, we heave the sacks over our shoulders and climb a ladder to the top of the wagon. There's a long plank laid across the wagon eight feet up from the bed. When the wagon's fairly empty, it's a little scary because we have to walk across the plank to empty our sacks. I empty mine as carefully as I can and pick my way across to the other side. Mily loves to sneak up behind me and give me a little shove to knock me off balance or, better yet, jump up and down so the plank bends and quivers. Mily can be a devil. In fact, that's our nickname for him, "El Diablo."

Once the wagon's half-full or more, we decide to have some fun. On my next trip up, I'm filled with anticipation because I know that now there's a lot of soft cotton in there. I empty my sack and look around. None of the grownups are paying attention. They're getting their sacks weighed or walking over to the faucet for a drink of water. I jump. Instantly, I'm buried up to my neck. It feels as if I'm floating on a cloud. Then a body crashes down on me. It's Mily. He couldn't resist the opportunity. We start to wrestle. I try to get away but he pulls me back. We tumble all the way to the edge of the wagon. I try to work my way back up the mountain of cotton, but he keeps dragging me back down.

On a good day, five or ten of us kids may end up in a free-for-all. It's not unusual for one of us to get hurt and for the cotton to end up stained with pink. Whether we get hurt or not, playing in the cotton is a real blast until the grownups spot us and yell at us to get back to work.

Toward the end of the day, I keep looking for Apa to signal us to stop picking. If there's still a lot of daylight, he won't give the signal and we'll start a new row. That's what happens today. Our shoulders sag. Now we know we'll be working until dark. No going home early and watching cartoons or *The Three Stooges*. By the time we get back, those shows will be over and only the stupid news will be on. We're resigned to our fate.

After a while, when we see the end is in sight, our spirits revive. We start working faster until Apa finally signals us to stop.

CHAPTER TWO

Oranges

T HE FIRST DAY OF CHRISTMAS VACATION! I'm eight years old and in second grade. Today I wake up earlier than on school days, but not because I'm eager to enjoy every minute of vacation. Today we're going to be picking oranges in Porterville, thirty miles away. The day is cold and the ever-present tule fog of winter in the Central Valley hovers thickly over our town.

I dread going outside, but I have to get my chores out of the way before breakfast. We're having one of those cold snaps when the morning temperature dips down to thirty degrees. I step outside. The cold blast hits my bare face and head. Bill, our unofficial barber, finds it easiest to give us crew cuts, so he's shorn me almost bald.

My first job is to feed the rabbits. I reach into their cage and find that the water bowl has a layer of ice on it. I open the attached box with the litter of baby rabbits. They've frozen to death overnight. The doe didn't provide enough fur to cover them. I don't have any gloves, and by the time I finish my hands are red and stiff. I blow on them to warm them up. Puffs of vapor rise from my mouth. I still have to feed the pigs, chickens, and goats.

As I'm heading into the house to warm up before we have to leave, my feet crash through the ice in our yard. My tennis shoes are worn out. The soles are flapping loose and fill with ice and slush. I'm wearing my only good pair of socks, so I'm going to spend all day with wet feet.

I get back inside, warm my hands and feet at the small electric heater near the back door, and grab a bean-and-egg tortilla for breakfast. I hear the Chevy sputtering in the driveway while we get ready. On days this cold, it takes quite a while for it to warm up. I put on as many layers of clothes as I can to ward off the cold, including an old pair of socks to use as gloves. "Let's go!" Apa yells, and hurries us out the door.

We crowd into the Chevy, with its torn upholstery and exposed springs, and sit on each other's laps. The headlights barely cut through the fog. It's so thick that the trip will take us an hour instead of the thirty or so minutes it would take in clear weather. Rosa's driving. There's no center line on the road, so she cranks down her window and sticks her head out trying to see. Apa does the same on the passenger side. "Watch out!" he yells. "You're too close to the edge!"

"I can't see anything!" she shouts, and steers back to the middle of the road.

They keep the windows open not just so she can see but also so they can listen for oncoming cars. The fog muffles sounds, and a car could hit us head on before we hear it. Every year, farmworkers die in early-morning accidents on their way to the fields. These are tragedies because the cars are usually packed with adults and children like ours is.

By the time we reach the orange groves, the sky is starting to brighten. The fog is burning off closer to the foothills of the Sierra Nevadas. A pinkish glow appears over the horizon. I can't help but admire the majestic beauty of the scene as the sun climbs slowly over the mountains, highlighting their snowy caps in the frigid air. I really enjoy coming up here and getting out of the fog, but I wish it wasn't for work.

It's still too early and too cold to start picking. We have to wait until the oranges thaw out, or they'll bruise. Some of us gather around a bonfire, while others stay in the car to keep warm until the contractor tells us we can get started.

By now the sun's shining brightly above the mountain peaks. I finally feel warm enough to start peeling off my extra layers of clothing. From my perch atop my ladder, I can see that the valley floor is still obscured by the fog. Goshen will be gloomy and foggy all day. The fog won't even burn off until afternoon, and the sun won't come out at all. At this time of year, we sometimes don't see the sun for days. Then our moods can get as gloomy as the weather. Porterville's elevation is less than two hundred feet higher than Goshen, but coming up here has at least gotten us out of the fog.

I like to start by picking the oranges at the top of the tree while my canvas sack is still empty. I have a small knife similar to the ones we use for grapes. We cut the stem as close to the fruit as possible. When we're in a hurry, we just pull the oranges off the branches and hope the stems come with them. My sack is draped over my left shoulder and hangs down on my right side. In no time, it's bulging, but the bin we're filling is still almost empty. How many trips will I have to make before it's full?

One thing I like about picking oranges is how spectacular the groves look. From my perch, I can see hundreds of trees that seem to stretch up the hillside forever in their green glory. The shiny oranges in their abundance add their color to the landscape. The clouds are fluffy and hang above the mountains as if framed. The air is heavy with the fragrance of the oranges.

Sometimes I come across an orange so big and colorful that I have to hold it up and admire its size with the mountains as a backdrop. I clutch it against my chest so I won't drop it, and I climb down the ladder. This one's going home with me where I'm going to savor it at my leisure because I know it'll be sweet and juicy. Most people never experience biting into such a truly wondrous specimen because oranges like this one never make it into the stores. As I hide it in the car, I wonder why not.

After I pick all the oranges right around me, I grab for one that's slightly out of my reach. But my ladder is a little unsteady. As I stretch out as far as I can, my half-full bag throws me off balance. The ladder slips out from under me and gets wedged into the tree. Waving my arms helplessly, I fall into the tree and dangle in the branches. The thorns on the branches rip my skin. My bag is weighing me down and I can't regain my balance. Eventually I manage to grab hold of it and bring it in front of my chest and stomach, but I'm not strong enough to free the ladder. If I weren't afraid of the ribbing I would get, I'd call for help. Somehow I manage to get myself, my bag, and the ladder under control. I climb down with no one the wiser.

One year runs into another, and after a while they all seem the same. Christmas vacation comes, and so does another season of picking oranges.

One year it's different. It rains. I've never seen so much rain. We have pans and pots collecting the water that seems to be dripping through our whole roof. The empty lot where we play is flooded. The edges of our street are submerged for as far as I can see. Whenever the rain lets up, we make little boats and float them in the flooded street. At first I'm glad we don't have to work, but the rain also keeps us pretty much confined to the house.

We kids try to keep ourselves occupied by playing Monopoly. No game goes without arguments or someone feeling slighted or cheated. With so many of us, we use all the markers and even make some up so we each have one. I like the little car and always grab it as soon as we start playing. Days like these are really the only time we get to play for hours.

There's nothing else to do except watch TV. All the shows are about Christmas and presents and families gathering around the tree and opening tons of gifts—nothing like our house. The closer it gets to Christmas Day, the emptier I feel. There's nothing to look forward to. By this time, we usually have a Christmas tree with at least a few presents under it. Even though no one in our family ever gets more than one or two gifts, there are so many of us that the pile looks impressive.

Not this year. No crops means no Christmas. I get the connection. We must have been through bleak winters before, but this is the first time I'm aware of how little we have. I can tell that Apa and Ama feel terrible because they can't give us any presents, but they can't think about anything except keeping us fed and getting by one day at a time. We eat mostly beans, rice, and potatoes with tortillas. Ama had bought hundred-pound sacks of beans, rice, and flour, but these are almost empty, and we still have to make it through the rest of the winter. If the weather doesn't change soon, we'll lose the orange-harvesting season completely. And then I don't know what will happen.

Ama's and Apa's faces are furrowed with worry lines. They don't know where to look for answers. It's not as if they don't work hard. I never see Apa doing anything but work, twelve hours a day, day in and day out, in the fields or irrigating. After that, he cares for our animals and we help him. He takes every opportunity to make ends meet. He looks years older than his age, and I feel so bad for him. I never ask him for anything extra because I don't want to place any more strain on him.

I get mad when I hear other kids at school whining and pouting about having to work in the fields. Sure, we have nothing, but it isn't for lack of trying.

Apa doesn't drink or smoke, and as far as I know he has no real vices. He takes care of us. On rainy nights, he's the one who takes us to the outhouse or holds a newspaper over our heads to shelter us when we pee on the dirt.

By the time December 24 arrives, I know for sure that we won't be having a Christmas this year. It'll be just like any other day. Not a special day. I won't be jumping out of bed early so I can open my presents.

Ama makes us go to the Catholic church for the Christmas Eve service. We're supposed to sit and pray and count our blessings and listen to a service that lasts for what feels like hours. I wonder what we have to be grateful for.

We have no Christmas presents, no turkey, a house that leaks all over us as we sleep, no hot water in the mornings. And no furnace, so we don't have heat either.

As I sit there in the pew, I get mad at God. What have I done to deserve this? Even though I'm only a little kid, I work my butt off. I carry my own weight. I'm not asking for anything special, only for what we've earned. Why should I pray to a God who doesn't care for my family? I feel like walking out of the church, but then I'd have to walk home, and at least it's warm in the church.

When the collection plate is passed around, the priest tells us, "Give what you can." All I have in my pocket is a couple of pennies. I'm very tempted to take some money from the plate instead of giving any, except that I'm afraid of being struck down by a bolt of lightning. I'm mad at God, but I still believe He could strike me dead.

I look around at the rest of my family. They're good people. Every one of them would give you the last cent they had. In fact, the only gifts we'll get tomorrow will be ones we've been able to get for each other, like comic books from the flea market.

After the service is finally over, we start walking home. Many of the houses have Christmas lights hanging along the edges of their roofs. The rain is clearing. The lights sparkle crystal-clear in the cold, biting air, but I know that Christmas for many of the people in those houses will be as bleak as ours.

When we get up the next morning and open the front door, we're astonished to find a couple of boxes full of food and clothes on the step.

23
Oranges

This won't be such a terrible holiday after all! We wonder who left them, and when. Whoever it was had to have done it late at night or before dawn on this freezing morning, because Ama and Apa both get up early. But they're as surprised as we are.

One box is full of staples like rice and beans, cans of vegetables and fruit, and even a canned ham—enough to last us for several weeks. Also, whoever left the boxes had a fairly good idea of all the younger kids' ages and sizes. I'm beside myself going through the stuff and trying on clothes. There isn't much for the teenagers, but they seem happy watching us enjoy our gifts.

⪻ ⪻
⪻

Another disastrous year hits when I'm in sixth grade, a couple of years after we move into our new house across from my school. The weather's too bad for us to work. It seems we'll have to do without Christmas again. It's not our fault that the weather's so bad. We want to work. The whole family depends on the orange harvest to carry us through the spring and into the summer. But there really isn't anything else to pick to get us by.

By now I'm not a kid anymore, and I know that we may lose our house if we can't make the mortgage payments. Our phone's already been cut off. We're getting notices that our gas and electricity may be disconnected if we don't make some sort of payment arrangement.

If it were summer, I could do yard work. At this time of the year, there's nothing. In the summer, I can usually get some work from our neighbor, Jim Drake. He always has some small job for me. Sometimes he and his wife, Susan, will go away for a week or two and let me take care of their house. He also puts me in charge if Joe or any of my cousins want to work, too. We do their mowing and weeding and watering after we get home from working in the fields all day. We also wash their windows and do anything else we can think of that needs doing.

When they get back and I tell him how many hours we worked, he pays us without question. He treats us like responsible kids. He knows that the money we earn in the fields is for the whole family and that we kids get nothing for ourselves unless we earn it doing other work.

Looking back, I realize how genuine and caring the Drakes were. Jim listened to me and taught me how to treat people with respect. He made me feel important, and he was one of the few Anglo people who gave me some sense of my worth. I wish I'd had a chance to thank him. Years later, I gained a better understanding of him when I stumbled upon a remarkable bit of history.

Jim Drake was the first organizer whom César Chávez enlisted when he started the United Farmworkers of America. César used to take Jim with him to the churches and farmworkers' homes. Jim died in 2001, a few days before the September 11 terrorist attacks. I also never knew until recently that he'd been an ordained United Church of Christ minister.

Susan also went to work for the UFW. She was César's secretary for a number of years. She later wrote a book, *Fields of Courage*, that talks about Goshen and even mentions my family. I never knew about their involvement in the movement until then. Now I understand why they were so kind and decent. They showed me what genuine, caring people were like.

Still, in the dead of this winter, even Jim Drake has no work for us. I feel responsible for helping the family, so when I hear that a new weekly paper is looking for delivery boys, I apply. I get five cents for every paper I sell. It turns out, though, that Goshen isn't a good town for trying something new, or something that involves reading. Within weeks, the paper shuts down. I'm lucky to break even. Joe and I manage to make a few bucks collecting discarded soda bottles.

During yet another poor harvest season a year or two later, I hear footsteps on our front walk on Christmas morning. When I open the door, my classmate Elaine's mom is standing there with some boxes. Elaine is Anglo, and she and I have been in the same class ever since kindergarten. Since fourth grade, we've been rivals for the spot of top student. I see her waiting in the car and she waves at me.

"Merry Christmas!" her mom tells me. "Our church passes out food baskets to needy families, and we're dropping some things off for your family."

"Thank you," I tell her.

"You're welcome!" She walks back to her car. Elaine waves again as they drive off. I'm embarrassed that Elaine knows how poor we are. I wonder how I can look her in the eye when school starts again, but to her credit she never says anything to me. We do appreciate the food boxes, but I never tell her that.

A year or two after that, a prolonged freeze sets in a few weeks after Christmas. We've picked all during the Christmas break and we continue every weekend until all the crops are harvested, but the freeze costs us half of the harvest season.

This is a worse disaster than usual, because if we'd known what was going to happen, we could have stocked up on staples to get us through the winter instead of spending any money on gifts. Since we live day to day, this is one of the worst periods we ever go through. Even though communities hold food drives for the needy during the holidays, they tend to forget about the post-holiday hard times.

Although we have only a small lot, Apa always has a garden, goats, sheep, chickens, rabbits, maybe even a steer. Somehow he finds a way to feed us. This year, though, all the community food pantries are soon empty, so we're forced to eat all the rabbits, chickens, and goats that

Apa keeps, not just for food but also to breed for the future. We also stand in lines for hours in freezing temperatures to get whatever government surplus foods are being handed out. We take home big loaves of cheese, packages of powdered milk, and large glass jars of peanut butter, all stamped "USDA," so we don't forget where it came from. The bakery outlet store sells bread at a fraction of what we would pay otherwise. We make do, hoping that something will come up. Somehow we always make it through.

When I look back at my childhood, I record the years by what crops we were harvesting, and how dire our circumstances by how bad the seasons were. A bad year for grapes meant no extras for school. A freeze or a poor orange crop meant no Christmas.

CHAPTER 3

Families . . . and Innocence Lost

ALOT OF THE HOUSEHOLDS IN GOSHEN are like ours—farmworker families with lots of kids who live at the mercy of the crops and the weather. But my friend Eddy Jimenez, who I guess is my best friend (or at least he allows me to be his best friend), and his family are different. The Jimenezes have only four children. His dad works full-time for the same farmer Apa used to work for until he got too old, and his mom works full-time at our school cafeteria during the school year.

Eddy and I have known each other since before kindergarten, when Apa and his dad worked together irrigating and used to take us with them. We would spend most of our time playing in the dirt and canals, and catching crawdads and frogs and earthworms. Apa and Mr. Jimenez would give us little shovels and have us dig and pretend we were really helping. I guess that's how most kids learn to imitate their dads' work.

Whenever I go over to Eddy's house, I'm amazed at all the food and snacks they have. Eddy can go to the refrigerator or the cupboard and get whatever he wants. He's always offering me sodas, chips, or cookies, and I can have as much as I want. His mother never scolds him for wasting food. At my house, I feel I have to ask for permission to eat anything because almost all of our food is for work or school lunches. I never invite Eddy to visit me because I can't reciprocate.

"Come on," Eddy tells me. "What would you like?"

"I'm not hungry," I say, even though I am.

Mrs. Jimenez says, "Nonsense! You go ahead and eat! There's plenty." So I do. And if they let me, I stay there all day.

Eddy's family looks like the ones I see on TV—a mom and a dad who live in a relatively nice house with hot water and an indoor bathroom, and four good-looking kids with clean, new clothes. And Mrs. Jimenez always seems to be in the kitchen cooking or baking cookies. What more could you ask for? Those TV families aren't anything like mine. For one thing, there are so many of us and we're so varied in age. I guess that Ama and Apa were pretty much obligated to take us in because it must have been obvious to them early on that our mother wasn't going to take responsibility for us.

It's complicated to describe how we're all related to each other. Ama and Apa essentially have two sets of children—the ones I grow up with in their house, and the ones who are already married and living on their own with their own kids. We kids who live with Ama and Apa are very close in age, with only about ten years or less between the oldest and youngest. In our household, some of us are brothers and sisters, while others are actually aunts and uncles and cousins. Also, Ama and some of her daughters have sometimes been pregnant at the same time, so a lot of us kids have uncles who are younger than we are. For example, Joe is nine months younger than I am, but he's my uncle because he's Ama's youngest son (and Frances's youngest brother). This makes for quite a bit of confusion when we try to explain our family

Families . . . and Innocence Lost

Ama and Apa in their yard in New Mexico, before the family
moved to California in the early 1950s

relationships, so we just refer to everyone as "brother" or "sister" unless they're twenty years older than we are.

My "brother-uncles" Bill and Mercy are about eleven years older than I am. My "sister-aunt" Rosa, Ama's and Apa's daughter, is ten years older. My "sister-aunt" Lily is next, about six years older, and my "sister-aunt" Elia is three years older. My "brother-uncle" Esmael (Mily) and my brother Al are next, at four years older than me. My brother Domingo is three years older, and my "sister-aunt" Delma is only about fifteen months older. I'm second-to-youngest, and Joe is the youngest.

We probably have lots of other relatives I've never heard of or met. At some point I learn that Ama's given name is Sofia and that Apa's given name is Bonifacio, but I'm never clear on how many brothers and sisters either of them had, or how many children Apa fathered. I also find out that he had another family in Texas, but we don't know much about them. I don't know who my grandfather is, any more than Marina and Josh do. . . . Interesting how history repeats itself.

We also have lots of relatives and other extended family members who live in Goshen—on our street, in our neighborhood, or close by—including Frances and Cruz and their children (my half-brothers and half-sisters), and some of Ama's other daughters, my aunts Matilda, Helen, Anita, Lucinda, and Catalina.

In the early 1960s, Goshen's population is about eight hundred. It's just a dot on the map along California Highway 99 between Fresno and Bakersfield. Now it's mushroomed to almost three thousand. I call it a town, but according to the United States Census, it's only a "census-designated place," an "area with a settled population."

If our family isn't much like Eddy's or the ones I see on TV, neither is our house. The first place I remember living in is a tiny clapboard house with a separate casita, a small shed, next to it. The family moved to Goshen from Carlsbad when I was about a year old because crops and jobs were plentiful. One family would make the initial move, and when they would report back about all the work that was available, one family after another would pack up their belongings and make the move, too.

Our house is right next to the railroad tracks—literally, because the only thing between us and the tracks is a road. Trains go by all the time. If we're watching TV when one passes, we have to wait patiently while the screen wiggles and the TV rattles on its stand. Sometimes this can take five to seven minutes. I get so mad when I can't hear my cartoons. Also, if we're trying to talk and we hear a train coming, we hurry to finish what we're saying while we can still hear each other. Most of our clan—my aunts with their broods of kids and my mother and my step-siblings—live nearby on either side of the tracks. Only a couple of my mother's brothers and sisters don't live in Goshen.

The rooms are so tiny that there's no room for furniture, only mattresses that cover most of the floor space. The casita is a hangout for us boys and also where Al and Bill sleep. Everything in the casita, and what little furniture is in the house, comes from the dump. The dump is our shopping center. We go there every week to get rid of stuff, but we usually came back with more junk than we take. We don't consider it garbage. To us, it's treasure. Apa, not one to pass up a possible bargain, has us climb up and down the mounds of debris searching for anything of value. If a chair has three legs, we salvage it because we have no problem finding a fourth leg. It doesn't matter if they don't match. We're not into décor, only function. Dishes, utensils, mattresses, couches . . . we load it all up and take it home.

My bike is made up of discarded bike parts from the dump. We find whatever books we have at home there. I'm into comic books. I enjoy Superman and other comic characters so much that this is one of the main reasons I learn to read. I find tons of good comics at the dump. I can't believe that anyone would throw them away.

We know that the best time to go is on Saturday afternoons, after people have dumped off their rejects but before the caretakers cover what's there with more stuff. They consider themselves "dump connoisseurs," so we want to get there before they start scavenging themselves. If they spot us with something that looks valuable, they want to be paid off and we have to negotiate a price with them. However, Apa has come up with a system. If we find something good, he takes one of us with him to the "office" so we can bargain, but while we're in there keeping them busy, someone sneaks the find around the back of the office and hides it in our car. This plan almost always works.

(Going to the Goshen dump was such a big part of our lives and so much fun that when Debbie and I were dating, we always took the trash to the dump and then spent time "shopping" there when we visited my family. She enjoyed finding the great stuff that people threw away, and she still remembers the day we found a purse for Ama. Unfortunately, the Goshen dump "mall" has closed down and people aren't allowed to "shop" there anymore.)

We have no indoor bathroom, only a ramshackle old outhouse. Until I go to Eddy's for the first time when I'm seven or so, I've never been inside a house with an indoor toilet. I think outhouses are the norm. The outhouse is stifling hot and foul smelling in the summer and freezing in the winter when the wind blows in through the cracks and knotholes. We frequently "end" up with splinters in our rear ends because there's no toilet seat. We have to sit right on the boards. It's dark and gloomy, and it's hard to go caca when you're trying to hold a candle. The many crevices in the old wood are perfect hiding places for black widows. We're always careful to check around the edges of the hole before we sit down, especially after Great-Aunt Natalia, one of Ama's sisters, got bitten on her behind.

We kids hate to go to the outhouse because it seems as if the roosters and turkeys wait in ambush to attack us if we go out on our own. So needless to say we hold off going to the bathroom as long as possible. Being kids, we pee wherever we are in the yard, but by some unwritten rule we don't poop on our playground. We step in enough dog crap as it is. We have a pile of newspapers in a box to use as toilet paper. Why buy toilet paper when newspapers are free at the dump?

When I head out to do my "business," I grab a couple of sheets, one for wiping and one to read. I open the door but don't see any of the "killers," so I take a tentative step out. So far, so good. They must be out feeding or terrorizing someone else. I'm halfway there when the turkey and I spot each other at the same time! What should I do—make a dash for it now or turn back? But I really have to go since I've been holding it all day. I take off. The turkey is after me in a flash, but I manage to fly into the outhouse a second ahead of the dumb bird. I win. Now I can relax and go about my business. Until I remember I have to make it back to the house.

The stupid dogs are just as bad sometimes. Late one night during a rainstorm, I wake up. I have to go the bathroom but I won't go to the outhouse in the dark and rain. I wake Apa up. He leads me out the back door and down the two steps, and holds an umbrella over me. It's hard to go caca when the rain and cold wind are hitting your bottom. And then the dogs come sniffing around. "Go away, stupid dogs!" I yell. They do this every time, and you don't see them until they're licking your behind.

Right next to the house is a big tumbleweed-filled lot that we kids turn into our personal playground. We make forts out of the tumbleweeds and play cowboys and Indians. The forts protect us from the rocks we're always throwing at each other. Once, we set a pile of bone-dry tumbleweeds on fire and stare at the flames in awe until Apa starts yelling, "What are you *pendejos* doing? Idiots!" We scatter in all directions and don't show our faces again for hours.

The lot is our baseball field, too. Our bases are scraps of cardboard or metal. We even try using our dog as a base, but she wanders off, and bases are supposed to stay put. One day, Joe and I get a rope and attach our German shepherd, Lobo, to our wagon. We're enjoying having him pull us across the lot—until he spots a cat. Before we can react, Lobo is off and running, and we're hanging on for dear life and screaming at him to stop as the wagon bounces and careens all over the place. Lobo always obeys us except in this one situation, when he's chasing a cat. We make it across the weed-covered lot but not the asphalt road. Lobo makes a sharp left turn and we make a flying exit to the right. Joe and I pick ourselves up, brush the dirt off our clothes, check our minor scrapes and cuts, marvel at our luck—and agree that we need to do this again.

We routinely have twenty to thirty kids of all ages from five to sixteen playing out on the lot. In our games, anyone can play, no matter what their age or skill level. But we do not take it easy on anyone. You want to play, you take your lumps. "Crybaby" is a frequent taunt when someone gets hurt or starts bawling, and running home crying is a common occurrence. But we always come back for more abuse.

When I'm in third grade, we move from our old house into a newly built one right across from Goshen Elementary School. We won't have to walk across the highway anymore or listen to the train rumble by our house. We've never had anything new, so this is one of the most exciting things that's ever happened to us. We have a yard, a bathroom with a toilet and hot and cold running water, three bedrooms, a living room, and a kitchen. Compared to our old house, it's gigantic. Although I'm very shy, I can't wait to tell all the kids at school about it. "Our house is so big!" I brag. "It has an indoor toilet and hot water and it cost almost ten thousand dollars!"

One day, my teacher, Mrs. Wheeler, takes me aside. "Raymond," she tells me, "most houses have toilets and running water, and cost a lot more than ten thousand dollars." I don't know why she has to tell me all that. How am I to know that everyone else takes all these things for granted? They're new to me.

With so many of us, we always have people milling around. The chores never end—tending the garden, caring for our meat animals, repairing tools for the next day's work. At any given time, Apa may be sitting on an old chair salvaged from the dump sharpening our grape knives, while my aunt Lucinda is washing clothes in the barrel-shaped washing machine with the wringer. (One of my cousins got his arm caught in it and ended up maimed for life.) Aunt Anita may be sweeping the floor while aunts Helen and Catalina gossip over the fence and a neighbor father is beating up his kid.

Alcoholism is rampant in our family. Most of the neighbor kids are also our relatives, and they're constantly getting beaten up by their drunken fathers. My cousin Ricky's father once came at him with a knife. Another time, he threatened him with a gun. When I see things like that, I wonder if maybe I'm lucky not to have a father.

My married aunts have a hard time with their husbands' constant drinking. After working in the fields all day, the men usually gather in one of the backyards, pool their money, and buy as much beer as they can afford. They offer some to us boys, and if we decline, they call us babies.

As the night progresses, they get more boisterous and belligerent. My aunts, who have spent the evening cooking and cleaning after toiling in the fields, too, try to coax the husbands into going home, but the men start screaming at them, "We're the men and we give the orders!" If the aunts persist, the beatings start. We kids often intervene to protect them. We swarm all over the men and knock them to the ground. Luckily, they're mostly slightly built and too drunk to shake us off. We sit on them until they pass out.

If the men don't pass out, the aunts often pay the price in other ways. I know this because I'm often exposed to my relatives' sex lives in our house and when we visit our aunts and uncles. Sometimes I have to sleep in the same bed with them, and I see and hear them having sex. "Leave me alone!" the aunt pleads. "The boy will hear us!" But the uncle just gets rough and more or less rapes her while I pretend I'm asleep.

I don't remember any serious beatings or physical abuse when I was growing up. Getting whacked on the head doesn't count. That's a normal, everyday event. Someone's always getting hit. It's just part of life. But there are other kinds of abuse that are much worse—the things I have to keep secret. Once in a while, Al, Domingo, and I go over and spend the night at Frances's. We all sleep in the same bed with one of Cruz's sons from a previous relationship. He is fifteen or sixteen, and a lot stronger than I am. In bed, he pulls down my underwear.

"Don't yell!" he warns me in a whisper. "Or we'll get in trouble."

Afterward, when I'm crying, he says, "I'll give you some money if you promise not to tell," and he crawls out of bed to get it.

The next day, as we're passing one of the corner stores, he announces, "I'll buy everybody some ice cream!" We get excited and hurry inside to pick our favorite flavors. He pays for everyone, then turns to me. "You've got money." So I buy my own ice cream with the money he gave me last night.

CHAPTER FOUR

Grapes

G RAPES ARE MY LEAST FAVORITE CROP. The harvest starts in late summer, so the grape fields are like ovens. The work is also dirty, because the juice from the grapes makes the dust stick to us like glue. At the end of the day, we can't wait to get home and clean up.

We drive our old truck to the fields. It looks like something straight out of *The Grapes of Wrath*. The adults crowd into the cab and we kids scramble into the bed. Apa has fastened planks on the sides to increase its capacity.

Even though it's summer and the temperature will climb to over a hundred degrees later in the day, we have to leave so early that it's still cold. Just as in fall and spring, we huddle under our blankets for warmth and try to get a little more sleep.

We work at a number of vineyards within about a half-hour of Goshen, but mostly in Kingsburg, about twenty miles north of us. When we arrive, Apa divides us up by age and ability into several more or less equal-sized groups. We take our metal grape pans and cutting knives, and, still feeling cold and sluggish, grudgingly position ourselves at the end of a row.

"Get moving, or no lunch break for you!" he threatens us.

Picking grapes right involves a lot of steps. Today we're picking Thompsons, which will be dried for raisins. The vines are staked in rows with a layer of smooth sand between each row. The sand is mounded up slightly so it's higher in the center. The grower provides us with rectangular wood forms and large sheets of butcher paper. We lay a sheet of the paper on the mound of sand and set the form on the paper to anchor it in place. Then we crawl into the vines, cut the bunches of grapes so they fall into our pan, empty the pan into the form, and spread the grapes out to dry for several weeks.

If you're really good at picking, a spreader is assigned to you. This is usually the youngest or slowest picker. Their job is to smooth the sand by dragging the form over it, lay down the paper, and set the form on the paper. When you empty the grapes into the form, the spreader spreads them so you can get right back to cutting. I like having someone to boss around, but I don't have a spreader today.

The good foremen give us plenty of forms and make sure that the vines are free of weeds. This lets us set out a lot of forms ahead of time, which makes for an easier flow of work and lets us build up speed and momentum. We get paid by the tray, not by weight, so we try to distribute the grapes as thinly as we can in order to fill more trays. But if the layers are too thin, the grower makes us go back and add more grapes to our trays so he doesn't have to pay us as much.

On a typical day, I can fill a hundred trays. At seven-and-a-half cents a tray, I make seven dollars and fifty cents—after a full day of backbreaking work in the hundred-degree-plus August heat. Although picking grapes is far down on my list of favorite crops, I do admire how the huge, luscious clusters look, and I can't resist eating them as I work. I cram them into my mouth and the juice drips down my chin.

But first I wipe off the white powder that covers them. We know it's some kind of pesticide, but that doesn't keep us from devouring grapes by the handful. Even though we wash when we get home, the chemicals have been settling on our clothes, mixing with our sweat, and seeping into our skin all day.

We work far enough apart that we seldom talk. We ignore each other until one or the other of us finishes a section and leapfrogs over us. We also keep an eye on how many trays everyone else is filling. That lets us keep track of how much we're earning, not because we get to keep the money for ourselves, but just out of plain old competitiveness. Apa and Rosa realize this and use it to spur us on to work harder and faster by yelling out how everyone's doing.

Today, Mily and I have a rivalry going. We both get caught up in the game and pick furiously, our knives flying and bunches of grapes dropping into our pans.

I come across a bunch that's so big and heavy that when I slice it off the vine, it fills my pan. At this point, I'm three forms ahead of Mily, and this is going to guarantee my lead.

I crawl out from under the thick, dark-green vines and heave the pan out to the mounded sand. I grab a new sheet of butcher paper and set it down, but as I start to lay the form on top of it, the wind flips the paper and I have to start all over. Mily's watching me struggle. I know he's hoping I'll have a stroke of bad luck that'll give him a chance to beat me. The wind's making me lose a lot of time. I straighten out the paper, place the form, dump the huge grape cluster into it, toss my pan aside, and quickly spread the grapes out.

Years later, while Debbie and I are attending UC Santa Cruz, she comes to visit one summer, and the family takes her out to pick grapes. Everyone tells her how to pick and spread the grapes just right so she can make the most money. Of course, the grower comes over and makes her add more grapes to her form. She learns fast, though—as soon as he leaves, she takes off the extra grapes and uses them to start a new form. That night she tells me, "It was such miserable work that I'd never do it again. It's not worth it. I spent all my money on sodas on the way home because I was so thirsty."

Another time, I'm a couple of trays ahead of Mily. The end of the row is just ahead. I have victory almost in the bag. I start a new section, but as I toss the dangling vines over the support wires, I hear a buzzing sound. It's a nest of wasps. All thoughts of beating Mily fly out the window. All I care about is survival. I take off running. The wasps come after me, but I'm lucky and manage to outrun them.

"What's going on?" Apa calls.

"Wasps!"

"Get rid of them and get back to work!"

I'm not going back over there. A year or two ago, when I was only four or five, Apa would have helped me, but I know he feels I'm old enough now to handle it myself. Mily comes over. "I'll help," he says. He may be my biggest antagonist, and a pain in the butt sometimes, but he always has my back and everyone else's in the family, too. We know we're going to have to burn or smoke them out. We crumple up some sheets of butcher paper into a torch and light it.

Mily hands it to me. "Here! Go on!"

He's older, so of course he makes me the torchbearer. We creep toward the nest. Some of the wasps are still agitated and are flying around among the grapevines, but most of them are settling down. I wave the torch at any wasp that tries to sting me. As I get closer, I see more and more wasps buzzing around. I want to retreat, but that would be the biggest mistake I could make because they'd come after me again.

The paper's putting out gray smoke. The flames start shooting up under the vines. I hope I've hit the nest dead on. If I've missed, the furious wasps will come after both of us and we'll end up with many stinging reminders of our failure. Luckily, I do hit the spot. The nest burns up, and the smoke suffocates the wasps.

At some point, the growers begin spraying for wasps, maybe because they get tired of being stung themselves. I can't imagine them spending money on insecticides just to protect the workers. In any case, we stop having problems with wasps—and start having more problems with black widows, which are not only venomous but hard to spot. Sometimes they hide above the grapes waiting for prey, or in the middle of clusters. I know that every time I cut a stem or grab a bunch of grapes and guide it to my pan or spread the grapes out on the form, a black widow can strike.

One day as I'm reaching up to cut a big bunch, I spot one. I freeze. What should I do? First, I stall. I cut all the bunches near that one. But now I'm out of excuses. I can't leave a big cluster like that because it'll fill half my tray. However, the spider herself is such a marvel that I stare at her for a while. She has a gleaming, perfectly round black body and a red hourglass-shaped marking on the underside of her abdomen. As she sits in the middle of her web waiting patiently for her next prey, I can sense that she's extremely alert. When I reach out tentatively and touch her web, she immediately disappears from sight among the grapes.

I peer through the grapes trying to spot her. Where is she? I can't see her among the grapes and the dark leaves. Maybe she's escaped out the other side. Finally I take a chance. I cut the stem. The bunch falls onto my tray, but I don't guide it with my hands as I usually would. She might still be in there somewhere. I watch for a moment. I use my knife to poke around the smaller stems and clusters. There's no way I'm going to put my hands in there.

Then I see her! She crawls out onto the tray right near my left hand. Now that I can see her, I relax a little. With the tip of my knife, I flick her onto the sand, which has to be over a hundred and twenty degrees. She scurries as fast as she can to get away, but within seconds she slows down. Her legs collapse. She shrivels up into a ball and dies. Still spooked, I go back to work.

Most evenings, we're in high spirits when we head home because we've had a good day. We've made a hundred dollars among us. We stop in Traver, about halfway home, and Apa lets us buy a soda to celebrate. We don't get rewards like that every day. Sometimes the grapes are scarce on the vines, other days we're just sluggish. But today everything went right, especially my escaping the black widow.

After we climb back into the truck and head down Highway 99 toward home, we start yelling out. "First!" "Second!" "Third!"

This is the start of our daily game to determine who gets to take the first shower. The first and most important rule is to know when it's time to call out "First!," except that there's no real cue like a set time or a landmark. We just know. But if you yell out a second too early, you have to take last place. No arguments, no discussion. Somehow— maybe it's just a thing that happens among kids who are growing up together—we all end up agreeing when the rule's been broken (except for the person who was stupid enough to break it.)

The crazy aspect of this daily ritual is that just seconds after we deny the offender's claim, we all start shouting out our numbers. The trick is to shout out the right number in the right order, not too soon and not too late. Again, there's no argument. I'm not good at this game, but I never jump the gun, and I get my share of second place.

Today I have to settle for second to last. This means a long wait before I'll be able to shower. The towels will be dirty and wet. I'm hot, sweaty, sticky, and covered in grime and the lingering white stuff. While I wait, I sit outside and eat grapes. I'm so tired I don't even bother rinsing them off with the hose.

Most of the growers and their foremen look at us as second-class citizens, but that's how they've been raised to think. Although Apa's been living in the United States for decades, he's still considered a "guest worker." He grew up in a small Mexican town across the border from Juarez, in a society where the bosses are god and control your life. Ever since he's been here, he's kept the subservient manner he learned long ago. He speaks softly and keeps his eyes lowered and says, "*Sí, sí*" to whatever the *patrón* says, even if he doesn't understand. He tells us to be respectful of *el patrón*. Even if we want just one cent more a tray, we don't ask for a higher wage.

Sometimes when we arrive in the morning, the foreman tells us the rate is eight cents a tray. Then, toward the end of the day, he says it'll be only seven cents. "That's all the grower can afford," he tells us. Apa never argues or storms away. He just goes back to work.

One day, one grower calls immigration just before the harvest is finished. Most of the other workers are undocumented, so they scatter and end up not getting paid at all. But when he refuses to pay us, too, Rosa stands up to him. She's only a teenager, but she's always been a spitfire. "We're not illegal!" she yells at him. "You have to pay what we've earned!"

He goes into his house and comes back out with a shotgun. "Get off my property!" he threatens. She stands her ground, and eventually he pays us what he owes.

Not all the growers are that way. One year, we work with a grower who's younger than most and who seems to go out of his way to make our work easier and more comfortable. He thanks us every day for harvesting his crop and tries to talk with us in broken Spanish. When we laugh at him, he laughs right along with us. We crowd around and pepper him with idle chatter. We're not used to speaking to Anglos because we're never around them. We live in one part of Goshen and they live elsewhere.

One day, just as we're finishing his harvest, the clouds let loose. It's been threatening to rain for the past several days. We kids are thrilled because now we'll get to go home early and watch cartoons. We jump up and down trying to catch raindrops in our mouths. As we're loading up our pans and knives, the young grower tells Apa, "I'm sorry you can't get a full day in today. How about if I pay you one cent more a tray?" My grandfather humbly accepts.

"Thank you again," the grower tells us. "I hope to see you all again next year." But as we drive off, I notice that he looks dejected.

I ask Apa, "Why did he seem so sad? Why did he say he 'hopes' to see us next year?"

"You don't know?" He answers me impatiently, as if I've asked a stupid question. "The rain's falling on his grapes. They rot if they're exposed to moisture while they're drying into raisins. His whole year's work is going to be wiped out." Apa adds that the grower is relatively new to farming and didn't buy crop insurance because he couldn't afford it. "He was trusting to luck. Now he may not even have a farm next year."

My brothers and I feel sorry for the nice grower, but we're so young that within minutes we forget all about him and go back to anticipating how much we're going to enjoy the rest of the day. "Quiet down!" Apa keeps yelling at us. I don't understand why he's so irritable. Can't he enjoy the time off, too? I don't realize that he'd expected us to bring home a hundred dollars today. Instead, we made only fifty. And the rain means no work or money for the rest of the week, either.

⬿ ⸱⬿
⤨

Being boys, we're always looking for a chance to play, and the more dangerous the game, the better and the harder we compete with one another.

Late one hot summer afternoon when I'm nine or so, Joe, Mily, and I are playing after a full day of work in the vineyards. It's still about a 105 degrees out, so we decide to hose down our cement driveway and use it as a homemade "slip and slide." We never think of asking Ama and Apa to buy us a real one. (Years later, when Marina and Josh are growing up, I buy them one because I had always wanted one.)

Ama's inside. I don't know where everyone else is. We're slipping and sliding and having a great time seeing who can slide the farthest. We cross the street to get a running start and sprint as fast as we can toward the wet, slippery cement. Joe's feeling cocky because he's the only one so far who's managed to get off a great slide without falling.

I'm pumped! I feel a good slide coming! I'm going to wipe that smirk off Joe's face! I get great joy in having people underestimate me. I have to prove myself. If anyone challenges me, I gear myself up to win. Besides, I'm almost a year older than he is. Today's no different. When it comes to Joe and me, I'm usually top dog. I don't want him beating me this time.

I'm off and running, putting everything behind my effort. I've even made Joe wet down the driveway again because I want every advantage I can get. I'm on my way to victory—and the next thing I know, I'm flat on my back. Joe and Mily are crouching over me, calling my name and looking scared.

"What happened?" I mutter groggily.

"You slipped and hit your head and passed out," Joe says.

I try to get up but I'm too dizzy.

"You're bleeding," he tells me.

"I don't feel anything," I say, but I reach around and touch my head, I feel something sticky and warm. I look at my hand. It's covered in my blood. The sight of blood always makes me faint, and I collapse back on the wet cement. What are we going to do? We don't want Ama to see me like this.

Mily and Joe carry me to the back of the house and rinse my head off at the outdoor faucet until the bleeding stops. I have a huge gash in my scalp. I'm going to have to hide it from Ama. There's no question of saying anything or of going to the emergency room to get it stitched up. But I do wonder whether Joe only pretended to hose down our "slide" and deliberately skipped a section. Years later, he and Mily tell me that I knocked some sense into myself that day. "That's what led to you getting smart," they say. I still have that scar. It reminds me of our childhood games.

None of us ever ends up in the emergency room, though we should have many times, given the risks we're constantly taking. We play "chicken" with our bikes, jumping over large dirt mounds we make. We dare each other to jump off the roof of our house, and of course we jump. We play football in the muddy school fields with no pads or helmets or any kind of protective gear against guys twice our size because if we showed up wearing anything other than a T-shirt, they'd call us sissies.

I do end up with lots of cuts and bruises and sprained ankles and wrists because no matter how much we get hurt, our risky games are still the most fun we ever have growing up. And not once do I or any of us kids use an injury as an excuse to try to get out of work. That's out of the question.

⤫ ⤫
⤫

Even though Joe's younger than I am, he still gets the better of me sometimes. One day when we're still living in our old house, he says, "Let's dig for treasure in the backyard!" He's got a knack for getting money. Somehow he always has a couple of pennies, enough that we have an excuse to actually buy something, like a couple of pieces of candy, instead of just window-shopping.

"What do you mean? There's no treasure out there," I tell him. But we all know that Apa sometimes fills up coffee cans with change and buries them. We don't use banks, so we don't have savings or checking accounts. The local market or liquor store, where Apa can cash checks for a fee, is our only "bank." The money he buries is our emergency fund.

"There is so a treasure!" Joe insists. "Look over here!" Sure enough, he shows me a spot where the dirt looks uneven. "Dig here," he says. "I'll try over there."

I start digging away with my hands. After a minute or two, I feel something. I dig some more and find a bunch of coins! "Hey, look at this!" I yell. We divide up the money and head straight to the corner store, with its multitude of goodies. What should we buy? Bazooka chewing gum, with the little cartoon strip inside? Red or black licorice? Maybe even a big five-cent candy bar?

Lola, the clerk, eyes us suspiciously. "Where'd you get all that money?" She knows us well.

"Digging for treasure in our backyard," I tell her. She's obviously doesn't believe me, but she takes our money and hands us all our goodies. We eat some of our candy on the way home. When we get back and Ama sees us, she starts quizzing us. "Where did you get the money?"

I tell her, but she says, "I don't believe you! How much was there?"

"Three quarters and two nickels," I say.

"That's exactly how much is missing from my purse!" she screams, and Joe and I get one of our few spankings. He had taken the money from her purse and buried it because he knew I was gullible enough to fall for his scheme.

Years later, a group of us were sitting around one day reminiscing and someone brought up Apa's buried coffee cans. We started wondering whether any of that money might still be buried out at our old house, so we drove over to look around. The house wasn't even there anymore. It had fallen down. That day, we found a lot of memories, good and bad, but no buried treasure.

CHAPTER FIVE

Migrant Summers

S OME YEARS WE LEAVE GOSHEN FOR part of the summer and
work in fields that are farther away. Some people might call
us migrant workers, but I don't think of us that way because
most of the fieldwork we do is close to our home, and we go back to
our house every night.

The summer between second and third grade, I get to go with
the family to Marysville to pick plums. A couple of years earlier, when
I was only about five, I got up when it was still dark on the morning
I knew everyone was leaving, and hid in the pickup. I wanted to go
to Marysville with everyone else, but Ama found me before we got very
far. She pulled me out kicking and screaming, but it was boring and
lonely being left behind with only her and Joe. It was too quiet, too.
I'm not used to silence because the house is always full of people
and activity. Now there's no one I can curl up next to when I start
feeling scared at night.

This year I finally get to go. I've never gone to pick plums, and it
sounds exciting since we're going to be going about four hundred
miles. Our truck is so loaded up with everything we'll need, including bedding and food, that it looks as if we're going away forever.
We all climb in and get comfy as best we can. It's so early that the

sun hasn't warmed up the morning yet. I can just see the outline of the Sierra Nevadas beyond the railroad tracks. We're going in a caravan of trucks and cars because most of our neighbors and all our other relatives are going as well.

If a car won't start, that's nothing new. There are always delays. Our transportation is unreliable since nothing is new. I've never seen a new car or truck because we buy from used-car lots. I don't think we get very good cars because we keep having to replace them. Our yard is littered with discarded cars or ones that don't run anymore. We spend hours having fun pretending to drive them.

Once all the vehicles are set to go, we take off heading north on Highway 99. Because of Apa's age and knowledge, he's the head of the family, and whatever vehicle he's in always leads the way. This time, our caravan includes Frances and her family, along with Anita's, Helen's, and Lucinda's families and a number of our neighbors and all their families. I feel so important sitting in my car and looking out the back window at all the other cars that are following us, making sure that everyone's in their place and not trying to pass us.

Near Fresno, one of the cars blows a tire. We all pull over to the side of the highway. Fortunately it's still too early for there to be much traffic. I scramble out of the truck and scout the area for goodies. All the other kids are out too, and we're soon running around and crawling under the cars and trucks. We get on the adults' nerves, and they yell, "Get out of here!" at us.

It doesn't take long to change the tire because retreads are cheap and everyone always carries plenty of spares. We're soon back on the road—but before long an engine overheats and steam starts coming from under the hood. We stop again. As the men ponder this latest dilemma, the women get out and chat and try to keep us off the freeway. For some reason, we think it's great fun to try to dodge traffic and get to the other side. By now, it's almost lunchtime, so Apa calls out for the women to bring out the food. As I sit by the side of the highway eating my bean-and-chorizo burritos and drinking Kool-Aid, I see cars going by full of kids who stare at us and wave. I wonder what they think, seeing a bunch of old cars and trucks and what must look like hundreds of people eating and talking.

It takes us all day to get to Marysville. I'm excited because from what my brothers have told me, this is going to be a holiday away from home. We pull off the road and drive along a dirt path through a grove of plum trees laden with purple fruit. The air smells sweet from plums that have ripened and fallen to the ground. I see a lot of small, square concrete-block buildings up ahead. The area around is crowded with cars and trucks belonging to other farmworkers who have already arrived and set up their households.

Apa directs us to one of the buildings. I walk inside and see that it's divided into two small, bare rooms. No furniture, no tables or chairs, no sink or bathroom. The bathroom part is no bother to me. I'm used to outhouses or just going outside anywhere. The camp has a central area with bathrooms, showers, and sinks.

Work begins early the next morning. I'm not expected to do much because I'm still too small to climb a ladder and can only reach the plums that are on the bottom branches. I enjoy my freedom, and Joe and I run around among the trees playing hide-and-seek.

It doesn't take long before I stop thinking of this as a holiday camp because it's no different from picking grapes or oranges twenty miles from Goshen. We're here to work. The days pass in a blur. Up before dawn, working until sunset picking plums and filling the bins. We start out picking close to the concrete blocks and work our way out to the other groves. I can see nothing but plum orchards for miles and miles.

We work each day until Apa says it's time to quit. I empty my sack into the bin and set off for "home." I can't wait to clean up. Today was hot, with no breeze—a day made for jumping into a lake or river. But there's nothing here but the concrete showers. I don't know why I bother showering because as soon I wash off the dirt and sweat, I go back outside and start running around, not the least bit tired. The adults are lying around or leaning against trees resting, but no matter how hard we kids worked during the day, it doesn't keep us from getting together and playing hide-and-seek or cowboys and Indians and generally running around like fools.

The summer days are long, and even if we work late into the evening we still have lots of daylight. It's one of the best times of my life. I forget about the work and think only about how much fun I'm having because there are so many kids of all ages here and so many things to do. We wolf down our dinners—usually beans and potatoes with tortillas washed down with Kool-Aid with lots of sugar, like most of our meals—because we're antsy to get to playing.

There's nothing better than running, climbing, and jumping through the groves. We can wander for miles if we want to and no one cares. If any kid finds anything of interest, they yell out, and swarms of dirty, screaming, out-of-control kids come running to investigate. Poor parents, they can't rest with us running around.

"Dirt-clump wars" are our favorite sport. The ground under the groves is dry but uneven. Apparently, after the orchards are irrigated, the dirt dries in large, sun-baked clumps that break up when you throw them at your opponents. Hitting someone dead on and seeing the dirt explode is pure joy—unless it happens to you, because you end up with dirt up your nose, in your ears and mouth, and down your shirt and pants.

Some of the clumps are bigger and harder than others. We don't throw these because they would hurt, so we make things out of them instead. Our parents like this because when we're sitting down carving things out of the stones, we aren't running around making noise. We do things like making "cameras" by shaping the rock into a square, cutting an opening through the middle, and placing a piece of wax paper over the hole. Then we all go around snapping pretend pictures of each other. I would give anything to have actual pictures of those days because there was never another time in my childhood when I felt so carefree.

We don't quit until dusk sets in or someone gets hurt. With so many kids running around and climbing trees, they're bound to get hurt sometimes. I'm lucky and never get seriously injured.

But halfway through the summer, I develop a terrible toothache. It gets so bad that I can't eat or sleep. Apa tells me I don't have to work, and Ama finally drives me back to Goshen to see a dentist. He takes one look and tells her he has to pull the tooth because I have a cavity completely through it. Our family's dental hygiene is nonexistent. Toothbrushes and toothpaste are not necessities. I've never brushed my teeth or been to a dentist. We all develop cavities, and without dental care, our teeth rot. I don't learn how to use a toothbrush until I'm in third grade.

The dentist tells me to sit in the chair. He makes Ama wait outside. I'm afraid. I don't know what they're going to do. The dental assistant holds me and tries to calm me as the dentist approaches me with the biggest needle I've ever seen. It looms bigger and bigger as his hand gets closer and closer. How would he know that I'm deathly afraid of needles? I doubt that Ama warned him. As he starts to insert the needle into my gum, I pass out. All I remember is waking up with a mouth full of blood-soaked gauze and a hole where the painful tooth used to be. I'm sure the dentist is glad to get me out of there.

This is my second experience with needles, and now I'm afraid of them forever. The first time was when I went for my kindergarten physical at a clinic in the Goshen school cafeteria. Since we didn't have a private doctor, this is how we received our shots. As Ama and I wait in line outside the door, I hear crying and screaming. I can't see what's going on, but I'm starting to get concerned. I make it inside and freeze. The kids are getting stuck with needles! When there are only two or three kids ahead of me, a nurse comes over to me with an alcohol-soaked swab. I take off running and make it out the door with Ama and the nurse chasing me down. They catch me and try to drag me back inside kicking and screaming, but I grab hold of the door frame. It takes three people to pry me loose. All the rest of the kids are now in a panic, too. I've disrupted the whole clinic, and now other kids are trying to escape, too. But the medical staff catch on right away and block the door. They hold me down. As soon as I see the needle close up, I pass out. (You can see the irony of my having become a pediatrician.) When I wake up wondering what happened, Ama takes me by the arm and drags me out of there as fast as she can. I've embarrassed her, and she wants to get me out of there before I cause any more trouble.

A few days after my tooth is pulled, Ama and I go back to the camp. By the end of the harvest season, I hate the sweet, sickly smell of rotting plums. I can't wait to get home and go back to school. At least third grade won't be hard, sweaty work.

PART TWO

Schoolboy
(1959–1968)

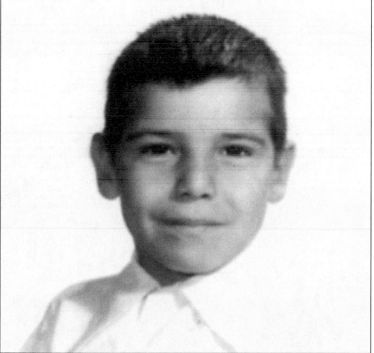

Me in fourth grade, the year that Mrs. Tobin changed my life

CHAPTER SIX

Goshen School

ACH YEAR IN LATE AUGUST, on the last day of the grape harvest, we get to go shopping for school clothes. We don't go
to J. C. Penney or Kmart, but to a little store on the road
back from Kingsburg. I don't know who owns it. I'm excited to be
getting new clothes because I wore the same pants and shirt to school
every day last year, and I'm sick of them. Ama lets us buy two pairs
of pants, two shirts, and two pairs of socks.

Although we have "work clothes" and "school clothes," the only
difference between them is how old they are and how many holes
they have. I usually get my brothers' hand-me-downs for work, and
since we have so little in the way of clothes, we wear everything out
very quickly.

But we're good at patching. We don't throw out anything that might
have a use. My clothes have patches that I've sewn on myself. If I tear
my pants, I know better than to ask Ama to repair them. What's more,
if they got torn because I tripped, and I'm bleeding because I cut my
knee, she's more concerned about the pants than about my injury. All
I get is a scolding. "You know where the bag of rags and the needle
and thread are!" she says. "Sew them up yourself!" I go off and do
what she says. Sometimes I wonder whether Mrs. Jimenez would talk

to Eddy like that, but I'm too young to realize that his mom has only four kids to deal with, not a whole houseful like Ama does.

Goshen Elementary School is a couple of blocks west of Highway 99 near the edge of town. The teachers there do the best they can with what they have. There's no involvement by parents since 95 percent of them are farmworkers who have no education. Besides, by the time they get home from work, they're too tired to attend PTA meetings. They aren't happy with the law that requires children to enroll in school, either. My parents have a hard time putting us back in school at the beginning of the school year because it's grape-harvest season, and we make a big part of our money at this time. They think we should be allowed to miss the first two or three weeks of school so we can finish picking the raisin crop. It is not unusual for us to start the school year a little late because making money to live on is more important than educating us.

I go to Goshen from kindergarten through eighth grade. I remember that in kindergarten we were kept separate from the other classes by a chain-link fence. Because we speak Spanish at home and because I stuttered, they felt I wasn't ready for first grade. Since my birthday is in August, I'm forever going to be one of the oldest kids in my class, and the idea of being kept back even in kindergarten made me feel like a dummy. Joe and I are in the same class, but he fits right in because his birthday's in the spring.

Eventually, I was allowed into first grade because my kindergarten teacher, Mrs. Barrios, came to my defense. She was the only Hispanic teacher at the school. She told the administration that if I didn't adjust I could always go back to her class. Years later, right before I started college, I ran into her. I went up to her and said, "Mrs. Barrios, do you remember me? You were my kindergarten teacher." I'm not sure she did remember me, but I got the feeling she was embarrassed to realize how long ago that had been and that she was now older.

When I start first grade, I feel like a big kid because I get to be on the other side of the fence and the teachers start treating us like real students. My older brothers and sisters and cousins go there, too, but I rarely see them even though the school isn't that big.

Although Mrs. Barrios was the first teacher who helped me, it's my second-grade teacher, Mrs. Lambers, who really inspires me. She's a small woman with a soft voice and a kind face. Maybe she knows about my family environment, but most of the kids in the school are in similar situations. I don't know why, but she makes me feel special. She takes an interest in me. She tells me I don't have to be like my parents and work in the fields all my life. She tells me I'm smart and that I need to go to college so I can get a good job. I don't know what "college" is—what second-grader does? But somehow the word stays with me. I become more aware of grades and want to be the best in the class. That one word shaped my whole life.

School is like living in two different worlds. We do our best to learn English as quickly as we can and to lose our native language, including using English versions of our names. We have to speak English in class, but when we hang out during recess, we use Spanish even though it's against the rules. Mr. Sims, our principal, has a paddle that he always carries with him, and he doesn't hesitate to use it if he catches us speaking Spanish. I often see him leading kids back behind his office. A few minutes later, they come back crying and looking ashamed. They think they're dumb because they're having a hard time picking up English.

We all struggle with English at first, but when the switch occurs, it seems to happen overnight. At least, that's what Mily says happened for him and his friend Ruben. "One day, when we were in third grade, we were walking home after school and Ruben asked me if I thought in English or Spanish," he tells me. "And we both realized we were thinking in English." It was as if their brains went instantly from one language to the other.

I expect the older kids in the family to speak to me in English at home or when we're out playing, but they don't. Because of Ama and Apa, we speak only Spanish at home and our broken English at school. I desperately want to learn English. I think in Spanish, and I want to make the switch the way Mily did. I try to get the family to speak it more at home. We watch English-language TV, but nobody seems interested. You'd think that with all of us living there we could teach each other.

I manage to avoid getting caught speaking Spanish by Mr. Sims because I never say much anyway. I'm more of an observer than a participant. When I do talk, though, I stutter. I have ever since kindergarten, and I almost wasn't allowed into first grade because of it. People keep asking me to repeat myself, so I decide not to talk at all. But that makes everyone think I'm slow.

When I'm in third grade, they make me start going to speech therapy. I hate it because it's only for dummies. When I get called out of class for my sessions, I hear the other kids snickering. The speech therapist is a nice lady, but I'm so mad and embarrassed that I sulk and refuse to do any of the exercises. The teachers tell me it's for my own good, but I don't believe them. I'm just mad about being singled out.

They make me go back week after week. A couple of other students in my class are also in speech therapy. I think they're dummies and that I shouldn't be included with them because I can read and write, and they can't. My stutter doesn't get any better. In fact, it gets worse, especially when I'm nervous. After a year or two, they finally quit giving me therapy because I'm not getting better.

I learn to sit at the back of the class and make myself as small as possible so the teacher won't call on me. I like school and I like to study and learn things, but I live in fear of getting called on.

"Raymond, will you tell the class what the answer is?" Mrs. Wheeler demands.

I mumble the answer.

"I didn't understand you," she says.

I try again, but in my anxiety I stutter more.

"I still don't understand you," she tells me. The other students snicker and laugh.

"Be quiet!" she tells them. "Raymond, take your time and tell me the answer. I know you know it."

By this time, I'm red in the face and so ashamed that all I can think about is sitting down or hiding. For some reason, she continues to hound me, and it seems like hours before I manage to answer her and sit down. I keep my head down and refuse to look at anyone. I know they're all looking at me and smirking, and that I'll have to listen to them taunting me at recess. I can't even avoid this by staying inside because we have to go out at recess. As soon as the bell rings, I run to the farthest corner of the playground. I sit by myself and let my shame run over me.

Most of the students are Anglos and Mexicans except for two families who are black. The Anglo kids in Goshen aren't that well off compared to the ones in Visalia, but they're still much better off than we are. And they never let us forget it. They're always teasing us because our clothes are dirty. We also feel singled out and shamed because we bring our lunches to school in brown paper bags.

Every morning, Ama and the girls line up a row of brown paper bags on the kitchen table and fill them with tacos made of beans and potatoes mixed with eggs or chorizo (which is a sausage made of chili and animal byproducts that you don't want to know about). My favorite is beans, eggs, and chorizo, but I feel ashamed because I want to be able to buy a hot lunch on a tray, the way most of the white kids do. Even the white kids who do bring their lunches bring real sandwiches made with white bread. They bring them in metal lunchboxes decorated with cartoon characters. The Anglo kids, and even the Mexican kids who are lucky enough to bring real sandwiches, look at us with disdain. We sit in a corner and try to hide our poor meal by eating as quickly as possible.

Aside from Mrs. Barrios, none of the other teachers speak Spanish. I'm in awe of the white kids because they talk back to the teachers and don't seem the least bit afraid of them, even if they're told to stand in a corner or sent to Mr. Sims's office. I'm intimidated by anybody white. We've been brought up to not talk unless we're spoken to, and even then I keep my eyes down and mumble into the floor. The teachers keep telling me, "Raymond, look at me when you're speaking," but that's hard for me. It takes me a long time to get used to looking my teachers in the eye, and it remains a problem even in college and medical school because I can't stop assuming that anyone Anglo is smarter than I am.

The other thing is that the teachers treat us differently from the Anglo kids. They seem astonished if we give a right answer, but they're not surprised if an Anglo kid gets things wrong. If we make a mistake, we never seem to get a second chance, but the Anglo kids get two or three.

When it's time for me to start fourth grade, I'm terrified that I'll end up in Mrs. Tobin's class. She's the most feared teacher in the school. I've seen her bully and spank kids for no apparent reason when she's the playground monitor, so I've kept my distance from her. Of course, I do end up in her class. Now I'm going to be at her mercy every day.

She's a short, stocky woman who looks like a fireplug. She has short, curly, dark-brown hair and wears horn-rimmed glasses. She has a mole on her chin with a thick black hair growing out of it. She always keeps her ruler in her hand so she can whack your knuckles if you so much as look at her wrong. We all tremble in her presence and she knows it. I wonder how I'm ever going to survive her. I'm sure she's going to ruin my life.

Instead, all she does is change me forever. After that year, I'm never the same.

From the first day of class, she starts riding me. She refuses to let me hide under the radar. She's hard on me. She's hard on all of us, actually, but especially on me. I don't know why she seems to be picking on me. At first I think she's after me for some reason I'm not aware of, but she never whacks me with her ruler, even though she doesn't hesitate to smack my classmates whenever she has an excuse.

When I fail to impress her, she makes me try again. She makes me stand up in front of the class and give my reports, and she whacks anyone who laughs when I stutter. Serves them right, I think to myself. When I'm done, she tells me, "Raymond, you did a very good job."

As time goes on, I start to realize that she's not going to make fun of me. She has a genuine desire for me to do well. She seems so tough on the outside, but when she looks at me I see a softness in her eyes that I've never noticed in anyone before. I guess I just wasn't expecting anyone to care so much about me. I try hard to please her because I'm hungry for positive words or gestures from anyone.

Up to this time, the only teacher I remember who ever showed any interest in me was Mrs. Lambers. As for anyone at home encouraging me . . . well, with so many of us, Ama and Apa are so concerned about surviving day to day that they have no time.

When I see parents on TV asking their kids what they learned in school that day, going to school games or performances, or helping them with their homework, I think all that must be made up. Nobody does that in real life. I wonder why TV never shows parents and all their kids out in the field picking grapes. That's what's real. And why do those families on TV have only two or three kids? And why do they need such big houses? What a waste. I think to myself that we should move into their house and they should live in ours. It doesn't make sense to me.

I get my first report card from Mrs. Tobin on a gloomy late-autumn day. The thick tule fog lingers over the town well into morning. I can barely see the school basketball courts from our living-room window, and they're only fifty yards away. We live so close that I never have any excuse not to go. I put on my flimsy jacket and bury my neck in the collar as best I can, but nothing keeps out the cold. The fog envelops me like a cold, wet blanket.

When Mrs. Tobin calls us up to get our report cards at the end of the day, I receive straight A's. I'm stunned. I've never gotten all A's before. I stare at my report card for a long time. Pride wells up in me. When I head home that afternoon, I feel such a warm glow inside that the day feels like summer. I walk slowly, enjoying the glow, taking my time as I cross the playing field and the basketball courts. I normally stop to play after school, but today I'm eager to show off my perfect report card.

Joe and some of his buddies are warming up on the basketball court. "Want to shoot baskets?" he calls to me.

"No."

"Oh, come on," Chongie teases me. "What're you gonna do, go read?" Although Chongie's one of our cousins, I always think of him as just a school friend.

All my buddies have taken to calling me "Bullwinkle" or "Professor," after the cartoons. They think reading's a waste of time and can't understand why it fascinates me. My family thinks I'm odd because ever since I learned to read, in school and from comic books, I read whatever I can get my hands on. When I was younger, I would read anything I could see. Road signs, store signs, anything. Now I always have my nose in a book.

Mily and I are the only ones in the family who enjoy reading. When times are good and we have a little extra money, Ama orders a subscription to the *Visalia Times-Delta*. He and I fight over it and then read it from cover to cover. Sometimes it's the only reading material in the house aside from the library books I check out. Ama likes to read the paper, too. I'm surprised that she can read English because she speaks it brokenly and avoids situations where she has to talk. She never went beyond third grade, and Apa never went to school at all. He doesn't know how to read or write, and when he has to sign his name it takes him a long time. I never let anyone know that reading is my escape. I may never be able to do many of the things I read about, but I can fantasize as much as my imagination will let me and dream about what I can do in the future.

I continue along the dirt path toward our house, then up the driveway. I know Ama's home because her car's in the driveway. I'm glad she's there, and I take my time getting to the front door. I'm feeling lucky because I won't have to wait long to see her reaction. She's going to be so proud of me! She'll probably get on the phone right away and call everybody, even my mother. She'll interrupt whoever's on our party line and yell, "I've got important calls to make!" After all, my getting straight A's is a momentous achievement.

When I walk into the house, she's sitting at our yellow metal dining table smoking a cigarette and reading the newspaper. The TV is tuned to a Mexican telenovela. We have two TVs, one stacked on top of the other. The older one no longer works, and we use it as a stand for the newer one. The TVs are surrounded by statuettes and pictures of saints—on top of the old TV, on top of the new one, hanging on the wall. Ama believes in the saints, and their images are scattered all over the house.

When I approach her, she looks surprised. I usually keep my distance so she won't make me run errands when I would rather read. I hand her my report card and hold my breath waiting for her reaction. "*Mijo*," she'll say, "I'm so proud of you!" Then she'll give me a big hug. But she does nothing. She just stares down at the card.

I say, "Ama, I got all A's."

She gives me a blank look. "Are you being good and not getting in trouble?"

I realize that she doesn't know what "all A's" means. "No, I'm not getting in trouble. All A's means I'm smart. Nobody else got all A's."

"Oh." After a few moments, she hands me back the card without another comment or glance. "Go get me some more cigarettes from the store. This is my last one."

"Ama, you need to sign it so Mrs. Tobin knows you've seen it." My voice is flat.

"I'll do it later," she tells me. "I need cigarettes now before the store closes." She hands me enough money to buy a whole carton.

I head out the door. The warm glow is gone. The cold wind bites into me. I feel dejected. Why isn't she proud of me? What do I have to do? Looking back, this was the first time I realized (although I was too young to actually realize it) that I wasn't going to get much encouragement from my family to dream of achieving more in life than becoming a farmworker. It took decades before I could let go of my anger, forgive them, and accept that they had done the best they could.

I think about how good I felt when Mrs. Tobin handed me my card and told me, "Good job! Raymond, you're the only student to get perfect grades this time." She said it loudly enough that all the other kids heard her. They looked at me with envy, especially Elaine and Rachel, who's Eddy's aunt. We've all been in the same grade together since kindergarten. They've always been the top two students, and I'm sure they never expected me to challenge their lead. I've always been too quiet. I never speak up eagerly the way they do to show off how smart they are. Until now, I've never thought of myself as smart. I've always envied Elaine and Rachel, but today it's their turn to be jealous. I enjoy seeing that, and I vow that I'll never let anyone get ahead of me again.

From then on, I'm not the same kid I used to be. I find myself wanting to be smart. I'm determined to read everything I can get my hands on. Whenever the bookmobile comes to Goshen, I check out as many books as they'll let me. Every night, after everyone's finished eating and goes into the living room to watch TV, I do my homework on our dining table. They make fun of me for being so serious and ask me why I don't come in and watch TV.

It's hard to study with so many people around and to not let myself get distracted by the TV. This past summer, Apa told us that if we worked hard all summer and made a lot of money, he would buy us a color set. We were so excited that whenever we slacked off, all he had to say was, "I guess you don't want a color TV," and we would start working like the devil again. The day we got it, we all crowded around as the technician set it up. We couldn't wait to see *The Wonderful World of Disney* and *Bonanza*, our favorite Sunday shows. At first the people looked all green, and I worried that the TV might not be any good, but when he finally got the picture right, we were thrilled.

I never thought twice about why TV shows always looked so blurry to me that I had to sit right on top of the set. I had no idea, nor did anyone else in the family, that I was nearsighted and needed glasses. I didn't find this out until eighth grade, when I was finally taken to an eye doctor. Until I got glasses, I had no idea what it was like to see normally. Unfortunately, I wanted wire-rimmed glasses like the ones Eddy and the other rich kids wore, but all we could afford were dorky black horn-rimmed ones. Al had these and hated them. The day I got mine, I left them in the case because I didn't want to wear them. Later that night, though, I got them out while I was watching *Flipper*. I couldn't believe how beautiful the color was. I didn't know what I'd been missing. I kept taking the glasses on and off to check the difference. I couldn't wait for

Sunday night to see what the Disney show looked like "in living color." I always thought that the blurry fireworks behind the castle at the start of the show were pretty, but with my glasses they were spectacular. Still, I didn't wear my glasses at school or for sports. By that time, I wanted girls to like me, but they wouldn't if I looked nerdy. I could see how they looked at Eddy, so I wouldn't wear my glasses.

After we get the color TV, it turns out that I'm the only one in the family who can manage to tune it and adjust the colors right. So at least once a night someone calls out, "Raymond! Come adjust the TV!" Everyone calls me "Raymond" now except Ama and Apa, who call me "Ramon." I do as I'm asked because I love being able to do something no one else can. I feel needed.

After I work my TV magic to everyone's satisfaction, I go back to my homework. I now study with a purpose. I try to ignore the distractions because I feel smarter and I enjoy learning. Maybe Mily and Joe were right and something did click in me after I cracked my head open on that wet cement.

I get straight A's for the rest of fourth grade and every year from then on until I graduate. I guess that the rest of the teachers realize my potential and expect nothing less from me. Mrs. Tobin turns out not to be the evil hag everyone said she was. I realize that she's a teacher who cares about her students and expects them to try their best. When they don't, she tells them she's not happy with their performance and gives them the grades they deserve, but then they blame her. That's why she has such a bad reputation. She's the right teacher for me. I end up in her class at the exact moment when I'm waking up to my potential. She sees my hunger and my desire to please and uses it for my own good. I'm lucky to have ended up in her fourth-grade class. Sometimes I wonder what my life would be like today if I'd had a different teacher.

When I'm in sixth grade, a traveling encyclopedia salesman comes to the door. He starts telling Ama about the books and how great they'll be for the children. She says she's not interested, but then he says she can use the easy-payment plan. A couple of years ago, she bought a vacuum cleaner from a door-to-door salesman on a payment plan. She's still paying for it even though we no longer have the vacuum.

I'm convinced that she's not going to buy the encyclopedia, but I'm looking through the letter "A" book and I'm mesmerized by the amount of information in it. Somehow the salesman convinces her to buy the annual update and to take the "A" and "B" books on trial. We end up with the whole set, and I read every volume. I want to be smart and go to college. I'm not quite sure what college is, but I know that only intelligent students go there. The encyclopedia books are the only books we own. We treasure them for years. They're never replaced or updated, and we use them until we finish high school.

CHAPTER SEVEN

Holidays

E ASTER IS ONE OF THE FEW TIMES that we do anything as a family. After Easter Mass, our entire extended family gets together—all the aunts, uncles, cousins, about fifty of us in all. We load all the food, snacks, Easter eggs, and eager kids into our cars and trucks and caravan up to the Springville area of the Sierra Nevada foothills where there's plenty of open land. The men stop at a grocery store on the way to buy beer for the feast.

We kids can't wait for the Easter egg hunt, but first we have to find a place to set up. It takes us hours to get going in the first place and then more time to find a place because every time we stop at a likely site, someone finds fault with it and we move on. By the time we decide on the perfect spot, everyone's cranky and the parents are fighting. The husbands and boyfriends have been drinking on the way, and they start complaining about driving so far from Goshen for an Easter egg hunt.

We finally pull over near a field. The grownups climb over the fence and do a hasty job of hiding the Easter eggs among the rocks and weeds. After we kids scamper all over looking for them, everyone sits by the side of the road and we eat our lunch of colored hard-boiled eggs, potato chips, bologna sandwiches, and Kool-Aid. Then we get back in the car and head home.

No Easter excursion would be complete without a car breaking down. I can't remember one trip when that didn't happen. The men are pretty handy with tools, and among all their cars they find the parts they need. By this time, though, we're all hot and tired, and impatient because we have to wait for the car to get repaired. Every year, we vow never to do another Easter picnic again because everybody always gets into fights, a car always breaks down, the men always get drunk, we never find the perfect spot, and we never have much fun. But the next year, we do it all over again.

Easter isn't Easter without the annual picnic, and Christmas isn't Christmas without tamales. Except during the hardest years, when we can't work and we have to eat all our animals, we usually have a sow and piglets, because tamales require pork.

One late-summer Saturday when I'm about ten, Apa takes me to the weekly flea market in Hanford, about fifteen miles west of Visalia. He takes rabbits he's raised, auctions them off, and uses the money to buy our Christmas hog. After we unload the rabbits from our truck, he goes to check out the hog pens, looking for one with a good appetite that might be a bargain. While he's doing that, I go looking for the comic-book vendors. If I'm lucky, they have lots of used copies of *Superman, Batman, Ritchie Rich,* and so forth for a nickel each. At the store they're a quarter. Today I'm in luck. I buy ten comics and the latest *Superman* to boot.

I get back to our rabbit cages just as the auctioneer comes up. I know that Apa's looking for another female rabbit to add to his brood so he can keep his stock at a certain number and add new blood into the mix. Two old men finally offer a price that satisfies Apa, and the deal is done. Sometimes, if the price is too low, Apa will buy back his own rabbits. He feels it's worth the ten percent auctioneer's commission rather than losing too much on them. With all the feed and time we invest in them, it would be stupid to sell them at a loss, even though our rabbit feed is free because we glean corn, alfalfa, and grain left in the fields around Goshen after the harvest is over.

We have so many animals that it's like living on a farm. Apa usually keeps a cow, rabbits, chickens, and even a goat or two. He even arranges with my school to let the cow graze in the soccer field when the empty field next to our house is grazed out. The teachers who teach the lower grades often bring their classes to our yard to visit our animals. Apa doesn't mind. He enjoys showing off his collection. There are always cute little bunnies to see and hold, and the children love petting them. He usually has fuzzy, yellow baby chicks that are irresistible. Apa keeps them in a box with a bright light on for warmth, and they chirp and scramble over each other for attention. The kids think the cow in the soccer field is cool, but I feel ashamed of our hand-to-mouth existence, so I ignore their comments and pretend I don't know anything about her.

I think Apa likes goats best. He's never without goats. He has a female for breeding purposes and milk. He makes a special goat cheese and sometimes he sells the goat milk to moms whose babies can't tolerate cow's milk. He always has ways of making a little more money here and there. The goats are constantly pregnant or nursing their kids. Goat and rabbit are the main meats we eat, but Apa's butchering method is so barbaric that I never get used to it. He'll make one of us—too often, me—sit on the bleating goat. It sounds like a baby crying. He has Frances or Rosa hold a bowl under the goat's head, and he then takes his knife and with one swift swipe slashes its throat. The blood pours into the bowl, and the goat's last bleat ends with a sad, terrible gurgling sound. Rosa takes the blood into the house to make goat stew with *sangre* sauce.

Apa then skins the goat, scrapes off the fat and remaining tissue from the hide, and dries it so it becomes soft and pliable and he can sell it as a rug. I never learned how he managed this.

Sometimes we butcher a steer for Christmas. Apa has a friend who works in a dairy and tells him if a male calf is available. I really don't know if this guy has the right to give away the calf, but we don't question it. We just go and pick it up in our truck, and Apa usually brings the friend something in exchange for the calf. We feed the calf milk from our cow, but we also have the chore of hand-feeding it. When it's grown and Apa butchers it, he makes a covering or rug out of its hide, too.

Joe and I are usually in charge of feeding the animals, morning and evening. I prefer evenings because I hate getting up early. We have a lot of chores every day, and I have no problem eating the animals we raise because they make a lot of work for me.

Apa is resourceful when it comes to providing for the family as economically as possible. I don't think he ever spent a cent on the cages for his hundred-plus rabbits. He made them out of discarded wood, metal, and wire scrounged from the dump. Most of the time our animals don't cost us anything to feed, either. We get hay for the cow, rabbits, and goats from an alfalfa field nearby. We don't own the land, but Apa's been irrigating it for years. There's another field near our house, and sometimes we just go and take some. We wait until late in the evening when the grower won't be around. Apa doesn't consider this stealing. He's just being resourceful. The grower won't miss the small amount we take, but just to be safe, we don't cut the alfalfa at the edges. We go in a hundred feet or so and rip off the top foot or so of the plants. We avoid pulling up whole plants by the roots because that would leave telltale signs of our "harvesting." We hide our tracks by taking no more than a two- or three-foot section here and there.

After the alfalfa is cut and dried, it's easier to harvest. But I hate getting the dry, flaking leaves in my mouth and hair. It's much easier to wait until after the baling machine has come through and wrapped the hay with strands of wire, because some bales come loose and are left behind by the truck. We're allowed to take what we want of what's not usable.

Because we also raise pigs and chickens, we glean corn, too. We bring our truck and toss corn cobs into the bed. The harvester misses a lot of the corn, so we easily fill up the truck. One of my tasks is to mill corn with a hand-cranked miller.

After dealing with the rabbits, we go into the auction arena. Lots of people are milling about. I watch the auctioneer in action and try to figure out what's going on. The hog that Apa's interested in is led in. I try to figure out how people bid on livestock, so I keep a close eye on Apa. But he doesn't look as if he's at all interested in that one hog. I guess he changed his mind. I look around to see who else seems to want it, but the auctioneer's gabbling so fast that I can't understand one word. A few minutes later, the hog is sold to someone for a fairly good price. I can't tell if Apa's disappointed or not. I'm still waiting for him to bid on a hog, so I'm surprised when he heads for the door. I know he usually has a backup plan, but he seems to be heading for our truck. We pass the food section and he buys some bananas and apples. I look at the chiles and tomatoes and think to myself that the ones from his garden look so much better.

Apa's a great gardener. I think he can grow anything he puts his mind to. He grows a very good Fresno chile, and he also makes a cow-milk *asadero* cheese that brings people running when they find out that he's preparing a fresh batch. (I don't like it myself because soft foods with slithery textures make me gag.) He uses a special ingredient derived from a plant that grows in the fields and looks like a weed. It has round yellow berries that he calls *trompillos*, and he says the *queso* won't curdle properly without it.

(Years later, Debbie tried to identify this plant from her botany books but couldn't. She took some of the berries to the local University of California agricultural office, but without the actual plant, they couldn't identify the berries conclusively. They did say that the berries came from the poisonous nightshade family. But Apa was a smart man even if he never had any formal education. He might not have known how to read or write but he had many survival skills. He used this plant many times and I'm sure was fully aware that it could be toxic. But he simply neutralized the toxicity by letting the berries dry and then submerging them to extract the ingredient he needed to make his queso. In any case, Debbie knew all about the plant but always ate the queso with relish because she trusted Apa's knowledge of botany. She and I both took college botany classes, but we never came close to the depth of information he had.)

Apa sells his queso, chiles, tomatoes, and other foods he grows or raises, but still, I get sick of always eating food that we've grown or raised ourselves. I eat our own hens' eggs, but I don't like them because they're brown and home-grown. I want store-bought white eggs, but I don't have any choice. If there aren't any eggs in the refrigerator, I go out and look for some. We always have plenty of fertile eggs from our chickens, though we usually have to search for the nests because the chickens hide them, maybe to protect them from predators.

I gather two or three eggs, heat up the lard in Ama's frying pan, and crack the eggs. But they're usually fertile, and if I see a small blood spot on the yolk, I feel terrible because the egg was on its way to becoming a chick. I can't bring myself to eat it, so I toss it in the trash or feed it to the dogs. Every once in a while, I'll crack an egg and see the chick's head and body. That's even worse.

I don't like the milk from Apa's cow, either. Ama keeps it in an industrial-sized mayonnaise glass jar in the refrigerator. The cream rises to the top in a two-inch layer of thick white gunk. Whenever I pour some out to drink or to put on my cereal or into my coffee, I stir the cream in so I can't see it. If no one's watching, I even spoon it off and throw it away, but usually I stir it in because otherwise the milk will look too thin.

I tell myself that when I'm grown up and have my own house, I'll never have brown eggs and I'll always buy real milk, the kind that comes in cartons. No more of this cheap stuff. How was I to know that one day people would gladly pay a premium for natural, homegrown foods like the farm-fresh eggs and milk I hated when I was growing up?

For me, though, these foods are daily reminders of our poverty. And I don't want to be living that way.

Rabbits are okay, though. Apa has to butcher at least three to feed our big family. He bashes them on the head with a hammer, then makes an incision around the necks and peels the fur right down the carcasses, like peeling a banana, until he reaches the feet. Then he makes a couple of incisions above the hind paws and hangs them up.

To me, rabbit tastes pretty much like the dark meat of chicken, but leaner. Apa is usually in charge of the cooking when we have meat, which he fries in lard from our last hog. It's very tasty. For years, the only way I eat meat is fried in hog lard. It takes me a long time to develop a taste for anything that wasn't cooked in lard. The first time I tasted eggs that had been cooked in water was at UC Santa Cruz. They had no flavor at all, and they made me gag. The same was true for how they served steak at the dorm dining halls. When I cut into it, it was red in the middle, and when I bit into it, it was bland and dry—nothing like the beef we had at home. I couldn't wait to get home and cook my meat with lard. (Even today, when I cook meat at home, I fry it in a layer of lard until it's almost black. And it's delicious.)

After we pass the food section and reach the truck, Apa keeps on walking.

"Where are you going?" I ask, surprised.

"To pay for the pig."

He had bought the hog after all, and I hadn't even seen it happen. We wrestle it into the back of the truck and drive home. I'm happy. We've gleaned plenty of feed, and if the hog doesn't get sick and die, he'll be huge and fat come the holidays. We'll have plenty of meat for our Christmas chili con carne and tamales, and Apa will also render the fat for lard to cook with. We have a five-gallon can of lard from our previous pig under the kitchen table.

By Christmas, the hog must weigh close to three hundred pounds. He's so fat he can barely walk. I'm not going to be sorry to see him go—he's a mean one. Every time I have to feed him, I'm afraid he'll charge me. A few weeks ago, I dropped the bucket into his pen. I couldn't quite reach it, so I had to climb in to get it back. As I grabbed it, he saw me and came snorting after me. I flew back over that fence just in time. (Years later, when Debbie and I were dating, I took her to a flea market. As we were walking around admiring all the animals, somehow she ended up on the other side of the fence from me. All of a sudden, a herd of cattle started stampeding toward us on her side of the fence. She screamed in terror and cleared the five-foot-high fence in one leap. I've never forgotten the pure terror in her eyes or the miraculous jump she made into my arms.)

A couple of days before Christmas, we guys all get together and lead the hog out by a rope around his neck with some of us pulling him and others pushing him from behind. It takes the whole crew of us. We have a fire pit going, and Ama's big black kettle, like the witches' ones I've read about, is already full of boiling water.

After we get the hog into the yard, Apa shoots him in the head with his .22 rifle. I didn't realize why we needed to get hogs out of the pen first until a couple of years ago when Mercy was given the honor of doing the kill. I don't remember whether Apa was inside the house or whether he had gone out on some errand, but he had told Mercy to go ahead.

"I'll be back to supervise the butchering," he said.

So Mercy took the rifle, walked up to the pen, took careful aim, and shot the hog right between the eyes. The hog fell dead in the pen, which of course was full of mud and pig shit. It took all of us to drag his carcass out. We all ended up stinking, muddy, and slimy from head to foot. Apa came back just in time to watch us trying to drag the hog out of the pen. "*Pendejos!* Idiots!" he laughed, shaking his head. We all had to wash up before we could continue.

A year or two after that, we thought we had learned our lesson, but Mercy wasn't very good at taking over for Apa. The next time he was called on, we all remembered to get the hog out of the pen first. Mercy waited for him to hold still, which we accomplished holding a corncob in front of him so Mercy could shoot him while he was eating with his head lowered. Just as Mercy shot, the hog sensed something and looked up. The bullet went into his mouth and he took off. Mercy got another shot off and wounded him in the shoulder. As we all scattered to escape, Mercy climbed onto the bed of the truck and took aim again. We tried to get the hog's attention so he would turn toward Mercy—who shot but missed again. When Bill climbed up on the truck and said, "Let me try," Mercy was only too eager to let someone else give it a shot, literally. Bill had no better luck. While the rest of us were trying to stay out of the hog's way and at the same time draw its attention, Apa calmly walked over to Bill and took the rifle. "Pendejos!" he muttered as he approached the hog and shot him square between the eyes. After that, we always did it Apa's way—tie the hog up and get him out of the pen before shooting him.

A hog slaughter is a festive occasion. Everyone comes, all the aunts and uncles and cousins and friends. Once the hog is dead, everyone gets involved. The men drag the carcass onto a sheet of plywood supported on two sawhorses. They pour buckets of boiling water from Ama's kettle to soften the hair, then we spend a couple of hours scraping off all the hair and bristles with sharp knives. When we're done, that hide is as soft and smooth as a baby's bottom.

Apa then slices off the hide in strips, along with a layer of fat underneath. He goes all the way around the hog up to the neck but leaves the head alone because it's reserved for the tamales, which are Ama's responsibility. We hang the strips of hide and fat over boards temporarily until he's finished. We have to keep kicking the dogs away

Apa and Frances cutting up a hog
(Debbie took this picture in the mid-1970s)

so they don't steal the choice pieces. When it's time to start cooking, Apa cuts the strips of skin and fat into two-inch squares and drops them into the kettle. After the fat is rendered off, the pork skin is set aside. Later on, it's fried into *chicharrones*—pork rinds.

Now it's time to cut up and cook the pork. We set up an assembly line. Everyone grabs a sharp knife and a slab of meat and starts cutting it into cubes. Most of the remaining fat is left on for flavor. Apa's very picky about the size of the pieces and how they're cut because if they're not uniform, they won't cook evenly. He's had his knives for decades. The handles are all worn and the blades are nicked from hitting against bone. People sometimes bring him new knives, but he complains that they don't cut right and goes back to his old knives. He frequently stops cutting to sharpen his knife on the large grinding wheel next to our chicken coop. If he sees that we're not cutting through the pork cleanly, he orders us, "Go put an edge on your knife!"

We use almost every part of the hog. At this point, the head is at one end of the plywood board with its eyes staring out lifelessly, with the feet at the other end. Slabs of meat are hanging over everything available, and scraps are scattered all over the backyard. We throw the entrails to the dogs, which finally gets them out from underfoot.

After all the meat is cut, we throw it into the kettle. The chilly December wind is bitingly cold, but for a change there's no fog. I can see abundant snow on the Sierra Nevadas. We huddle close to the pot and take turns stirring the meat with the three-foot-long wooden paddle Apa has fashioned so it doesn't burn. We can't stay close to the kettle for long because it's so hot. The smoke blinds us and makes our eyes water.

We love this part of the gathering. Everyone's here. Our street and the empty lot next to us, which Ama and Apa bought at the same time they bought our house, are filled with cars and trucks of all kinds. The men stand, squat, or sit on logs, drink beer, and comment on the proceedings as we all take turns stirring the meat. Someone always brings up Mercy's fiascoes. We all have a great laugh and reminisce about other mishaps, like the time we tried to butcher a steer but it got away and kept charging us, or the time Apa killed a chicken by wringing its head off, but it escaped and ran around for several minutes.

A couple of hours later, when the meat is almost ready, Apa sends me in to tell Aunt Lucinda that it's time to add the chili. Lucinda's in charge of preparing the chili, the mixture of red New Mexico chiles and other ingredients that turns the pork into spicy-hot carne asada. This is the moment we've all been waiting for. Apa pours the chili into the pot, stirs everything around, and tastes it for flavor and spiciness.

"*Poco más*," he tells Lucinda. "A little more." When he finally announces, "It's ready!," all the families and visitors who have helped bring out pots and other containers so they can get their share of the *asada*. It's a family tradition that we divide it among everyone who's there and who helped prepare it. Once everyone's gotten their share and the kettle's nearly empty, we're all allowed to dig in at will. We run into the kitchen, grab some homemade corn tortillas right off the gas stove, and rush back outside to eat our fill.

Decades later, I still don't know anything that tastes better than scooping a fresh corn tortilla into the kettle for a mouthful of hot chili with its metallic iron taste from the pot, especially outside on a cold, crisp winter day.

※ ※

The hog slaughter is Apa's show. The next day, when it's time to make tamales, Ama takes over. Our kitchen, which is tiny and cramped, is also our dining room. We usually keep the dining table against the wall with three of its eight matching chairs stored behind it against the wall and eat in shifts because the refrigerator, counter, and sink are opposite the table. Ama has a print of *The Last Supper* mounted on a piece of shellacked redwood hanging above the table. (When they died forty years later, it was still there. So was the table.)

Whenever we pull out the table so we can seat more people for holidays or special occasions, we can't open the refrigerator, get through the kitchen, or reach the door that leads to the side yard. Not to mention that the kitchen is always packed with people. It's all part of the holiday festivities. To get to the rest of the house, we have to go outside and come back in through the front door.

Before Ama went to bed last night, she put the pig's head into the oven to roast slowly all night. In the morning, we move the kitchen table out from the wall, and the girls and women set out all the ingredients—chili, cornmeal, corn husks, and the meat pulled from the head.

They take their seats, forming an assembly line. Making tamales is difficult and time-consuming, so the more hands are available, the more they can make and the faster they can make them. Even some of the boys help. This year, we end up with twenty-five dozen. Ama has a habit of disappearing while the tamales are being made. "I have something to do," she says. Or, "I need to go look for something." Then she leaves and we don't see her again until the task is finished.

After the tamales are ready, they're stacked in a large pot. Water is poured into the bottom of the pot so the tamales can steam. As they cook, the house fills with the smell and we can practically taste them in the air.

Tamales are an annual holiday ritual. I helped with them for so many years that I almost feel I can make them by myself. In fact, in the spring of 1974, during my sophomore year at Santa Cruz, we Chicano students decided to make a Mexican meal for about five hundred minority high school students who were visiting the campus. We thought this would help recruit them. Since all of us had helped make tamales in our homes, we decided by an overwhelming vote that that's what we would serve. Five hundred tamales.

But who was going to lead the effort? We all started looking around at each other, but it turned out that none of us actually knew how to make them. We'd only watched and helped out a little. So we all got on the phone to our families to get the recipes and instructions. We did end up making five hundred tamales and serving them to the students. But we stacked them so tightly in the pot that the steam didn't reach them all and some of our potential recruits got sick.

(I've never forgotten that when Marina was about five, we went to Goshen for a family feast that involved a hog butchering. We had visited a few weeks earlier, and she had admired the "big pig." The fog made us so late the we missed everything but the end of the butchering. When we arrived, Marina took one look at the pig head, feet, and miscellaneous bits of meat strewn on the improved plywood table and exclaimed, "Put it back together! Put it all back together!" She didn't cry or get upset. It was more that she was bewildered because the pig wasn't all in one piece. She didn't make any more fuss and just went about playing with the other kids. Several days later when we were at dinner at Debbie's parents', we recounted the scene. Debbie's mom was upset that we'd let Marina witness such a grisly scene and started telling her about the Native Americans' winter holiday traditions that she had heard about while growing up in Minnesota. "In the old days, the Indians would go out in their canoes to gather wild rice," she said. "They would bend the stalks and beat them so the grains would fall into the canoe." Suddenly Marina burst into loud sobs. "Honey, what's the matter?" her grandma asked. "I don't want them to beat the wild rice!" Marina wept. She grew up to be a vegetarian.)

Tamales are one of those dishes that can serve as the entrée of any meal. I like to eat them with home-grown eggs or beans on the side. In fact, when we do make a batch of tamales, we eat nothing else for as long as they last. I like to fry my eggs in a layer of Apa's hog lard an inch thick, but my favorite meal when I'm really hungry is to cook refried beans in a ton of lard and eat them with flour tortillas. They taste fantastic in lard, and any time I cook beans my brothers and sisters hang around like vultures waiting to grab what's left.

CHAPTER EIGHT

Almost Valedictorian

END UP WITH THE HIGHEST GRADE point average in my eighth grade class. I've kept my vow to myself to be the top student. I'm looking forward to graduation but also feeling apprehensive and nervous about giving the valedictorian's speech although I'm already practicing in front of the mirror.

I imagine the look on my family's faces and how proud of me they'll be when my name is called and I stroll across the stage to the podium. I'll look out over the audience, and when I spot my family I'll give them a slight nod in acknowledgment. I hope I don't stutter and mumble too much. I'll give a wonderful speech, and everyone will cheer and clap after I finish. Then I'll walk off the stage and back to my seat, where I'll sit down and humbly accept my classmates' acclaim.

Several weeks before the big day, I'm told to report to Mr. Sims's office. I think they're finally going to tell me I need to start working on my speech.

"Good morning, Raymond," he says. "Please sit down. How are you doing?"

"Good." I'm lying. Actually, I'm nervous.

"Are you excited about going on to high school?"

"Yes."

"I guess you're wondering why I asked you to come in."

"Yes."

"Well, it's about graduation day. I know you're our best student, and you've done a great job here. And we're proud of you." He pauses. I wait, and he finally says, "Well, I'll get to the point of why I called you in. We're going to have Elaine give the valedictorian's speech. She's right behind you grade-wise, and we feel she'll do a better job because people will be able to understand her better. With your stutter and accent, people have a hard time hearing you, and Elaine has a very good voice. You do understand, don't you? We know you thought that being the best student . . . well . . . we want you to be the salutatorian and welcome everyone. All you have to say is 'Welcome.'"

But I've stopped listening. I say, "I understand," and I leave his office. Actually, I think I do understand. I've been wondering myself how I was going to pull off the valedictorian's speech. My friends and teachers are always asking me to repeat what I said or telling me to slow down. The more excited I get, the more I stutter. When I'm in a crowd or in front of the class, I'm hopeless. I can barely get the words out. I speak faster and faster so I can get done as fast as I can and end my misery. Deep down, I do understand. But that doesn't stop me from being pissed off.

I've already told my friends what I'm going to say and that I've been practicing my speech. Now when they ask me what Mr. Sims said, I'll have to tell them. No, I decide. I won't. I end up saying I didn't want to do it, that Elaine worked harder and that she really wanted to speak more than I did. I almost convince myself that it's the truth. But this was my one chance to feel like somebody, to make my family proud of me. I've worked so hard for it. I blame it all on my stuttering. I tell myself it would have been different if I didn't stutter so much.

A few weeks later, the guidance counselors from Redwood High School in Visalia arrive to advise us on what courses to take. I know I want to go to college, and I'm going to ask about college prep courses. I learn that Mr. Moss, who was my older brothers' counselor, will be mine too. But Al, who's now a senior, warns me, "If you want to go to college, don't listen to him. He's going to try to place you in wood shop."

Bill, Al, Domingo, and Mily all took wood shop. They've made a lot of the furniture in our house. Bill made a large china cabinet that dominates the living room and a hope chest made of fresh-smelling cedar. Ama is proud of it and stores all our valuable papers and keepsakes in it. Domingo and Mily built a stereo cabinet for the living room, and Al's chest of drawers contains our underwear and socks. I know that Ama's proud of all the furniture they've made. She's happy that they're going to be carpenters because they'll be able to make a lot of money and can always fix things around the house.

"I'm going to tell him I want to go to college," I say.

"He'll say you should forget college and do what we did."

"Why won't he let me take college prep?"

"He doesn't think Mexicans belong in college. He thinks they should be carpenters or workers."

"Well, I won't let him do that to me," I insist. I'm not going to let myself be bullied into becoming a carpenter.

When Elaine and I are ushered into Mr. Moss's presence, I see a big Anglo man, over six foot four and maybe two hundred and fifty pounds. He has our transcripts on the desk in front of him. "So, you two are the top students," he says. "Is that right?"

"Yes," we answer.

He turns to Elaine first. "So, Elaine, what are you interested in studying?"

"Nothing."

"Aren't you interested in college?"

She shrugs. "No."

"Well, with your grades, you should be." He tries to convince her to think about college, and Elaine reluctantly agrees to consider it.

Then he turns to me. "Raymond, I know your brothers, and they're doing really well in wood shop. We'll sign you up for the same classes they had."

"I'm interested in going to college, and I want to take college prep courses."

"I don't think college would be a good idea for you. It'll be really hard and you won't like it. Why don't you just take wood shop? It was good enough for your brothers."

I wonder why he's so insistent that Elaine should go to college, but when I tell him I want to, he tells me the complete opposite. For once, I don't back down. Thanks to Al's warnings, I know about the kind of "counseling" he gives students, especially Mexicans. If it hadn't been for Al, I probably would never have dared confront this Anglo man twice my size.

Finally he says, "I'll put you in the college prep courses on trial. But if you have any trouble, I'll pull you out of them immediately." I don't say anything. I've won this battle.

But now I start wondering whether what Mr. Sims told me about the valedictorian's speech was true, or whether there was some other reason. I've been aware of favoritism toward the Anglo students for a long time. I knew that as a Mexican I was facing an uphill struggle, but I had never believed that it had anything to do with race. Today, thanks to Mr. Moss, I've learned very clearly that racism exists.

Graduation is an anticlimax. Ama and Apa don't show up even though the school is right across from our house. I didn't expect them to come.

To them, my graduating from eighth grade at the top of my class isn't an important event. Not like a funeral. I wonder if they would have come if I'd been valedictorian. Probably not.

The graduation is held outside in the schoolyard. The early June weather is scorching. I'm wearing a new white shirt and a tie that Bill has lent me. It feels tight around my neck, even more so since I've never worn a tie before. As I walk to the podium to deliver the salutatorian's welcome, I'm sweating from the heat and my nervousness. A breeze almost blows my speech out of my hands. I'm shaking as I look out at the audience. As quickly as I can, I mumble my words and get off the stage. When Elaine gives her speech, I have no idea what she's saying because all I can hear is the noise of my blood pounding in my head.

During the rest of the ceremony, I get called up several times. I receive the award for being the top student in my class, as well as certificates for best student in English, math, and history.

A few days later, I'm invited to a Rotary Club of Visalia awards ceremony for outstanding students at all the schools in our district. I'm the only one from Goshen, but I have to tell the principal's office that I probably won't be able to attend. They assure me that they'll arrange a ride for me. On the evening of the ceremony, I'm astonished when a squad car with two white cops in it pulls up in front of our house. My first thought is that Elia or one of the other girls has gotten into trouble, but the cops tell me they're there to take me to the ceremony. I jump into the backseat and they take off at about ninety miles an hour to be sure I get there on time. Or maybe they do it to give me a thrill.

I'm happy to be getting another award, but when I find out that it includes a trip to an LA Dodgers game that Saturday, I'm ecstatic. The Dodgers are my favorite team. I've never been to a live college or professional baseball game, and I can't wait to see some of my heroes . . . Tommy John! Ron Cey! Steve Garvey! Davey Lopes! Maury Wills!

I just hope Ama and Apa won't make me work that day. But they let me go, and Ama actually drives me to the bus, which is waiting at the Visalia courthouse. As I climb on board with the other kids, I realize I've forgotten my glasses. I can't believe I made such a stupid mistake. I step off the bus and ask one of the Rotarians if I can call home to see if someone can bring them to me.

"It's probably too late," he says. "There's a pay phone over there by the courthouse, but I can't promise the bus will wait." I use one of my precious dimes to call home. Mily answers. I tell him my glasses are on top of the dresser and ask him to hurry and get them to me. "I'll try," he says, and hangs up. I pace back and forth outside the bus waiting for him. Fortunately, one of the Rotarians hasn't shown up yet. Otherwise the bus would have left by now. I pray he won't arrive before Mily gets here. Then I see a gray-haired man walking toward us.

"Here he is, late as always," someone exclaims. I lose hope. I'm not going to be able to enjoy the biggest event of my life because the players will all be blurs. All I can do is climb onto the bus—but just as it's about to pull away, Mily roars into the parking lot in his and Domingo's gray '64 Chevy. He spots me at one of the windows, leaps out of the car, and races over. I open the window and he hands me my glasses. I've never forgotten that he was willing to risk a speeding ticket that day to make sure I got them.

CHAPTER NINE

Daredevil Irrigators

IRRIGATING IS A RITE OF PASSAGE FOR the guys in our family. As we get older and make money irrigating during the summers, there's less need for us to make the journey to the migrant camps. We also find local jobs picking tomatoes and other crops. (The rite of passage for the girls is working in the fruit and vegetable packing houses.)

Apa starts taking me out to irrigate when I'm about four years old, and I continue doing it for more than fifteen years, all through high school and even into college. He drives me to the irrigation fields in an old Jeep. He always drives very slowly, with his hands gripping the steering wheel at two and ten o'clock and his head jutting forward over the steering wheel. He avoids the paved roads as much as he can, and I don't learn until years later that he never had a driver's license. When he gets older, he quits driving for some reason, so Ama drops us off at six in the morning and takes off in a cloud of dirt.

I tag along behind him as he walks the dirt paths through the fields to his first plot. He eyes the area to be irrigated and begins moving the curved siphon pipes by hand to the next section of the field. They're about three feet long and one to five inches in diameter. He sets them so one end is in the irrigation ditch and the other end is at the end of the crop row, so the water can be pumped through them and flow down the rows of crops by gravity. It's hard, heavy, monotonous work. We finish each plot, walk on to the next one, and repeat the process. I carry my little shovel slung over my shoulder just the way he does, but I'm so small that I can't get my hands around even the small two-inch pipes so I'm not much help. Still, I carry as many pipes as I can hold. Apa never yells at me or tells me to hurry. Maybe he's just glad of the company.

By noon the temperature's over a hundred degrees. We're done with our morning rounds, so we head to our favorite place to rest, in the shade under a giant oak tree. I'm hungry and looking forward to my lunch of beans and potatoes in a flour tortilla. We've walked more than three miles this morning and have been on the go the whole time except for a short break at ten. We don't carry water with us. When I get thirsty, I kneel by the ditch, cup my hands, and scoop up handfuls of clear, cool water from near the pump, where it hasn't yet mingled with the chemicals that are pumped into the ditch a bit farther along.

Sometimes, if we're lucky, Ama will come by at lunch and bring us a cold Coke, but she doesn't do this every day. Usually we have only water. I'm lucky today because my lunch includes a snowball cake that Ama bought at the bakery outlet store.

We're tired but we have time to relax in the cool shade of the tree. Apa warns me, "Keep an eye out for *el patrón*." He means Sam, the foreman. Then he closes his eyes for a little nap. For a while I dutifully keep looking left and right, but I get bored and wander off chasing a butterfly. Then I hear a car coming. I run back to the tree and see Sam driving up. Sam looks at Apa asleep, then at me. He shakes his finger at me and, smiling, drives away.

The hardest thing about irrigating is the long hours. (I recently found one of Apa's hourly work records from 1955 that showed he worked from six A.M. to six P.M. seven days a week for one dollar an hour—probably the most he ever made in his life.) Six to six is the schedule growers expect. Because irrigating is a family tradition, the growers automatically hire us as soon as we're old enough to work on our own. They expect us to start working the day after school lets out for the summer and to work until the day before school starts again, and so does my family.

⚡

By the time I'm eight or so, Apa's too old to continue irrigating and his oldest son, Mercy, takes over. Mercy didn't make it out of high school because he got his girlfriend pregnant, so he had to take the only job he's qualified for—irrigating. Mily works with Mercy as his paid assistant and Joe and I get passed along as unpaid summer helpers. Our only payment is a lunchtime soda. I guess Apa feels it's better for us to keep busy than to stay home being bored.

But because we younger kids are only helpers, we can have fun when there's a lull in the work. If we finish all our morning work in time, we can relax and find ways to cool off. Carrying and setting hundreds of pipes all morning leaves us hot and sweaty, and, with the irrigation ditches right there, we're constantly jumping into the cool, fresh water. We soak our T-shirts and put them back on dripping wet. By the time we get to the next field, the scorching sun has dried them, so we dip them again. We do this all day long so we don't get heatstroke.

Our favorite place in Mercy's irrigating plots is a square concrete collecting pool with a pump. It's about four feet deep and has a conduit that lets water flow into a nearby canal. It isn't a swimming pool, but we use it as one all the time. When we're caught up with work and there isn't anything else to do, Mercy drops us off there for an hour or so. The pool isn't deep enough to be dangerous, except that none of us knows how to swim. We dog-paddle and frolic and wrestle and hold each other underwater. We try to float but don't get the hang of it. We have contests to see who can hold their breath the longest or who can swim the farthest.

Being kids, we get bored after a while, so we come up with a game. The canal is a lot deeper than the pool, and it's fed by water from other sources upstream, so the water flows strong and fast through a large concrete pipe—we call it "the tube"—that runs under a dirt road, then out of the pipe on the other side of the road, where it drops like a waterfall into a deep, dark pool. We enter the section of the canal nearest to the pump, take the biggest gulp of air we can, and lower ourselves into the tube. The rushing water carries us through it, then down the waterfall and into the pool.

The pipe has screens at both ends to keep out large objects (like us), but over time—and with our help—the screens have been pulled aside enough that we can squeeze through them. The trick is to stay to one side of the pipe so we don't get snagged in the screens. Needless to say, this game is exciting. It's also dangerous and stupid. I've played it many times, but I always feel a little scared every time I take the fifteen- or twenty-second trip through the pitch-black tube before I'm carried to the end and get swept over the waterfall and into the pool.

Today I take a deep breath and let the water sweep me away at a good speed. I keep to the right, away from the screen. Everything's dark and terrifying, of course. We wouldn't do this if it weren't a little scary. I feel myself reaching the other side and glimpse daylight as I near the narrow opening at the end of the tube. Suddenly my shorts catch on something. A twig? A piece of metal? I don't know what it is, but I'm stuck. I panic and grab at whatever's snagging me. I know I can hold my breath for about a minute, but if I can't get loose . . .

I'm sure that Mily and Joe are scared because I should have come out by now. My air is very short. I'm feeling panicky. Am I going to die? I yank at my shorts one more time. They rip, and suddenly I'm free. Seconds later, I pop out of the tube and down the waterfall into the pool.

As I bob up to the surface, I see that Mily and Joe both look terrified.

"I hung on to the screen just to see how long I could stand it," I tell them casually. "No problem." I'm not about to let them know I barely escaped with my life. Unfortunately, this episode doesn't teach any of us a lesson. We continue swimming, or pretend-swimming, in the canals all the time. I have another narrow escape another time when I get snagged at the bottom of a canal, but again I manage to avoid hurting or killing myself. How none of us ever drowned is still a mystery to me.

Actually, the dangers we create for ourselves by our games and horse-play aren't the only ones we face out in the fields. There are other ones that aren't our doing. We aren't aware of them, though they may affect our health in the future, and they're caused by how the ranchers and farmers run their business.

For example, there are ammonia tanks near the water pumps that spew ammonia fertilizer into the water. The pumped water gouges out deep, round pools where we can swim and cool off. But the area around the ammonia pumps has a terrible acrid smell, and the water is stained a dirty yellow right where we swim. Do we pay any attention? No. We avoid drinking the water, but we also just go on swimming and dunking each other to cool off in the searing heat—even if we sometimes gag and choke from the smell.

Then there are the crop-dusting planes. One day while Mercy and I are laying down pipes, I see a crop duster spraying a field some distance away. I don't pay much attention. I know the pilots usually have a spotter to show them where they left off and where to start spraying next. But this guy doesn't seem to have a spotter. Maybe he's trying to keep track of where he needs to be by some landmark on the horizon.

Mercy's across the ditch facing the other direction when I hear the plane engine getting louder. I stand up to see what's going on. Everything goes into slow motion as I see him looking right at me, seemingly unconcerned as the plane gets closer and closer and the sprayers on the wings start releasing a white powder. Before I can jump into the ditch, I'm covered. I dive under the surface and wash off as much of the powder as I can. I also rinse off my clothes. As soon as they're dry, I put them back on.

That's the extent of my "decontamination." I don't give it any more thought. I've been exposed to chemicals all my life. We just wipe the powdery residue off the crops we pick and then eat them. I can't think of any crop I've harvested that hadn't been treated with some kind of chemical, but I learned to not even think about it. Debbie, on the other hand, has always been very careful about studying the ingredients in the foods and buys bottled water because our well water tested out with high levels of nitrates. As a doctor, I have some concerns about exposure to environmental toxins, but because of my experiences in the fields, I personally don't take this too seriously. I respect Debbie's concerns, and I don't mind her paying more for organic produce. And I do test my patients' exposure levels if their families are concerned.

I don't know if the pilot sprayed us on purpose that day, but when I was growing up I often saw dusters spraying over fields filled with pickers. In those days, farmworkers had no benefits or even toilets for privacy. When a woman had to go, one of her friends had to block her from view. Although I may sound offhand about the dangers we were exposed to when I was young, I'm glad that over the past thirty or so years, ranchers and growers have been forced to treat farmworkers better and to limit the use of pesticides. These changes are good because they were taking advantage of the farmworkers and just didn't care about their welfare.

Hunters are another danger, because it seems as if they have no regard for farmworkers or irrigators. They hunt in packs like jackals and often shoot right over us. Their shotgun blasts scare the hell out of me. When we know there are hunters around, we scramble to get our work done so we can get out of the fields as fast as we can.

Not that I don't do a little hunting myself. I get a BB gun soon after we move to the new house, and I take it with me when I'm irrigating with Mercy. Joe and I shoot at blackbirds, which are plentiful. We see lots of pheasants, quail, jackrabbits, and crows. The male pheasants, with their bright, iridescent purple-and-blue collars and tail feathers, are too beautiful to kill. We rarely see the females because they blend in with the dull, dry grass. I feel for the pheasants because there seem to be fewer and fewer of them every year. The quail, scurrying through the fields with their flocks of babies skittering along behind them, are funny and touching. I don't shoot real game birds, maybe because I admire and even envy these animal families and the parents' protectiveness toward their young.

One day right after I get my BB gun, Mily, who thinks he has Superman powers, tells me to shoot him so we can see if the BBs bounce off his chest the way they would off Superman. "Go on! Shoot!" he orders me, facing me and sticking his skinny chest out. Being a dutiful little brother, I shoot him squarely in the chest. He grabs at his chest and screams in pain, so we discover that he doesn't have Superman powers after all. (And Superman wouldn't cry, either.)

I'm still exploring what the BB gun can do, so I decide to look for a likely target. Our rooster, *El Gallo*, is strutting around the yard. He's huge and cocky, and I dislike him because he's come after me and pecked me dozens of times. But Apa will kill me if I shoot him. I'd better look for another target.

Our rabbits? There are plenty of them loose in the yard, but they're Apa's too. I finally decide to look for an inanimate target and take aim at one of our neighbor's fenceposts. I miss the post but hit the fence, so I walk over and see that the BB didn't penetrate very far into the wood. I need to pump the gun more to increase the force, but as I'm doing that I hear a sparrow above me. It's perched on the power lines that run behind our house. Without really thinking about it or expecting to hit it, I point straight up and shoot at it. The BB hits the bird solidly. It falls to the ground at my feet, quivers slightly, and dies. I feel terrible. I pick up the frail little body and cup it in my palms. It doesn't move at all. I've really killed it. I've never killed anything in my life other than flies, ants, wasps, and black widows. But this was a careless, random act on my part. This poor little sparrow was at the wrong place at the wrong time, and I killed it needlessly. I no longer feel any joy about my BB gun, and I never shoot at anything alive again.

A year or so after I start working with Mercy, I become his "real" assistant. When he picks me up, before six A.M., the weather's still chilly even though it's the middle of summer. I don't own a windbreaker, so all I wear is a T-shirt. I'll be cold for the first hour or so, but I'll warm up once I get to work and the sun heats up the day. (Even today, Debbie, Marina, and Josh tease me because I have windbreakers, jackets, and sweaters for every kind of weather. They don't realize how uncomfortable I was most of the time growing up, and that I never want to feel that way again.)

I also wear the heavy black-leather irrigating boots that Apa got for me. I'm thrilled because they keep my feet dry—except when I try to jump an irrigation ditch, come up short, and land in the muddy water. Then I have to spend the rest of the day sloshing around wearing wet socks and clammy leather.

I hate working with Mercy because he gets mad when things go wrong and he expects me to do more than I'm capable of at my age. Unlike Apa, who moved the siphon pipes by hand from field to field, Mercy and the younger irrigators pile the pipes in the bed of their truck. Then, while the driver heads down the road alongside the ditch, the pipes are tossed out so they land with one end in the irrigation ditch and the other end in the crop furrow. This lets the irrigators cover a lot more territory, and calls for great timing and precision.

I get my first driving lessons when Mercy makes me drive the truck while he throws out the pipes. This is fun, but he yells at me if I make the truck lurch. He doesn't realize that I can't help it. I'm so short that I can barely reach the gas pedal, much less control it. And I'm not too good at braking either.

Learning to drive is a huge perk of working in the fields, and, before long, Mily, Joe, and I come up with all kinds of horseplay where we can pit ourselves against each other. Of course, they're all spiced with danger. First we argue about who's going to get to drive and who has to do the hard work of throwing the siphon pipes across the ditch while standing in the truck bed. We also vie to see who can drive the truck the most slowly, the most smoothly, and the closest to the ditch. As soon as we load the pipes in the bed, the driver—usually whoever manages to get to the cab first—gets behind the wheel. The loser has to climb into the back and throw the pipes out while the truck is moving.

It's the driver's job to steer as smoothly and slowly as possible so the guy in back can do a good job, which means throwing the pipes across so they land right where they should. If any of them end up in the ditch, we have to fish them out, which delays us. If the truck makes any sudden stops or starts, the guy in back will lose his footing. And if you're the one driving when that happens, you'll have a fight on your hands.

Of course, we manage to make a game of this. It starts when we get close to the end of the section we're irrigating. Today, I won the race to drive and Mily's in back. I keep my eyes on the rearview mirror to see how many pipes he has left, and he knows I'm watching because we both know that the game is on. He's making sure he's got his balance. I'm driving so slowly that the truck is barely moving because Mily's throwing the pipes across very slowly. He's down to his last four or five, as far as I can tell, but I think he's hiding one under his foot or to the side, out of my line of vision. The moment he lets the last pipe fly, he dives for the bed of the truck to keep from being flung off as I gun the motor to try to send him flying into the ditch. That's the essence of the game.

One day when Joe's driving and I'm in back, he's so busy keeping an eye on me that he forgets to look ahead and runs the truck into the ditch, where it gets stuck. Mercy gives him hell. I deny any responsibility and say, "I was just minding my own business tossing the pipes down." But the truth is that I had faked Joe out several times by making him think I had reached for the last pipe. So he had gunned the motor to toss me off when I still had some pipes left, which meant he had been losing the game. Although we play this game all the time, no one ever gets seriously hurt. Banged knees, heads knocked against the truck's sides or rear window, bloody gashes from the tailgate or protruding metal—for us these are just part of the action. We engage in this kind of childish behavior well into our late teens.

Like Apa, Mercy likes to take naps after lunch. "Don't let Sam catch me," he warns me, "or we'll be in trouble." I get sleepy, too, but I don't dare doze off. After he falls asleep, I keep myself awake by sitting in the truck reading the books and magazines that he gets from the dump and keeps hidden under the seat.

The magazines have pictures of naked women, and the stories are all about people having sex, or girls being raped or molested. By now I know how to read, and I also know what the people in the pictures are doing. I never wonder why he leaves these things around for me to see. I don't know whether it's normal for him to do this because, except for the TV shows I watch, I have no idea what normal families are like. For all I know, most kids my age are being exposed to material like this. Still, I also sense that I shouldn't be looking at them, so I hide them if Sam or anyone else comes by. To be fair, Mercy also keeps a stash of detective and crime magazines under the seat, and I read those as much as I read the sex magazines.

PART THREE

High-School Boy

(1968–1972)

Running cross-country,
Redwood High School, 1971

CHAPTER TEN

First Days

SEPTEMBER 1968—MY FIRST DAY at Redwood High School! I've never seen so many people! There were only about forty of us in my graduating class, and I felt overwhelmed there. Now I'm going to be in a class of five hundred. And almost all the kids in my classes are white. I see only a few Mexican kids like me.

I step off the school bus that takes us from Goshen to Visalia. My first class is French. It's the height of the Vietnam War, and if I'm going to get drafted and sent over there, I should learn French. Maybe it'll give me a better chance of surviving. I have no doubt that I'll be drafted. I'm determined to apply to college, but what are the chances of my going, or even getting in? Except for Bill, Al, and Mily attending College of the Sequoias (COS), our local junior college, no one in my family has ever gone beyond high school.

How am I going to compete? I don't feel cocky anymore. I start wondering whether I should be taking college-prep courses after all. And because of Mr. Moss, I'm on probation already. I can't forget his threat to put me in wood shop if I have any trouble. My classes for the first semester are French, Algebra 1, college-prep English, world geography, and some other required classes, plus running cross-country after school. When am I going to have time to study all this stuff?

After my academic classes are over, I head to the gym for sixth-period physical education. This is considered the jocks' PE period. We get the bigger lockers as a perk. I'm running cross-country because I have the endurance to run three-mile races. I ran track and long-distance races at Goshen Elementary and usually came in first or second, not because of any outstanding natural talent but because I practiced. I knew that to win, I had to practice and have determination and not rely only on ability or heart.

John Pitman, the Redwood coach, saw me in a junior-high meet, realized I had potential, and recruited me. Besides, cross-country is a family tradition. Bill, Al, Domingo, and Mily all ran cross-country for him. Bill started the tradition. He won a lot of races, and when we saw his picture in the yearbook, we all wanted to emulate him. Now it's my turn.

Coach Pitman's very much into winning. His team hasn't lost a meet in six years, and he doesn't intend to let us spoil that record. He picks us up before seven every school morning for practice and also has twice-daily practices the first two weeks of the season. The team is made up of ninety percent Mexicans with only two white guys. One's a senior and our top runner, but the other one isn't very good.

I first meet Ernie Moreno and Adolph Nava on the morning runs at the Visalia golf course. They're my competition. They know I'm Coach Pitman's top recruit, so they make fun of me, calling me the "next great hope."

Ernie is an outgoing jokester with a good sense of humor. He comes from a farmworker family like me, but there are only two kids in the family, Ernie and his brother. I'm envious of him because he has a mom and a dad, even though his dad's a heavy drinker. Ernie went to Green Acres Elementary in Goshen, so we had never met each other before.

Adolph's quiet and I don't get to know him very well until he and I end up at UC Santa Cruz. Like Ernie, Adolph has two parents, one brother, and three sisters. His dad is a drinker like Ernie's, and his brother uses drugs. Adolph's been put into wood shop, maybe by Mr. Moss.

Practicing after school during track season is hard for me, just as it was in elementary school, because fall is cotton harvesting season and Apa wants us out in the fields. Every hour and every dollar counts. I try to work and train at the same time by running from school to the cotton fields while my brother Joe rides his bike.

A couple of weeks into freshman year, Ernie, Adolph, and I start hanging around with a group of other Mexican kids who are also thinking of going to college. Until now, my family has been my whole world. These friends are my entry into the world outside my family, and we stick together all through high school. Some of us even end up at Santa Cruz together. We become friends for life even though we rarely see each other after college. I'm still in touch with some of them today, forty years later. And weeks and months later, when I sink into black depression and am fighting for my emotional survival, they become my anchor.

The boys are Ernie, Adolph, me, and Eddy. The girls are Pata, Elaine, Amparo, and Magda. Except for Eddy and me, everyone else is from Visalia.

Eddy is part of our group off and on. Once in a while he joins us during lunch breaks. He quickly becomes very popular because he's a complete jock. He does every high-profile sport and is the star of them all. He's so well known that he even gets elected to the student council as our freshman representative. He can come and go as he pleases. I envy his ability to fit in anywhere. Although he's been my "best friend" since grade school, I know he doesn't think about me the same way. Eddy has always done what was best for Eddy, and if it was to his benefit to be my friend, he was, and if not, he wasn't. Me, I'm known as "Eddy's friend." I'm in his shadow and may not be noticed, but at least I'm there. I hear a lot of "Ray, you can come, too, if you want" from him.

Of course, he's also a big hit with all the cute girls and has dates every weekend. I end up never going on a date until my senior year, and if I try to stammer out a conversation with a girl hoping I'll get up the courage to ask, I fail miserably. The girls only want to find out about Eddy and what he's like, and they ask me if I'll tell him about them. Some girls don't ask about him, so I think I have a chance with them, but by the time I get around to asking them what they're doing on Friday, they've somehow guessed what I have in mind and have already given me an excuse.

Pata's a vivacious, fun-loving tennis player who's always up for anything. She's also smart and opinionated. She comes from an intact family. Her family isn't rich, but they're better off than mine. Both her parents work, and she has to help out a lot around the house, but she also gets to go out with her best friend Elaine whenever she wants.

This Elaine isn't the one I competed with in grade school and whose mother brought us the Christmas boxes that one year. Her family is Japanese and has a tomato farm. She doesn't have it as easy as most of our group. She often mentions that she has to go home after school to help, but she never sounds as if she's complaining. It's just a fact. Elaine has a wacky personality and never appears to take anything seriously except her studies. She and her younger sister, Janie, play tennis and are excellent students. I respect both of them because I know how hard they work.

Amparo's a real leader—outgoing, dynamic, outspoken, even militant. Her parents own a small family grape farm outside of town. She knows all about picking grapes and laying them out to dry. The difference between her situation and my family's is that hers gets to keep the profits of their labor, but we get paid only for our labor, while the owners get the profits. She's a hard worker and deserves what she gets. I don't begrudge her anything. She understands fieldwork, but she doesn't know what it feels like to be poor, either. She has a couple of older brothers who are already away at college, and she knows she's going to follow in their footsteps because her father is determined that all the children get an education. She and Magda are the only ones in our group who have older brothers or sisters in college.

Magda's the cutest and smartest girl in our class. In fact, she's probably the cutest girl in the whole school. I first meet her in my French class, and I soon learn that she's very different from the rest of us in our group. She's the first person I've met who's half-white and half-Mexican. I'm astounded to learn that her dad, who's Mexican, has a college degree and is a professor of French at COS. I've never known a Mexican college professor. Magda speaks Spanish and English, and we all think she's rich.

I actually meet Magda's father one day the following summer when I get up the courage to ride over to her house on my bike because I once told her I would visit. When he answers the door, I can barely speak because I'm so intimidated by him.

"May I help you?" he asks.

"Is Magda home?" I croak.

"What's your name?"

"Raymond."

He opens the door wider. "Come on in. I'll go get her."

I walk into the nicest house I've ever been in. The living room is spacious and tidy. The carpet looks new and clean. There are bookshelves filled with lots and lots of books. The sofa and armchairs are arranged with the sofa against the wall and the chairs facing it. A coffee table completes the setting, and there's still room for more stuff.

In our house, the cheap carpet is falling apart and stained from the dog urinating. The living room is small and cluttered. If you stand at the front door and look around starting from the left, the first wall has the china cabinet that Bill made, a foot or two of space, a small sofa and a table with a lamp. The second wall has a large sofa and another table, then an armchair, which stands right next to the door that leads into the kitchen. Next to the kitchen door is a large stereo cabinet, then a short hallway that leads to the three bedrooms. The third wall has our two TVs, a tiny closet, and the front door again. The walls are covered with religious pictures and fake flowers.

Magda's house looks sparse to me. I can't believe that she lives in this gigantic house with only her mom and dad because her brothers are away at college.

"I'm in my room!" she yells to me. I head down the hallway. I pass the dining room, with a dining table in the middle of it, and then a spotless kitchen with no pots or pans piled helter-skelter. Nothing's out of place. The hallway's lined with family portraits and photographs. It looks like the perfect family. It really does.

Magda has her own room. It's twice as big as the one the four girls share in our house, and it's super-clean and orderly like the rest of her house. I compare it to the two bedrooms where we kids sleep. At our house, it seems we sleep wherever there's room. Five of us boys sleep in one room. At one point, Al and Bill sleep in one bed, and Domingo (except when he's in the hospital), Mily, and I sleep in another. Later on, Domingo and Esmael improve the situation by making bunk beds for us, and Al's chest of drawers also helps, but we still have to use every inch of space—under the beds, on top of the dresser, on the floor. We all share a closet and one set of drawers. At various times, I slept at the foot of Ama's and Apa's bed and on the sofa. Joe used to sleep at the foot of their bed, on one of Apa's hides on their bedroom floor, and later on in the living room. After I move into the boys' room, I eventually get a rollaway cot and sleep on that until I move out of the house.

Rosa, Lily, Elia, and Delma share two double beds in the other bedroom, and that's all there's room for.

The girls also share a closet and dresser, but they have a lot more "girl stuff."

We all have to share the one bathroom, so school mornings are a real zoo. We boys have it easy—we comb our hair and wash our faces, and we're set. Not so for the girls. They have to get everything just right, which can take hours, but they never have enough time. They have a mirror in their room, and they try to keep all their makeup there, but there's not enough room, so they monopolize the bathroom.

"Let's go outside," Magda tells me. "I'm going to do some gardening." After I help her for a little while, she offers me some lemonade. I drink it and I tell her it's time for me to go. "Don't leave on my account!" she protests. But I think she's wondering why I showed up in the first place. Maybe she forgot that I had said I was going to. I feel I'm taking up her time and she's too nice to say so. As I ride away, I think how nice she is and that she was just being nice to me the way she is to everyone.

I've been in only a couple of white families' houses. One is my classmate Nancy's. She lives several blocks away from the library. Actually, since Magda is Anglo and Mexican, Nancy's house is the first time I see the house of an all-white family. It's immaculate. The sofas and armchairs have plastic covers that look molded onto the upholstery. I must look surprised, because Nancy says, "We aren't allowed to sit on that furniture. We use the other room." So they have a whole room that's just for display. I leave thinking that all white families do this to their furniture, but later on a friend from tennis invites me to her house, and I see that her family uses their furniture instead of keeping it on display.

It is true that Magda gets along with everyone. She's comfortable around the rich white kids, but also with the *vatos* who hang out along "the wall." This is a group of disaffected Mexican guys who are only in school because it's the law. They gather in groups of fifteen or twenty and squat on their haunches or slouch against the wall of the administration building. With their dark clothes and sunglasses, it's easy for us to believe they're as cool and tough and sinister as they're trying to look. Even we Mexican kids go out of our way to avoid them. And if we're afraid of them, imagine how the white kids feel.

I'm astonished when Magda goes right over and starts talking with them, and even more astonished when I see them stand up straighter and try to make themselves look presentable. They look down at the floor and scuff their feet and speak politely to her. When she says goodbye, they watch respectfully until she walks out of sight. Then they resume their posturing as budding tough guys.

The *vatos* pretty much leave me alone because a lot of them are from Goshen. It's amazing how, when someone tries to better themselves, their own kind can put them down. I decided a long time ago that I wasn't going to let myself be pressured by the other Mexican kids. When I became known as one of the few Mexican "smart kids," they made fun of me and called me names like "Bullwinkle" and "Four Eyes" and tried to get me to avoid studying. I didn't back down or give in, and I didn't let myself show fear. They eventually learned to leave me alone to follow my own path.

Before long, Joe becomes one of the wall kids. He hangs out there and eyes me when I walk by. Although we've always been in the same class in school, and when we were younger we used to work and play together, I'm not "cool" or part of his world anymore. I know he thinks I'm a sellout because I've opted to try to make it in the white world. He and his gang don't think much of us "uppity" Mexican bookworms. Joe takes the basic required classes and wood shop, just like Bill and Esmael.

What he's doing is foreign to me, and what I'm doing is incomprehensible to him. His friends and mine are like night and day. I'm trying to assimilate with the white kids and the middle-class Mexicans.

As always, we're in the same class because of our birthdays, but our paths are so different that it's as if we aren't even related. Up until fourth grade, Joe and I were pretty much equal in ability. At that point, though, we started to go our separate ways. Thanks to the encouragement of Mrs. Tobin and my other teachers, I began to believe in myself. But Joe never got any positive reinforcement. He got labeled as one of the dumb, uncaring students. He couldn't compete with me, and when he would show Ama his report card, with all C's, she would compare it to mine and call him "Burro! Stupid donkey!" just to make him feel bad. As I look back on it all, maybe she thought that ridiculing him was the best way to try to motivate him to improve. Or did she even care? I have no idea.

He starts getting into trouble. Any kind of attention is better than none, so he and the other wall kids get into fights, disrupt classes, and torment the other students. Eventually he gives up trying to learn and just sits slumped at the back of the classroom with all the other "dumb kids."

All these kids had potential at one time. What happened? Maybe their parents are apathetic, or no teacher ever takes an interest in them or makes them feel special. How can kids in that situation envision a successful future? So they give up and just mark time in school until they can quit. In the meantime, they scare anyone who comes near their turf.

I see how Joe, and my cousin Chongie, and Robert, who's the younger brother of my sister Rosa's boyfriend, Raul, and the others, do try. For a while. I notice them looking at the teachers for a kind word, or an "Atta boy!" pat on the back, or any kind of encouragement. I see the hunger in their eyes.

They never get it in school, and it's a given that they don't at home either. Chongie's and Robert's fathers are big-time alcoholics who roam the streets of Goshen drunk. Robert has older brothers who are in gangs, and most of them have already served prison sentences, including one brother in San Quentin. The teachers know all about his brothers, so they dismiss him as a troublemaker and he becomes a marked kid as far back as third grade. Every little thing he does is wrong, and when any other kid would be ignored, he's sent off to Mr. Sims's office for a spanking. I see him begging by his actions for some form of acknowledgment, but he doesn't stand a chance. He eventually gives in and lives up to the teachers' expectations of him. Then they say, "See, we knew he was just like his brothers. It was only a matter of time." And their self-fulfilling prophecy plays out.

Too Late Now

They look with eager eyes
They sit and wait for
One kind look
One little gesture

They beg without words
They scream without a sound
"I exist"
They seem to say

With the passing of time
They fade
Still present
But never acknowledged
Even if hope still lives in them

Others give them up for lost

Beyond salvation
They asked for so little
And that is what they are given
Now they give back
Pain, horror and fear
Always fear
A lineage unbroken

The time has passed

One little gesture
One kind look
That is all it would have taken
Those many years ago
To make a difference in a life

Too late now

CHAPTER ELEVEN

Teen Years

ONE MORNING WHEN I STEP OFF the school bus, I see a crowd gathering around a commotion near the entrance. I hear screaming and yelling, and I see four girls clawing at each other, pulling each other's hair, and tearing at one another's clothes. Two of the combatants are my sisters. I look away and walk off, embarrassed and hoping nobody realizes they're my sisters.

I'll do anything to avoid fighting. The only people I've ever had fights with are Joe and Mily. Maybe there's nothing I feel I need to fight over, or maybe I'm just chicken. Or maybe I see Rosa, Mercy, Elia, and Delma all settling their problems physically, and I want to stay out of the way if I can.

I'm lucky in a sense because most of the time I seem to be invisible to them. Or maybe I make myself that way. This morning, I'm ashamed to see the girls fighting in public, and I start to feel that if I'm going to create my own life and be who I want to be, I have to minimize my ties with my family members and almost cut them out of my life. I live in a bubble of my own making and isolate myself from everyone related to me. I let them be and they let me be.

I never talk about my family situation or have anyone come over to our house. I also distance myself more and more, not just from

Joe but from my other brothers and sisters at Redwood. I don't interact with them at home or at school. At school, they don't exist for me unless they intrude into my world, or rather the world I'm trying to break into. In all my four years of high school, I have no memory of seeing Domingo, who's a senior when I'm a freshman. And I don't see Joe because I take the sports bus home at six, while he takes the regular bus that leaves around three and then takes off with his friends on their bikes. I usually stay home reading or doing homework.

Delma is only one class ahead of me, but I never see her either. Elia is a senior like Domingo and with luck may graduate this year. But for all the girls in the family, school is like most things in their lives—something they're being forced to do, like working, but not really their idea. They're not getting anything out of it. They see no future in learning. After all, they're just going to get factory jobs anyway. So they constantly ditch school. They become adept at forging Ama's name on absentee slips. Of all the girls, I get along best with Lily. I think of her as "the quiet one" because she's the nicest to me. She's also the only one of the girls who avoids getting into trouble in school and at home.

Now that the girls are in high school, though, they're forbidden to date, see boys, or even talk with them on the phone, as if even talking may lead to trouble for the girl and bring shame to the parents.

These restrictions don't work, at least in our family, because starting with my "mother," almost every girl in her generation and mine becomes an unwed teenage mother. The girls understand that they aren't going to be able to get the rules changed because they've been in place for generations. So they do what comes naturally. They sneak out to see their boyfriends and lie to Ama about where they're going.

Ama makes the rules and tries to enforce them, but it's a losing battle, as I learn one day when I'm eleven or twelve and Rosa's sixteen or seventeen and she tells Ama that she needs to go the store. Ama insists that she needs a chaperone, and I'm elected. After we finish our errand, Rosa goes looking for Raul, the boyfriend she isn't supposed to have.

I don't like him because he wears dark shades, dark pants, and a white T-shirt bunched up at the shoulders to show off his tattoos and muscles. *Vatos* like him are scary. They'll hurt you if they even think you disrespect them. When I'm around them, I don't say anything for fear I might accidentally set them off. Raul is like a vicious dog, ready to attack the moment someone makes a wrong move. I once saw him beat up a guy on the street. He left the guy a bloody pulp, and he didn't care who saw him. (In his later years, though, after he and Rosa were married, he became one of the nicest, most settled, and most stable members of the family. He and Rosa have been married for more than forty years now.)

I don't like Rosa placing me in this situation. While she's talking with Raul, I sit silently in the passenger seat and hope she remembers that Ama's going to start wondering what's taking us so long. After she finally says goodbye to Raul, she puts the car in gear and turns to me. "You better not tell, or else," she warns me in her most menacing voice.

"I won't," I reply. I'm not stupid. I know her. She's fierce and fearless. No, I won't tell anybody.

But what Ama tells the girls and what she does are two different things. I don't know when she sleeps because she goes out to dances in the nearby towns three or four nights a week. She puts on makeup and her dressy clothes, takes her car, and out she goes. Apa never goes with her. After working all day, he's tired and goes to bed. She usually doesn't get back until at least two in the morning. I know because at this point I'm still sleeping on the sofa and she wakes me up when she comes back. She often leaves an unopened can of beer on the kitchen table. She doesn't drink, but when the men she meets offer to buy her a drink, she accepts and then brings the beer home in her purse. Why she flaunts the beer in front of Apa, I don't know. He seldom drinks except for half a beer on special occasion like weddings.

After she gets in at two, she wakes me up again at five with her Mexican folk songs. I get to where I hate her music. I also resent her going out four times a week. Her behavior makes me feel bad for Apa, and I have very confused feelings about her. Not only that—Frances often joins her on her outings. I think it's strange for a woman in her fifties who's raising a houseful of kids to act like a teenager, going out to dances with her thirty-year-old daughter who also has school-aged kids at home.

Unlike the girls, the guys in the family can basically do whatever they want. Al and Mily can stay out all night and not a word is said. When I'm a freshman, I go out cruising Mooney Boulevard with them until two in the morning. Ama either isn't aware of it or doesn't care, but then most of the time she isn't home herself.

Our car is full of teen guys all looking cool. Somebody scored beer that day, so as we cruise up and down the main drag eyeing all the girls, we all have cans in our laps. I have one, too, but I only pretend to drink. I want to look hip but I'm not going to get into trouble by getting drunk and doing something stupid. I keep a close eye on the driver in case he's drinking too much, but I'm lucky because he stays sober.

As the oldest of the guys, Bill's probably the only positive male role model in our family. It's his example that we follow, and that's probably why the guys stay out of serious trouble for the most part. Even Joe, who, despite being a wall kid throughout high school, does end up going to COS and studying carpentry.

For me, Bill is more than just an older brother. He's also a father figure. He's ten years older than I am but seems much older and smarter. I look at him as someone I can rely on and look up to. He's responsible for most of the outings we have as a family. Maybe he remembers what it's like to be a kid stuck at home with no way to get out and have any fun the way regular families do, so he makes every effort to include us in fun activities. If he sees that there's an Elvis double feature at the drive-in, he'll say, "Anybody want to go?"

Of course we want to go! A drive-in movie on a summer Saturday night? What could be better? We've been working all day, so we rush to shower and clean up. We pile into his cherry-red '57 Chevy. He spends all his spare money on it. He and Al are constantly under the hood. It does seem to break down a lot and require a great deal of work. We take our own snacks along because the snack bar is too expensive. On our way, we stop off at the A&W to pick up a gallon of root beer. To this day, I still associate A&W root beer with drive-ins.

The drive-in charges per head, so Bill pulls over a few blocks before we get there and three of us climb into the trunk. It's hot and stuffy, and we hold our breath so we don't make any noise when he pulls up to the booth. I'm always afraid I'll sneeze or cough and give us away.

"How many?" the attendant asks.

"Six," Bill tells him, not counting the three of us in the trunk, of course. He pays for six and we're in.

The minute he parks, all the kids in the front and back seats jump out and cluster around the trunk. Bill glances around to make sure the attendant isn't looking, then opens the trunk. We climb out and join the crowd with no one the wiser. We know this is cheating, but it's either this way or not at all. We pull out blankets and sit in and all around the car. We don't dare sit on the Chevy because we might scratch it. Bill's nice, but he'd probably get mad about that.

Bill also organizes the only trip that I remember us boys taking with Apa. When I'm about twelve, he convinces Apa to take us guys up into the Sierras. Apa makes all kinds of excuses about why he can't go, but he finally gives in, and Bill, Al, Mily, Domingo, Joe, and I pile into Bill's Chevy.

I'm excited because we hardly ever go up into the mountains. Bill's good about stopping frequently so we can enjoy the view. I can tell that Apa's enjoying himself for maybe one of the few times in his life. His face looks so relaxed, and he's really impressed by the giant redwoods. We all are because we find it hard to believe how old they are and how high they tower above our heads. I think about the fact that we live and work so close to such a beautiful area, and yet many of us never get to appreciate its majesty and beauty.

On the way home, we're all feeling relaxed, talking and rehashing what we saw, when—typically for all our family excursions—the brakes start acting up. We sweat the trip home, and Bill has to keep using the emergency brake to get us back.

He spends time with us when he could be with his girlfriend, Kitty. She's the first white person any of us have associated with on a personal basis and the first Anglo girlfriend to come into our house. Her mom, Lola, is the clerk at the store who didn't believe Joe and me the day we came in with the money he had stolen from Ama and buried for me to dig up. Sometimes Bill even takes us on his dates with Kitty, and she never acts annoyed.

One day when Mily, Joe, and I are riding around with Mercy in his truck, we spot Bill's Chevy out near the pool where we go through the "tube." Mercy drops us off and we join them. They're kissing, and Kitty blushes when she says hi to us. I can't tell if Bill wants our company or not, but they both act as if we're perfectly welcome. We tease them no end, and then after an hour or so, Mercy picks us up again and we leave them alone.

I always look forward to seeing Kitty. She's so nice, she has a soft voice, and she really seems interested in listening to my ideas and hearing about my desire to go to college. She believes in me. She tells me I'm smart and that I'll go a long way.

CHAPTER TWELVE

Darkness and Light

BEING IN HIGH SCHOOL IS EXCITING and challenging. I like belonging to my circle of new friends. But during the fall of my freshman year, I slowly sink into a dark period that I'm unable to shake. I don't realize I'm depressed. No one ever tells me that, and I've always thought that depressed people are crazy. I wake up every morning. I go out and do my chores with the animals. I catch the school bus to Redwood. The weather's cold and the fog is thick, but not thick enough to cause a fog delay. Too bad. I wish I could stay in bed longer. Maybe tomorrow. I trudge into French class. Madga says hello. Normally this would make my day, but today I'm barely able to mumble "Bonjour" back to her. I can't wait to get out of class. I need to escape.

My next class is algebra. It's on the other side of campus, a miserable walk on a cold day like today. I started off well in algebra, but as the school year progresses I start to slip. My brain can't seem to grasp the formulas. It's as if some barrier has been implanted in my brain and I can't think clearly anymore.

I dread what comes after algebra, a fifteen-minute break when our group gathers near the senior quad and we talk about the morning's events. I stay away again, as I have for the last week. I find a place out by the art building where I know my friends don't hang out, and I stay there until my next class. All I have to do is make it through one more day. Another day.

I can't fail. I need good grades if I'm going to get into college—if I make it that far. I have my doubts. I don't see myself living past high school. Why? I don't know. I'm in so much conflict and yet so detached that I feel as if I don't exist. I'm in a fog, drifting above everything below me. I escape into my schoolwork and withdraw more and more into myself. Although I go on functioning at school and manage to keep my grades up, I no longer have inner peace. Not that I've ever felt content, actually, but so far I've coped with whatever life's thrown at me. Now I find myself thinking more and more about the bad things I've endured and dreading the bad things that may yet come.

I envy my friends because they have the security of knowing that their parents will be there when they need them. It seems as if no matter where I go when my friends play or perform, I see involved parents. That's what normal, wholesome families do. The more I see what the norm is, the more resentful and envious I become, and the more I withdraw.

I feel isolated, without a foundation. Most people have their family, church, or friends for support. I don't have anyone. I lost my faith years ago. The Catholic Church didn't protect me from the abuse or the hunger. Ama and Apa hardly ever go to church, so why should I? Maybe my brothers and sisters would be there for me, except that I don't let them into my life anymore. They have enough problems of their own to cope with. How can I burden them with mine?

My friends are the only foundation I have, but I feel unworthy of being around them. I can't stop thinking, "I don't belong around these nice, clean, wholesome kids." I don't want to contaminate them with my ugliness. All the things that have happened to me make me unfit to be around them. I think they can look right into my soul and see how filthy it is.

I'm not sure why, but I know I'm facing some kind of identity crisis. I don't know who I am. I've never had "the conversation" with Frances—the one where I would say, "Why haven't you ever told us who our father is? Why do you treat us like nephews instead of your sons? You had five kids by the same man and you've let him be a complete mystery to us. Why?" I know that Al and Domingo haven't asked her either. We don't even talk about it among ourselves. What are we afraid of? I'm not sure.

I feel that maybe I would be better off not knowing my mother at all instead of her being right here in Goshen. Or if I'd never been born. I've gotten along fine without her all this time, so why is it bothering me so much now? I've also learned to live just fine without a father, or so I think until I see the parents of my friends and classmates looking so proud of them at open houses. I wish I could show off to my mom and dad, too, but Ama and Apa are too old to be there for me. Actually, they never went to any school events for my brothers or sisters, so I'm no different. But I yearn for someone to show they care—the way Eddy's parents are there for him.

Eddy's a big jock—a star football and basketball player. His mom always comes to the freshman team football games to root for him, and even though his dad works in the fields, he shows up at halftime. The other players' parents are also there cheering their kids on. I stay for the game because I'm third string for both football and basketball. When I see all those proud parents' faces and that even the parents of kids who aren't in the starting lineup are there, I wonder, where are mine? At home. They don't even know I have a game. I don't bother telling anyone anymore. I'll get a ride home with Eddy's folks. They're good about getting me back. If it weren't for them or the afterschool sports bus, I wouldn't consider playing sports.

I do get a taste of what it'd be like to be in a family like that at one basketball game when we're so far behind that the coach gives up on the game and decides to give the third string, including me, a chance for some real minutes. Somehow we get hot, and I make several baskets and steals. Eddy's parents are there and they cheer me on. I glory in the personal attention. I love it and wish my own parents were there so I could show off for them. That game is my day in the sun. (When we get to within several points of winning, the coach realizes he can win after all and puts the starters back in.)

I'm so aware of what's missing in my life that I often feel bothered when my friends or other students don't realize or appreciate how fortunate they are. One day, I overhear an Anglo girl complain to her friend, "My mom didn't let me go out to the movies Saturday afternoon! She told me I couldn't go until I cleaned up my room! I was really tired from the game and the dance Friday night and I didn't get up until noon and the movie started at two. She's so mean!"

"My mom's the same way!" her friend replies. "She makes me get up by eleven, and I have to make my bed! Can you believe that?"

As the two girls wander off, Pata comments, "Boy, are they spoiled! That's what rich girls do all the time. They don't realize how easy they have it. They're not poor like us."

What had my Friday night been like? I went to the game and the dance, since Eddy was my ride home. The game was fun because our group cheered him and our team on. I'm proud to be his friend because maybe his success and popularity will rub off on me, or at least I'll be somebody when I'm with him. But dances are another story. I'm a wallflower. When I'm standing next to Eddy, girls come by and say, "Hi, Eddy! You were so good tonight!" They mostly ignore me, but sometimes a girl is nice enough to say hi to me, too. Last night, two girls came along. Eddy asked one of them to dance, and off they went. The other girl looked annoyed that her friend had left her with me.

"Do you want to dance?" I asked awkwardly.

"No, I have to go. I see a friend I need to talk to." She hurried away. Then I saw one of the jocks stop her. They talked for a minute and then went onto the dance floor. I didn't ask anyone else. I just waited for Eddy to give me a ride home. And by nine o'clock on Saturday morning, while the two girls I had heard complaining were still fast asleep, I had gotten up at five and was picking oranges by six. By the end of the day, I was too tired to think of doing anything else. Besides, I didn't have the money to go out anyway. Not even to a movie.

One morning as I'm leaving algebra class, Amparo asks me, "Where were you all last week?" I can't say anything to her. My voice doesn't work. Every day that this depression goes on, I have a harder time managing to speak. She looks at me oddly. She's probably wondering if I'm mad at her or something. Maybe they're all wondering what my problem is, because it looks as if I'm avoiding them.

Well, I am. They're good friends, so I figure they must be talking about me and wondering why I act so moody at times, but I can't explain my feelings to them. I don't understand what I'm feeling myself. I refuse all their overtures of support because I feel that if I let them really know me, they won't want to be friends with me anymore. Sometimes Amparo comes over when I'm off sitting by myself by the art building. I've been tempted to open up to her because she seems to really care. But when she asks, "Are you doing okay?," I clam up and stare blankly into space until she gives up.

Sometimes I don't understand what's wrong with me. After all, I'm not the only kid I know whose family's living in poverty and who's going through stuff at home. Everyone else seems able to cope. Why can't I? Or maybe they're struggling just as much as I am, but I'm too overwhelmed to see it.

After an endless couple of weeks, I start to drag myself out of my funk. Slowly, I venture back to my friends. I feel ashamed of my behavior, but I can't give them any explanation. It's hard to get back into being with other people. I've gotten so used to my silence that my own voice sounds funny to me. My speech is soft and barely audible. I haven't lost my stutter, but I have learned to speak more slowly, and I don't have to repeat myself as often. No one makes a big deal about my absence. I wouldn't be able to handle that. The fact that they seem to take me in stride and let me slip back in as if I had never flaked out makes me feel better.

One day I'm sitting with the group. I'm almost back to normal. I buy my usual snack, a package of miniature powdered-sugar donuts.

Pata asks, "Can I have one?"

"Sure, but just one."

She pries out one donut. The white powder gets all over her hands. She takes a small bite and ends up with a cute little mustache on her upper lip. Then, with a devilish glance at me, she passes the package to Ernie.

"Hey, give those back!" I exclaim.

I grab for them, but it's too late. Ernie takes a donut and passes them to Magda, who's giggling. She makes a big show of taking one out very slowly, and then, putting on a grandiose manner, stuffing the whole thing into her mouth. Powdered sugar flies all over the place.

That leaves only three donuts. Magda gives one to Amparo. Only two left!

"I want one, too!" Elaine says. She grabs the second-to-last donut, then hands me the last one.

I pretend I'm mad and make a big deal about them taking my donuts, but inside I'm feeling pure ecstasy. The cloud that's been hanging over me lifts completely. They've done what no amount of money or therapy could've done. They've made me feel accepted. Even more importantly, they treat me no differently than they do each other. To me, being teased this way is proof that I belong, that I'm part of this group. And I do so want to belong.

I finally decide that if I've lived with my misery this long, I suppose I can go on living with it as long as I have to. I hang on to the only thing that keeps me going—college. That's the only way out of my dilemma. I may still be depressed, but at least I'll be in college. I can't see any way out of my sadness other than to keep on pretending I'm happy. Every few months, the dark feelings keep coming back. They're so strong that I have to disappear again. Eventually they go away, and I go back to being with my friends.

At home, no one notices.

CHAPTER THIRTEEN

Tennis with the Rich Kids

N THE SPRING OF MY FRESHMAN YEAR, Mr. Inamine, my PE instructor and the tennis coach, urges me to go out for tennis. I decide to try it, much to Coach Pitman's disgust. He wants me to keep running track and work on increasing my endurance for next year. When I show up for the first tennis practice, I'm in for serious culture shock. Most of the players are white and have been playing for years. They're not only white kids, they're the school's rich white kids. I've seen some of them in my classes, but I've never even spoken to them.

I'm going to be associating with kids who have known each other most of their lives and live in the richest neighborhood in Visalia. They're totally out of my reach socially. They belong to the country club. Their dads are the judges, lawyers, doctors, and city leaders in Visalia. Even the Goshen kids I think of as "rich" don't compare. Little do I know that the Visalia kids consider the Goshen kids "poor whites" and that the Goshen kids themselves are intimidated by the money and prestige that the tennis kids enjoy.

People like us never associate with people like them except when we have to get a lawyer because of drunk driving or domestic abuse, or when we have to go to court because of those charges, or when the doctors deliver one of our many babies. The only Goshen student I know who seems to mix with them is Eddy, maybe because of his athletic prowess.

It takes me no time at all to learn how much distance exists between them and me. I'm always overhearing conversations that prove it, such as when one player tells the others that his dad bought him a new racquet but he doesn't like it that much and is going to ask for another one. Meanwhile, I'm playing with a school racquet.

I also learn that however supportive my friends' parents are of them, the parents of the Anglo tennis kids are involved in every aspect of their lives. When I see these mothers and fathers in the stands, they have an air about them that I see only in the movies. They look at you as if you're not there, but when it comes to their kids they'll do anything they need to do. They have no qualms about complaining to Coach Inamine if they feel that their precious son isn't getting to play varsity or in singles. They say they'll hire a private coach to give their son lessons so he can play varsity next match. And the son looks on and acts as if this is a perfectly normal thing for his parents to do.

I'm very respectful to Mr. Inamine. That's one thing I've been taught at home—don't speak to your elders unless they speak to you first, and always treat them with respect. I do respect him because he takes time to give me specific instructions. I get the feeling that I'm a project of his and that the other players are a bit miffed.

But I'm an outsider. On the courts, they're very snobbish and essentially ignore me. I decide to quit, but when I go to tell Coach Inamine, I'm floored by his response. "I want you to stay and let me teach you how to play," he tells me. "I think you've got the potential to be a good player, and I'm sick and tired of coaching these rich, spoiled white kids. They don't know the meaning of hard work. I want to coach someone I'll enjoy teaching." I agree to stay.

Still, at a certain level, I realize I'm setting myself up for future turmoil. Something's driving me farther and farther away from the world I grew up in. Playing tennis means having to relate with a culture vastly different from anything I'm familiar with. I don't understand why I'm doing this. I'm already suffering from low self-esteem, yet here I am putting myself into a situation that's guaranteed to make me feel even more inadequate. The only bright spot is that Pata and Elaine also play, so at least they're around.

I listen silently as the tennis kids talk about the trips they've just taken and where their parents want to go next summer. I hear about New York, Europe, Hawaii, and going to San Francisco or Los Angeles for football games, about tennis camp in Monterey, and about playing golf at Pebble Beach.

I realize how much I'm missing, how little I really have. I don't take part in their conversations. I have nothing to contribute. The only trip I've ever taken was to that Dodgers game after my eighth-grade graduation, and that was only to Los Angeles. I do learn that Rotary is a very exclusive club and that most of the tennis kids' fathers are members. The disparities between us are amazing and sad. How is it possible that in the America of the late 1960s, with all the advances that have been made in our society, I and people like me can be made to feel so unequal? So beneath contempt?

I sometimes think about what I would say if one of them ever asked me about my plans for the summer. I would reply, "Work, doing irrigating." But they don't ask because they don't really care. Once in a while, someone throws a question my way, but I feel that my answer is immaterial because they just look past my shoulder and nod. I know they aren't listening.

What I want to tell them is, "I'll be working all summer, starting the day after school lets out. I'll work twelve hours a day, seven days a week, for a dollar and seventy-five cents an hour until the day before school starts again. My family will let me keep a little of the money I earn so I can pay for all my own school expenses for the year."

One day, one of the boys overhears me telling Pata something about an incident that happened in the grape fields and chimes in, "I picked grapes a couple of years ago. My uncle has a winery, and when we went to visit, my dad had us go out and work for an afternoon. It was fun picking my own grapes. I didn't think it was so hard." I hate condescending comments like that. To work one afternoon for your uncle and think you know anything about working in the fields burns me up. I wish that he and I could trade places for just one week.

I fantasize about this quite a bit. I know that my only way out is by getting into college. Someday, I think, if I'm lucky and manage to improve my economic situation, maybe I'll be able to experience what their lives are like.

During the summer between my freshman and sophomore year, I enroll in summer school so I can get some of my fall classes out of the way. I don't know why Ama and Apa are willing to let me out of field work, but they do. I'm excited, and most of friends are going too. It's one of the easiest, nicest summers I ever have because all I have to do for that six weeks is attend classes for four hours a day.

Of course, a lot of the other students complain about wasting all summer in class when they could be home lounging around the pool or going off to their families' beach homes or mountain cabins. The temperature soars to over one hundred degrees every day and the school has no air conditioning, so everyone is irritable, not just because of the heat, but also because they're in school. I'm in heaven. I'm indoors in the shade and not out in the fields. What could be better?

Except for the jerk who sits behind me and decides to pick on me. James is a big, burly lineman. Every day he kicks my chair. He outweighs me by a hundred pounds, so I try to ignore him. But the more he harasses me, while his friends egg him on by snickering, the more I feel I probably should have spent the summer working rather than putting up with this humiliation.

One day, I've had enough. I turn around. "Cut it out!" I tell him. He's obviously shocked that I've had the courage to confront him, and he actually stops. His friends seem to be impressed, too. A few days later, my stock with them goes up even more after the teacher warns another group of bratty white kids who are acting disruptive to stop, or she'll make everyone stay after class. Sure enough, they ignore her warnings, and when the bell rings to dismiss us for the day, she announces that we all have to sit there for twenty minutes as punishment. We all yell that we shouldn't be punished for their bad behavior, but she tells us that the whole class has to suffer to teach them a lesson.

Being kept late means I'll miss my bus back to Goshen. That means no ride home, and I can't call anyone to get me. I surprise even myself by standing up and telling her, "I don't think it's fair for all of us to be punished, and I'm not going to miss my bus because of some idiots." I then walk out, with most of my classmates following suit. For some reason, I don't get into trouble for that, and for the rest of my high school years, James and his friends never pick on me again.

After summer school ends, I go back to irrigating with Mercy. This time I start getting paid by the hour. I make the same wage he does, a dollar and seventy-five cents an hour. I've been working all my life, but until now I've never seen any of the money I've earned. I'm thrilled to be getting an actual paycheck with my name on it. We used to get one check for the whole family's work, and it was always made out to Apa or even to Rosa. But I'm shocked when my first check is less than I expected. No one ever told me about taxes. Still, even though I have to give most of it to Ama, it feels like a lot of money.

By now, all of us kids are in our teens or married. We have jobs and essentially pay rent and board (not that she gives us a bill, but if we try to hold on to more of our money, she lays a guilt trip on us).

As we start bringing home more money, Ama lets us keep a little more, but if we run out, we're stuck. We know she won't give us anything back, so we borrow from each other. If Elia or Lily or I don't have work and run out, we can go to Mily or Domingo or Al. With their carpentry skills, they almost always have work.

I can't even think about dating, even though I'd like to ask someone out to the drive-in, because first I need a car, and second I need money. I have to save whatever Ama lets me keep so I can pay for my school expenses. This means pinching pennies and budgeting so my money will last all year. I can only buy essentials. When my gang wants to go out for pizza or to a movie, I make an excuse to get out of going. I would love to join them, but that would mean giving up something else, and the only thing I could skip would be lunch—that's how tight money is for me.

I really resent those white kids and the soft lives they lead.

CHAPTER FOURTEEN

Sophomore–
Junior Blur

MY SOPHOMORE AND JUNIOR years go by in a blur, punctuated by summers spent irrigating. In my sophomore year, I go back to running cross-country, and I continue playing tennis after the running season's over. Coach Inamine keeps telling me that I can get good if I practice and play weekend tournaments. "I can't," I reply. "I have to work."

"I'm sorry to hear it," he sighs. "You have the potential, but you have to put in the time practicing."

Coach Pitman is excited to have me back. He works on getting me to live up to the potential he sees in me. He lets me run varsity in our first match, and I think he hopes that the competition will bring out the desire in me. I do better than most of the runners from the other school, but I'm no match against my teammates.

"You need to have more desire if you want to keep on running varsity," he tells me. His disappointment's obvious, but I don't care. I'm going through the motions, but my mind isn't there. I get involved in school activities like the Rally Club, the French Club, and so on. I run cross-country but have no heart for it. As we near the finish line and it's time to kick into high gear and I have a chance to finish in the top three, I can't find that extra boost, and I fade. I want to win. I know I've trained hard enough to win. In the past, I would never have let anyone get the best of me if I felt I was the better man. But now I don't know how to make myself care. The blue moods come on more and more frequently. I learn to hide them better. I sit with my friends and joke around and join in their laughter, but I feel like giving up on everything because I'm not going to amount to anything anyway.

I don't normally identify with music, but at some point in high school the Smokey Robinson and the Miracles song "Tears of a Clown" reaches me. I listen to it whenever I hear it on the radio because it's about a guy who feels he has to keep a clown's happy smile on his face even though he's crying inside. I'm trapped in three different worlds. I can't stay in my family's world because I know it'll destroy me, but I'm not part of my friends' world. And I certainly don't belong with the rich kids.

So I accomplish nothing special in cross-country or tennis. I don't live up to Coach Pitman's or Mr. Inamine's expectations. I like tennis but I can't tolerate the other players. I only stay with it because I keep hoping to break through and show Mr. Inamine that he was right about me.

I don't know why this is happening to me again. No one's said anything to make me feel inferior. Why am I feeling dejected? I have an overwhelming longing to let my sadness flow out of me, but instead I play the role of happy, well-rounded, college-prep student. I keep going on. My friends are my only anchor, and they don't even know how much I need them. Every time they show me a kind gesture or include me in an outing, I feel worthwhile. When I sit with them at football and basketball games, I'm part of something.

I know I can't explain my feelings to anyone, so I don't even try. I close myself off from my friends again. I try to go on hanging out with them, but even though I laugh and joke, I feel like crying. Sometimes when they start complaining about this and that, I get too angry to want to be around them. I have to take off by myself until I can get a grip on my feelings. Then I wonder whether my anger's due to my inability to cope. Maybe it doesn't have anything to do with what they're complaining about. I'm sure that other kids, like the *vatos*, are having the same problems I am. I guess they're coping by quitting school or by not bothering to study or care.

After a while, I start feeling that no one will blame me if I don't make it into college after all. They'll just say, "Well, what did you expect, considering the way he was raised? Poor and mixed up, no father or mother . . . " The problem is, I care too much. I want to prove I can make it. I want to show Mr. Moss that he was wrong about me. I want to make something of myself for those teachers who showed me they cared. If I quit, I'll be just another promising Mexican kid who ends up disappointing them. "We thought he had potential," they'll say. "But he folded when the going got tough."

I don't want to fold. If I give up, I'll be giving up for everyone who ever believed in me. I feel the need to show that with the right input and motivation, kids like me, and kids like Joe, have as much ability as anyone else.

Even though Mr. Moss realizes that I'm not going to fail my college prep courses, he makes no effort to spur me on, and he still refuses to give me any information except to send me to the career desk at the library. I fill out the questionnaires, and, although it isn't clear what career would be best for me, the results show that I can be anything I want and that I have the aptitude to attempt any field. I don't go to him for advice anymore.

However, I do find a woman who is 100 percent behind me. Her name is Pat and her daughter, Paula, is in my class. Pat works at the school district office. I don't really know what her job is. I only know that when I go in to see her, she always has time for me. She has a college education and is one of the few Mexican role models I have. She's also the only person I can begin to share my feelings with. When I tell her about my struggles and that every time I bring up going to college Ama tells me I can't go, she replies, "Nonsense! Of course you'll go to college!" She says she'll speak to my parents on my behalf, but she doesn't understand that they're totally ignorant of what an education can do for you. When I tell her how lousy and lonely I feel, she says that if things get really bad, she'll be there for me. She is the first adult I've known since grade school whom I really believe in and begin to trust.

Actually I don't know any other Mexicans with a degree other than Frank Padilla, the assistant cross-country coach, and Manuel Encinas, a Spanish teacher. I'm not taking Spanish, so I have no contact with Mr. Encinas. I do have some contact with Mr. Padilla, and he's a nice man but, as with Mr. Inamine, I don't talk with him. Maybe it's because they're men, and I don't know how to relate to men as father figures. Except for Apa, who's too old to do fatherly activities, I have no one who even comes close to a father.

Mr. Inamine is great, but I can't tell him my troubles. It isn't that he wouldn't try to help. He has tried before, telling me that I need to enter weekend tennis tournaments to get better and that he'd be willing to give me private lessons for free if my parents would let me off work. They don't even know that I'm playing tennis after school, and as long as it doesn't interfere with working, they don't care. Free lessons would be a big help because I would like to get better and to show those rich kids how good a poor Mexican kid can be, given half a chance, but I have to thank him for his offer and decline. I've told him about my having to work all the time, but I'm not sure he understands how much Ama and Apa depend on me to make my share of the money.

Even though I'm mad at them for not allowing me to enjoy my high school experience in its totality—the games and going out to movies with friends on Saturday afternoon and just hanging out with them—I know where they're coming from. We've experienced so many hard years, and I don't want any more of them if I can help it. I don't want to see the defeated look on Apa's face again. He has aged so much in the last year, and I know that working in the fields his whole life has taken its toll. I want to succeed and make his last years as comfortable as I can. He's one of the reasons I can't give in to my despair. I have to fight it or else I'll fail in my resolve for him.

I spend the summer between my sophomore and junior years irrigating with Mercy. Sam is well aware of Mercy's love of napping and has made numerous attempts to catch him in the act. When I've worked with Mercy before, part of my job was always to look out for Sam while Mercy napped in one of his many hiding places. One morning after Sam has finished his morning rounds and driven off, and we've finished our morning work, Mercy tells me, "I haven't been over to that grove of trees east of Goshen for a while. Sam won't think to look there." We take off, secure in the knowledge that Sam has already come by and will be none the wiser if we catch an hour's sleep.

But as we're driving on the dirt road that separates a field of corn six or seven feet tall from another one planted with cotton, Mercy comes to a sudden stop. Sam is waiting at the end of the cornfield. He and Sam are face to face and only a few feet apart. Mercy looks taken aback. Sam, on the other hand, just looks amused.

"Where are you headed?" he asks Mercy.

Mercy stammers, "I was going to go look for you and ask you if we can leave twenty minutes early today because Raymond here needs to get to a meeting about college." This is an outright lie, but I admire his ability to come up with that line so quickly. Only a couple of days ago, I told him I had seen a flyer a few months ago announcing the annual fall "college night" held in Visalia. I planned to go because the only information my counselor, Mr. Moss, gave me was to send me to the career desk at the library.

"So you want to go to college?" Sam asks me. He sounds surprised and rather doubtful, probably because in all his years of working with many Mexicans and Okies, not a one has ever finished high school, much less gone to college.

"Yes," I say meekly.

I've been uncomfortable around Sam ever since I was four and started helping Apa irrigate. He's been with the Shannon Ranch for many years. I don't know how old he is. He's lanky and tall and wears the same hat year after year. His face is ruddy, with wrinkles that keep getting deeper and deeper. His voice is gruff, as if he's smoked for years, though I've never seen him with a cigarette. I can never tell whether he's upset or not because his face doesn't change expressions unless he's pissed off (which he was the following year when Eddy and I got into trouble on our first day of work and had to shut down the pump).

"What college d'you want to go to?"

I hesitate. "I like USC and UCLA."

"Those are tough schools to get into." His comment catches me by surprise. I didn't think he knew anything about colleges, but I actually know nothing about him. He never volunteers any information, and I'd be afraid to ask him. I only want him to leave us alone.

Finally he tells us, "Sure, go ahead and leave early. Just make sure all the work is done."

⚔

The only high point of my sophomore and junior years is earning my letter jacket for cross-country in my junior year, although this almost doesn't happen. At the start of that year, I'm running so well that I make varsity. I'm the last one Coach Pitman names to the team, but I make it and I'm proud of it. Also, I can list it on my college application. We have such a good team that in most cases we run right over our opponents. Even as their last man, I'm better than their first, so we never have any real competition. My teammates let me catch up with them so we can all cross the finish line together. Redwood has a six-year history of not being defeated, and we don't want to be the first squad to lose.

Then I come down hurt after the fifth race of the season. I can't run anymore because the fronts of my legs are hurting right below my knees. I don't know what it is and I don't tell my coaches for fear of losing my varsity position, but they find out when I can't catch up with the team so we can cross the finish line in a group.

When Coach Pitman comes over to me one day and asks me if I'm having problems with my knees, I have to admit I am. I'm limping so badly that I don't even bother lying about it. It's due to picking walnuts. After the family finishes the grape harvest each year, we move on to walnuts. In the fall, the growers knock them out of the trees with machines, and we spend all day kneeling on the damp ground gathering them up. I've been picking walnuts since I was five or six, along with all the other crops we worked on, so by now my knees have been through ten years of abuse. I've known all along that I shouldn't be stressing them by running because they ache all the time.

But I want my blue-and-white letter jacket. Once I get it, the jocks and the other students will see me as a real person and not as a nobody. All the rich kids have already earned theirs as sophomores. It wasn't hard for them because they've had the luxury of playing tennis and getting private lessons ever since they were kids. I have to admit they're good, but I wonder how they'd do if they ever had to face some real competition. I know that if those of us who grew up poor were given the same advantages, we could beat the pants off them.

In tennis, when we run to build up our endurance, I can lap them, and when the weather's hot they quit practicing before Coach Inamine wants them to, and he can't make them go back out. Sometimes he and I are the only ones out on the court. Heat doesn't bother me at all.

They marvel at my ability to withstand the 105-degree heat. Hell, I work in temperatures higher than that. Here, on the courts, I have water and shade whenever I need it, so playing tennis is a piece of cake.

"It could be shin splints," Coach Pitman tells me. "I think you'd better lay off running and see if you get better." I take him at his word. After all, he's been coaching for years and has seen shin splints before. But when he suggests that I get checked out by a doctor, I know that's not an option. Even though I can hardly walk across campus and my legs are killing me by the time I get to my classrooms, I can't think about seeing a doctor if I can still walk and get around. The bottom line is, we don't have the money. Our family has Medi-Cal, a medical care program for poor families like ours, but I'm too ashamed to admit I need it, so I suffer instead.

Thinking about Medi-Cal reminds me of other things about being poor, like the fact that I'm eligible for our school's free lunch program, too, but I'm not going to take advantage of it. I've heard other students make fun of the kids who do. They call them "freeloaders" and add contemptuously, "They're as bad as people on welfare." I never tell anyone, not even my friends, that we've sometimes had to apply for welfare and food stamps to make it through the winters. I'm too ashamed. I remember hating going to the grocery store with Ama when she pulls out her food stamps. I once hear a woman behind us groan about having to wait behind "these welfare people." "After all," she comments loudly, so we're sure to hear her, as she takes out her checkbook. "I'm paying with my *own* money."

I'm determined to never accept assistance from anyone again if I can help it.

⚡

I follow Coach Pitman's advice and drop out of varsity. He replaces me with a sophomore "phenom" named Juan. This is hard to take, but after about a month, my knees are so much better that I decide to start running again and to compete in the seven-school East Yosemite League championships at Monache High School. Unfortunately, I'm in the junior varsity division along with the rest of the kids who can't make it into varsity. In my race, I start off tentatively and linger toward the back. I'm not really expecting much from my knees, and I don't think I'll have much endurance because I haven't been practicing.

But the closer we get to the finish line, the more I realize that my knees are feeling strong. I'm not feeling any fatigue. I move up to the middle of the pack. I pass them one by one. Now all I'm expecting of myself is to finish respectably. I start running a little faster. The lead runners are only about two hundred yards ahead of me. We're nearing the end of the race and there's not much distance left, so I pick up my pace even more. I'm feeling something I haven't felt in a long time—the desire to win. The heart. Finally! It's been so long since I've felt this good! Has my enforced inactivity had a positive effect on me emotionally?

I start my sprint about a quarter-mile from the finish line. Normally this is suicide because I can't hold this pace for long. But today I have wings. I pass all the runners but the leader, and I'm gaining on him with every step. The yellow tape is flapping in the breeze just ahead. . . . I give one last push. . . . The finish line is only yards away. . . . He can feel me breathing down his neck as I eat up the yards behind him. I lunge toward the yellow tape . . . and come up short by one yard.

My second-place showing and the return of my heart makes Coach Pitman put me back on varsity for the Valley finals, where more than three dozen schools compete. This means I'm going to get my letter and my jacket. But my desire and emotional high don't last. The Monache race turns out to have been the best day of my junior year. My blues return, and in the finals I end up finishing way back in the sixties. For us to win, I needed to be in the top fifty. Afterward, Coach Pitman comes over to me. "I blame you for losing us the championship," he tells me.

I don't know what to say. I feel terrible that I didn't do better for my teammates. I take the loss personally, which only makes me feel more miserable. But when I feel lousy, there's is nothing I can do, no matter how much I want to or how hard I try. I'm helpless in the face of my depression. I don't know how to cope. I have no escape avenue and no one I can talk to.

We have our team party the week after the last race, where we won the league championship despite our losing Monache. I don't know if I'll get my letter since my knees kept me from running varsity for part of the season. I also don't know if Coach Pitman is going to hold my poor performance at Monache against me. I couldn't help getting injured. I hope he remembers that.

The party is at Steve's house. He's the only white senior on varsity. It's a huge ranch house out in the country. His parents supply the cake, which has "League Champions" written on it to celebrate our winning the league title again. When Coach Pitman announces the awards, Steve gets MVP for being our top runner and the captain. Juan gets best sophomore. I'm waiting to hear who's getting their letter. Then come the names of the entire varsity—Steve, Ernie, Adolph, Adolph's cousin Al, and Juan. That makes five. My name isn't called out. I try not to show my disappointment, but I feel like shit.

But then he announces, "Before we wind this down, I've got one more letter to give out. Due to injuries, Raymond had to step down from varsity for much of the spring. He turns to me and says, "I polled the team, and they voted to grant you a letter because of your dedication and perseverance." I'm thrilled as I thank him and the team. I buy my jacket as soon as I can and wear it proudly—except that the weather gets too hot a few days later, and I have to wait for my senior year to wear it again.

The end of my junior year takes me by surprise. It's spring 1971, and I find it hard to grasp that I'm so close to finishing high school. My thoughts are still focused on college, but I can't seem to see beyond high school. Although in some ways I'm preparing for the next phase of my life, I'm afraid of the future. I don't want to plan for it or even think about it. I know I want to do something to make Apa proud of me. He's in his seventies now, and he may die before I get the chance.

I don't understand what's going on in my brain. I'm full of contradictions. I'm haunted by thoughts and fears of death. I don't seriously think of killing myself, but I'm so sad so much of the time that I assume my depression will kill me. I can't seem to imagine any kind of future life for myself, but at the same time I can't let go of the goal of college either. So I need to prepare for it just in case I survive.

I've been preparing for the Scholastic Aptitude Test all during my junior year. Now the time is finally here. I plan to take it a couple of times because only my highest score will count, and I want to maximize my chances of getting into the better colleges.

I have to do well. I don't want to attend COS. I want to get away from here. I've always thought that USC or UCLA would be great schools, but my only reasons are that I'm a football fan and they're always among the top college teams. I also dream of Harvard or Stanford, but they're totally out of my reach. I'm not even going to apply to either of them. Besides, top schools like these demand A-plus averages and great SATs. My freshman and sophomore years, I was getting As and B-pluses, but now my grade averages are down to the B and B-plus range. I know that even though college admissions people will take my family situation and financial need into account, that probably won't be enough to offset my less-than-outstanding grades or SAT scores. Plus, I figure I'm not going to ace the SATs. I have too much trouble understanding the subject matter, especially math, although I do manage to get by with a C+ in Algebra 2.

On SAT day, I'm so nervous that I get up earlier than usual. I have to be at COS by ten-thirty to sign in and have my identification checked. The test starts at eleven. Ama's going to drive me. I've been reminding her all week so she won't forget, but when she gets up she tells me she has to run out to see her sister first.

"Relax!" she tells me. "We'll have plenty of time!" But I'm concerned because she's forgotten about me before, like the chilly winter night when I was working on a project at the library and she was supposed to pick me up after the library closed at eight. She didn't show up. I waited in the cold for twenty minutes and then called her. "Oh, *mijo*, I forgot!" she said. "I'll be right there!" I knew this meant at least a thirty-minute wait. So I sat on the cold concrete bench in the dark and wished I still had my warm winter jacket. I had bought a nice new one at the beginning of winter with some of my irrigating money. The first day I wore it, it disappeared from my locker. Several days later I saw one of the *vatos* leaning against the wall wearing it. There was nothing I could do. Confronting him would have been dangerous, and reporting the theft, useless. I didn't have the money to buy another one.

By ten-thirty in the morning, I'm frantic. Ama's still not back. When she finally drives up, I tear out to the car yelling, "We've got to leave right now! Or they won't let me take the test!" She doesn't say anything about why she was so late.

When we get to COS, luckily I know which building to go to. The moment she pulls up, I take off running. It's already five minutes to eleven. What if I'm so late that they won't let me in the door? I get to the room. Several students are still in line. I slip in right behind them. As I find a seat and sit down, the wall clock shows one minute to the hour. I'm sweating. My heart is racing. And I'm pissed off at Ama for not realizing what this means for my future.

After it's over, I know I've blown it. I can feel it. I didn't know anything, and I had to guess at a lot of the answers. At least it didn't cost me anything because I qualified for a fee exemption—one good thing about being poor. I'll have to try again in the fall, and those results will have to count. I didn't know that some kids could buy study materials and sample tests or take SAT prep courses, and I wouldn't have been able to afford them anyway.

I decide I'm never going to rely on Ama for anything again. Sometimes I wonder whether she's deliberately trying to sabotage me. Maybe she just doesn't realize the importance of education to us kids. It doesn't matter. Next time, I'll ride my bike from Goshen if I have to. This is my one chance to change the course of my life. I am not going to allow her to screw me up again. I am not going to take any more chances. From now on, my future will rest solely on my own resources.

CHAPTER FIFTEEN

Irrigator Again

SEVERAL WEEKS BEFORE WE FINISH our junior year, Eddy and I have already secured our summer jobs. Thanks to Apa's and Eddy's dad's connections, Sam offers us a job working together. We've always worked as helpers but we've never been in charge of "our own waters," the term we use to describe the areas we're responsible for. We'll have our own truck and be our own bosses.

I've always thought, given the chance, I could do a better job of irrigating than Mercy does. I don't think it takes much effort to get the water from one place to another. Since Eddy and I consider ourselves fairly bright, we're already calculating all the free time we'll have. Of course, we'll have to do the usual six-to-six routine, but we've only been assigned three fields, so the time in between will be all ours. When he picks me up in the work truck on our first morning of work, we congratulate ourselves again on what an easy summer we're going to have. How wrong we turn out to be.

We reach Traver, which is only seven miles north of Goshen, in less than twenty minutes. We could take Highway 99, which is faster, but we prefer the frontage road that runs alongside it because the truck we're using isn't freeway-worthy and we don't want to risk getting a ticket.

I was twelve the first time I drove the 99, and that was by accident one day during grape harvest season when we were hired to go work in Kingsburg. By this time, the older guys in the family had other jobs and weren't working with the rest of us anymore. We had an old yellow wood-paneled Jeep that looked like a Woodie station wagon but a bit higher. The girls had driver's licenses but couldn't drive a stick shift, and Apa was no longer driving.

So he told me to drive. I wasn't tall enough to see over the steering wheel, so I ran into the house and grabbed some pillows. As I backed out of the driveway, Apa reminded me to turn on the headlights. So far, I had only driven during daylight, and the sun wasn't up yet.

When I reached the left turn that leads onto the 99, I had to wait for a car that was coming from the opposite direction, and when I tried to turn, I stalled out. This was embarrassing because I'd just been bragging to Joe about how I was more responsible than he was and that was why Apa asked me to drive. I looked in the rearview mirror and could see him laughing at me. I got the Jeep going again, got onto the 99, and merged with the traffic. It was so early that there were very few cars. The only vehicles out were other farmworker cars and big trucks.

I was driving very carefully, and it occurred to me that I probably looked just like Apa, with my hands gripping the wheel at the ten and two positions and my head as far over the steering wheel as I could get. Massive trucks kept barreling down on me, looming larger and larger until they appeared to fill the mirror and were right on top of me. At the last moment, just when it seemed that they were going to crash into me, the truck drivers would suddenly honk their earsplitting horns and veer around to pass us. I was scared to death.

Everyone except Apa had fallen asleep. I felt put out because I could have been napping, too, if I hadn't been driving, and that I should have been getting paid extra or allowed to sleep later, but I knew I wasn't going to get any extra rewards for my efforts behind the wheel.

I got us to Kingsburg without any problems—but right before I reached the exit, a state highway patrol car rolled up behind me. He lingered there for what felt like forever, then drove up alongside us on my left, and looked me over. I noticed this out of the corner of my eye—I didn't dare make eye contact with him. After a moment, with a slight salute, he speeded up and drove on. He had to have known that I was underage and didn't have a license, but he let me off the hook. And in so doing, he did more than he would ever know. I never developed the fear of police that so many Mexicans like me feel. And my trust in the police was reinforced two years later when I graduated from eighth grade and those two white officers drove me to the awards ceremony in Visalia.

We reach our first plot of land at six-fifteen, just as the sun is popping up over the mountains to the east. The dawn colors and the majestic peaks captivate me, and I'm glad I'm up to witness the spectacular view.

We know that we need to get started by blocking the ditch about a hundred yards past the area where we're irrigating, the way we've seen Apa and Eddy's dad do it. Eddy raises the metal block above his head and slams it down, but it goes in at an angle. When I laugh at his feeble attempt, he tells me that if I think I can do better, I should go ahead and try. Sure enough, I get it up and over my head, but I overdo it and it falls behind me. We both crack up, but this is the first inkling we have that this job might not be the cakewalk we've been envisioning.

It takes us quite a while to set the block. It never seemed to take this long before. But once that's done, we can set the siphon pipes, an easy job. We calculate that we need about a hundred or so for this plot. We haven't turned the pump on yet, so no water is flowing into the ditch. We double-check. The pipes are set, the block is secure (as best as we know how), and everything looks in place. With great ceremony, we go over to the pump and push the big red button. Water cascades out of the huge pipe and flows down the ditch, filling it slowly. We take our places at each end and wait for the water to rise high enough that we can dunk the ends of the pipes and create the suction that will start the water siphoning into the rows. We accomplish this very quickly and efficiently, stand back to admire our work, and wait in the truck for a while to make sure we haven't miscalculated.

Just as we start to drive to the next plot, I notice a slight leak around the metal block—a potential disaster. We get out of the truck, shovel more dirt around the block, and tamp it down. Okay, now things look fine. Except that the water level has dropped and the pipes have stopped drawing water. We realize that the water level is going down too fast because we set too many pipes. No problem. We simply pull some pipes off the rows. Then we sit and wait just in case something else goes wrong.

By now it's almost eight and we haven't even finished our first section. The water rises to the proper level—but then it keeps rising because we took off too many pipes. We realize that we need somewhere between ninety and 105 pipes. We add seven more pipes and keep a close eye on the mark the rising water has left, making sure it stays level. We've done it! We've achieved equilibrium! But it's already eight-fifteen and we're far behind schedule.

Sam pulls up right as we're leaving. He saunters over to the truck and we get out. "Looks like you two are doing very well," he says. "Good job. Looks like everything's flowing smoothly."

We both thank him, but then he continues, "Did you have any trouble with the alfalfa or corn acreage?"

"We had some trouble getting this one going and haven't been to the others yet," Eddy replies.

Sam laughs. "You two better get on the ball! Otherwise you'll be here until dark!" This isn't funny to us, and we start to wonder if he's right. We're supposed to stop at six p.m., and it doesn't get dark until eight-thirty or so. There's no way we're going to be here that late! Sam says he'll stop back later. Then he leaves to check on Mercy and the others.

On our next field, we're feeling a little less confident. You'd think we had learned our lesson, but this pump is bigger and we have no idea how much water it should pump out. We figure that since it's bigger, we should set about 120 pipes. We make sure that the block is firmly in place by shoveling more dirt around it and stomping it down as hard as we can. Then we push the pump button. The water level rises. We start the siphon pipes and marvel at how well everything's going. It's nine-thirty. If we were still helpers, by now we would be sitting under a tree having our snack and anticipating lunch.

We keep a close eye on the water level, and the instant we see it change, we take some pipes off. But we take off too many and have to put some back on, then take more off. We play this game with the ebb and flow of the ditch but can't seem to get it just right. We can't figure out the formula, and our nerves are starting to get raw. This is not the fun time we were imagining only this morning.

Now it's ten-twenty and we still have another plot to handle. Plus we have to go back and check the first one before lunch. Fortunately, the block is working perfectly—until we see the water level suddenly drop. We check the block. It looks fine. There's no water going past on the other side. But when we look around where the pump is, we see that a damned gopher has dug a hole through the ditch all the way to the crop side, and the force of the water is making it bigger by the minute. By the time we run to our truck and grab our shovels, part of the ditch wall collapses and the water floods into the rows, ripping plants from their roots. We rush to bridge the gap by shoveling mud and dirt onto both sides of the hole, hoping to create a solid base that we can build on to close the breach. But as quickly as we shovel mud in, the water washes it away. Screaming and cursing, we work feverishly—and get nowhere. The break keeps getting bigger and more out of control. It's now eleven. We may as well kiss our break goodbye. And lunch, too, for that matter.

There's only one thing to do—turn off the pump. This is our last alternative, and no irrigator ever wants to resort to it. In Sam's eyes, turning off the pump is almost a crime, and we know that he's going to make our lives miserable. We know we're going to be in for three visits a day from him, with sarcastic remarks every time he comes around.

We have no choice. We turn off the pump and start filling the four-foot-long break in the ditch, which is about six feet wide and three feet deep. There's a large, fan-like area where corn plants were uprooted by the rushing water. It looks as if they were hit by a flash flood. They won't recover. This area will remain this way while the rest of the corn plants grow around it, a constant reminder of our failure on our first day of work. We can be sure that Sam will comment on it every time he sees it, and that he'll also let us know how much our mistake has cost the ranch.

When Mercy, who's working about seven miles east of us, hears about our misadventure from Sam, he comes over on his lunch break to see the damage for himself. He cracks up watching our futile attempts to correct the damage, but to our surprise gets out of his truck and pitches in. When we finish, he restarts the pump and helps us get everything going again. Just like that, the pipes start drawing water into the fields and the water in the ditch stays at an even level. It's picture-perfect, with the orderly rows of foot-tall corn running all the way to the other end of the field, the water trickling down every row at the same speed, and the thirsty ground soaking up its first taste of water since the spring rains. In that moment, I feel good about doing this work, and Eddy and I forget our troubles and bask in our accomplishment.

When Mercy asks us if we want to join him for lunch—it's already noon—we have to confess that we haven't finished our morning rounds yet. "What the hell have you two been doing all morning?" he scoffs. "I finished my parcels two hours ago and I'm all by myself." As we tell him about our various ordeals, he listens with a smirk on his face. He knows that we think we're smarter than he is, but on his turf we're the idiots. We're surprised when he offers to help take care of the cotton section so we can get caught up, because he's famous for his long lunch breaks and his naps afterward.

Eddy and I head for the cotton field while Mercy drives to the store in Traver to pick up a couple of sodas for us. "Give me some money and I'll be right back," he says. He's never been generous, and I guess that with three kids he isn't going to start now. We hoped he would stay and help us finish up the morning, but he has saved us a lot of time.

We have no confidence left, and we approach our next challenge warily—only to discover that when this ditch was dug, the driver didn't plow all the way. There's a massive four-foot-high dirt mound between the ditch and the pump. We're going to have to dig a trench so the water from the pump can reach the ditch unimpeded. The plus side is that we'll only have to dig down less than three feet, until the mound is lower than the level of the ditch, because the force of the water will push the rest of the dirt out of the way. The downside is that the mound is ten feet long. This is going to take a lot of digging, and it's well over one hundred degrees. We're almost at our breaking point, and we're barely halfway through our workday.

We see a plume of dirt rising behind Mercy's truck as he returns. At least we hope it's Mercy. If it's Sam, he may just fire us. Even though I'm having second thoughts about this lousy job, I have no other options. Thank goodness, it's Mercy. When we explain what we've been doing, he explodes. "Bastard!" he exclaims. "I've been through that kind of thing myself. That damned guy is damned lazy! Just to save himself a couple of minutes, he let the plow drag up. He doesn't care that it'll make the ditch block up because he doesn't have to unplug it!"

Unfortunately, he can't stay and help us after all. He gives us our sodas and drives off (without giving us our change). We wolf down our lunch tacos and guzzle our cold, refreshing sodas. So much for our thinking we would be able to have a leisurely lunch under a nice oak tree, followed by some time to sit and relax, and maybe even take a nap or a dip in the canal. Instead, it's already one in the afternoon and we have work to do that we should have finished by ten or so.

By now, we have no more illusions that this work is going to be easy, so when it isn't, we're not surprised. Everything is twice as hard and is taking twice a long as we thought it would. But to our shock, this next parcel goes very well. By now, we're so gun-shy that we don't want to move on because we're afraid that it we turn our backs, something will bite us on the ass.

What's more, Eddy and I aren't very happy with each other because we each thought the other one knew more than we did. His bragging had led me to believe that he was more experienced. The only reason I agreed to work with him was because he convinced me that we would have a lot of fun. He told me that his dad left him on his own a lot and that he did things by himself while his dad went on to another field. Obviously, this wasn't true because I can tell by watching him that he doesn't know much. I should have realized that his dad wouldn't have let him work on his own.

But Eddy has a bone to pick with me as well. "Didn't you work with Mercy all the time?" he says. "I was counting on you, since you've been doing this all your life."

"Yeah, but I was always just the help. I did what I was told to do. I never had to make any decisions. . . . I am sure when Apa and Mercy first started, they had problems, too."

"In that case, we're fucked," Eddy replies.

We finally finish our morning work at two in the afternoon. There's no time to relax or take a break. We have to go back and check the first parcel. When everything's in order, each parcel has water flowing all day long, and by the end of the day the entire length of the row should be submerged in water. We drive to the far end of the field and glance down every row. Of the hundred-plus rows, about twenty aren't showing water flowing. We stop the truck, grab our shovels, and walk into the field. Each row is blocked exactly in the same place about a hundred yards in. The damned tractor driver didn't plow evenly, and now we're paying the price. We hate that damned jerk, and we don't even know who he is.

Of course, Mercy's day is vastly different from ours. He arrives at his first tract around six and gets it going within thirty minutes. He moves on to the next one—another half-hour. If everything goes without a snag, he opens his thermos, drinks some coffee, and takes a fifteen-minute break. By now, it's only seven in the morning. He goes on to the last section and is done by eight. Then he goes back to the other tracts to check for problems—barriers, breaks caused by gophers, leaks around the blocks, and all the other things that can go wrong. Most days, though, he's done with his plots by ten. Then he doesn't have any more work to do until late afternoon, when he repeats the morning routine by moving the siphon pipes a little father down the rows. By staggering each tract, he pretty much knows how long it will take for each one to complete its circuit. If he keeps to his timetable, he'll easily finish by four in the afternoon. Then he just waits around until six to go home.

Eddy and I aren't even close. We're so far behind and have messed up so badly that we have no idea when the water will reach the other end of our rows. Sam was right. We are going to be here until dark. We can't leave until one parcel is finished and we've moved the pipes so the water can run all night on a fresh section. If we leave the pipes where they are, the rows will be flooded the next morning. We finally head for home at eight-thirty in the evening. We're tired, irritated, and humbled. What's even worse, we'll have to get to our tracts before six just in case we've miscalculated. The way things have gone today, we're sure we've screwed up, so we're dreading the morning. But for now, we can look forward to dinner, a shower, and bed.

The next morning, Eddy picks me up at five in the morning. It's still dark and chilly out, and we're sore and tired from our fourteen-and-a-half-hour first day. We arrive so early that we can't see the ends of the rows. Eddy turns the truck toward the field, and the headlights illuminate the shimmering water. Our timing is perfect. By the time we get everything set up to move the pipes farther along, the water will have reached the ends of the rows. We do know from our previous experience as helpers that we can't let the rows fill all the way to the edge of the field. We stop the run when the water is about fifty yards from the end of the row because the water still in the pipes will continue flowing down to the end of the row even after we turn it off.

Of course, we still manage to screw up. Moving the pipes turns out to be a struggle because when we blocked the ditch beyond the previous barrier, the water was still being pumped through, so we have to scramble to move the pipes and restart them before the ditch overflows. We know how many pipes we need, but we have to work as fast as we can because the water's getting extremely high. We don't dare let it break over the top of the ditch or we'll have a real disaster on our hands. This is as bad a no-no as turning off the pump. We run, grab a bunch of pipes, lay them out, start drawing water, run back, grab more, run back. . . . And the whole time, we try not to trip over the rows of pipes or bump into each other. When we manage to lay down the last pipe and siphon the water into the last row, the water is one inch from the top of the ditch. After a few minutes, the level slowly starts to drop, and we know we're safe for now. We breathe a sign of relief, open our thermoses, and toast ourselves with hot coffee.

The rest of the day brings no real disasters, but we work nonstop except for a quick lunch—no time for a soda run. That night we get home at eight. The next night it's seven. And so on until one day we finish all our work by six and stand staring at each other and thinking, "Can you believe this?" We still toil all day with no lunch break, but at least one of us can take the time to run to the store and buy cold sodas. It's amazing how much better lunch is with a cold beverage.

By the end of July, we're experienced irrigators and our days are much easier. We have our routine down pat. We finish our morning work by eleven and head off to the store in no rush. We linger, buying several sodas each and some snacks because we have time to goof off and swim in the canal. Life is now close to what we envisioned at the start of the summer.

Sam has noticed that we're not as busy, so he gives us a couple more plots. We're not fazed by this because we now know how to handle all aspects of irrigating and we'll still have a lot of free time.

One afternoon, he gets out of his truck and we get into a conversation. I guess he no longer thinks we're imbeciles. For some reason, he asks us about our college plans, and we both say we're going but we don't know where.

When he tells us he attended California Polytechnic Institute, Eddy and I look at each other in astonishment. "You didn't think I went to college?" Sam laughs.

We respond no.

"I got my degree in farm management. I majored in math and biology. In this job, you need to know both." He notices our skepticism and asks, "Have you two taken algebra?"

"Yes," I answer. I've taken algebra one and two. Eddy took one but not two.

"Then why didn't you apply it to the pipes and pump?"

When we look confused, he explains, "Irrigation is a simple matter of equations. Take the pump—it pumps out so many gallons per minute. The ditch fills up at a certain rate. Depending on the diameter of the siphon pipes, they'll draw out so much water per minute. All you have to do is the calculation, and as long as the amount pumped in equals what's being drawn out, you have equilibrium."

Eddy and I look at each other and think how stupid we were all this time. We never considered trying to think our problems through. We thought it was a matter of experience and not something we could have figured out. Sam is enjoying watching us catch on. "Yeah," he chuckles, "if you two had applied a little of the math you learned, you wouldn't have had all that trouble and had to stay working so late." Then he gets back into his truck and drives off.

We can't help thinking what dummies we were. Why didn't he tell us this a long time ago? I decide that he probably wanted us to figure it out on our own.

CHAPTER SIXTEEN

Senior Year

'M A WEEK AWAY FROM STARTING my senior year. The irrigation
season is winding down, the corn's been harvested, the cotton's
down to its last watering. The fields are down to stubble. One by
one, the growers and foremen let the summer workers go. Eddy has
already quit because he had told Sam at the start of the summer that
he'd be leaving early to start football practice.

Then Coach Pitman calls me. He wants the cross-country team
to start practice a week before classes begin. I tell him I have to work
right up to the day before classes start. I can't and won't quit early. I
need the money. I know he feels that if I really cared about running
and winning the Valley, I should sacrifice and start getting into shape
as soon as possible, but he doesn't realize that after working a twelve-
hour day, you don't feel like going out and running five miles.

I need to work as many days as I can. The more days I put in
now, the less I'll need to go back out to the fields to earn money during the school year.

Besides, I want to take part in all the special senior events that are
coming up, like buying my class ring, going to the prom, and going
on our senior trip to Disneyland. I've dreamed of going there ever
since I started watching *The Wonderful World of Disney* on TV with my

brothers and sisters when I was just a toddler and it was still in black and white.

I tell him I'll try to put in the time, but I don't have much desire to run this year. I need to get my grades up for college, and that has to be my focus.

The first day of class is a scorcher. Fall heat waves are nothing unusual for Central California. The calendar may read September, but daytime temperatures often continue to hit over a hundred even into October. And our classrooms have no air conditioning.

I take stock. I have nine months to go until I graduate, and I know I haven't done anything special to show what I may be able to accomplish. I've never ended up excelling in tennis or cross-country. I'm an average student or slightly above, but nowhere near the top. I have no special skills or apparent talents. I've left no mark on any class or club. I have nothing to brag about, nothing to offer anyone or any college. I'm about as nondescript as you can get.

Still, I've fulfilled most of my college requirements, and I'll finish the rest of what I need this semester. I have room for an elective, so I choose to be a lab assistant to our biology instructor, Don Nagel. I enjoyed his class last year. His classroom is filled with all kinds of plants, amphibians, and animals, including some rattlesnakes that he feeds mice to. Of course, we find this fascinating. He says he'll be glad to have me as an assistant but warns me that part of my job includes giving a couple of lectures to this year's juniors. That almost scares me off. I never speak in public if I can help it, not so much because of my stuttering—that's gotten much better—but out of plain nervousness, and because it's not part of Mexican culture to put ourselves forward.

Mr. Nagel reassures me that it won't be that difficult because I already know the material. When he tells me that my first lecture should be on the nitrogen cycle, I realize he's right. But the nervousness never goes away. I speak as fast as I can and get out of there.

But overall, this school year starts off better than most. I don't get

•

depressed as often, and when I do, I snap out of it more quickly. I don't go off and isolate myself as much as I used to. Our group is almost all together again except for Eddy, who has started hanging out with the jocks. Magda's back after spending her junior year in France with her dad and mom after her dad went there on a teaching exchange. Magda's French was fluent before, but now she speaks like a native. Instead of taking fourth-year French, she decides to work on her Spanish. She's very fluent in that, too. She's the only person I know who's trilingual. I still think of her as our number one student even if she has been gone for a year.

The area where the seniors traditionally hang out is now ours, and our group does venture over there sometimes, but the cheerleaders and the uppity seniors usually monopolize it. We don't associate with them much, nor do we want to. Most of their conversation is vulgar and nasty. Sometimes we tell racy jokes, but nothing like theirs. On the spirit bus that takes us to games at other schools, the cheerleaders spend most of the time telling dirty jokes.

If we're telling racy jokes (all of which are milder than the cheerleaders') and see Magda coming, we stop talking.

"What are you guys talking about?" she asks.

"Oh, nothing," Pata responds.

Magda can tell by how we're acting that we've been telling racy jokes. "Tell me!" she says angrily. Nobody wants to because for some reason we think of her as being so pure. This makes her furious. "I'm not as naïve as I look!" she bursts out. This makes us all laugh because we can't think of a more innocent-looking person. She walks away in a huff. Later on, I tell her that we weren't telling jokes. Pata was telling us which pages in *The Godfather* have the sex scenes. We all like that book, and especially those pages. "Good!" Magda tells me. "I'm going to get it and read it, too."

I discover I feel better so far this year. I don't know why, but I think it has to do with my future plans, that I'm getting closer to escaping and going out on my own, even though I'm still not quite sure how I'm going to make it happen.

One day a few weeks into the semester, I get a note from the principal's office telling me that instead of going to my one-thirty class, I'm to go to one of the library meeting rooms. When I mention this to the group at lunch, I learn that all of us have gotten the same notice. We have no idea what it's about.

We settle ourselves in the meeting room and wait to see what will happen next. None of the school administrators are there. The door opens and two men come in. They're obviously Mexican. One is an imposing-looking, dark-skinned older man, not too tall, but with wild hair like Albert Einstein, bushy eyebrows, and a thick moustache. With him is a younger man who looks familiar. His complexion is lighter, but he's clearly Mexican as well.

"My name is Roberto Rubalcava," the older man says. "I'm the director of the Educational Opportunities Program at the University of California at Santa Cruz. And this is Noe Lozano. Noe graduated from here at Redwood when you were all freshmen. He's a psychology major, and a psychobiology and education minor, at Santa Cruz. We asked to meet with you today because you're the top minority students at Redwood, and we want to tell you about Santa Cruz and about our program."

We look at each other, startled. How did he find out about us?

Roberto goes on to tell us that Santa Cruz is the newest UC campus. It's only ten years old and has made a commitment to recruit the brightest students of color. He and Noe are going to all the Valley high schools to meet with students like us because he's determined to make Santa Cruz the best and most receptive UC campus for Mexican students. He's very fired up and doesn't mince words. Apparently, only about five or ten percent of the entering classes are minority students.

"The representation of Mexican students in the UC system is so low that it's a travesty," he says. He tells us that because of affirmative action, colleges and universities all over the country have been ordered to open their doors to more minorities. "We're trying to recruit more minority students at all the UC campuses," he says. "The numbers of black students in college have increased, but too many talented students still aren't being given the chance to attend because of the color of their skin. And everyone seems to have forgotten Mexican-Americans. We've seen your grades, and I'm telling you right now that you all qualify for admission to the UC system. But it seems that nobody's bothered to inform you of this fact." He's right. The only advice our counselors give us is to go to COS.

(I know for a fact that even today, more than thirty years later, most Redwood students—even the top ones—are still being encouraged to settle for COS because it's easier and cheaper, and they can transfer out to the UC system later. In my day, if we really insisted on "reaching for the stars," we were told to think about Fresno State College, which in 1972 became California State University Fresno, because it was part of the UC system and also the closest four-year campus to Visalia.)

Roberto says he'll tell us everything we need to apply to any UC campus and that his assistant, Linda Cuellar, will visit us and help us fill out our applications. This is great news because I have no idea where to begin to apply and I need all the help I can get. He finishes by saying, "Now I'm going to turn things over to Noe so he can tell you what it's like to be a student at Santa Cruz."

Noe begins by telling us that, like many of us, he comes from a farmworker family. He decided to attend Santa Cruz after Roberto recruited him four years earlier during a meeting like the one we're having. Except that he was the only Redwood student present that day. (To this day, I still don't understand why no one at Redwood ever told us about EOP, because if Roberto had recruited Noe, the school administration had to have known about it.) After meeting Roberto, he took a recruitment trip to Santa Cruz, and later applied and was accepted. "I've never regretted it," he says. "In fact, I like it so much that I go on recruiting trips so I can give prospective students a firsthand account."

Just as I'm wondering how a farmworker kid like him can afford a place like Santa Cruz, he adds, "I bet you're all wondering how I can afford college, given my parents' economic status. The answer is Cal grants and scholarships." He explains that Cal grants are for financially disadvantaged students who wouldn't be able to afford college otherwise. The grants are based on family income, and if it's very low, the grant will pay the whole cost of college minus the student's summer earnings.

I know I might get some scholarship money but I've been expecting only enough to cover COS. Noe has just shown me the way out. I know I'll qualify easily because my family is way below the poverty line. When he adds that the grants are also based on family size and need, I know I have it made in more ways than one. As I sit there, I start to believe that I may actually make it to college. I'm thinking fast. Every year, the Goshen Mounted Police give a scholarship to the town's top high-school graduate, but so few Goshen students plan to go on to college that I can probably win it.

The session ends with Noe and Roberto inviting us to visit the Santa Cruz campus in a couple of weeks so we can see it for ourselves. I don't need the tour. I'm sold already. I want to go to Santa Cruz. I'm filled with exhilaration! This is a defining moment in my life. I now have the goal in sight, and it's up to me to make it happen.

Sometime later, Noe told me how we all ended up being called to that meeting that day. At the time, he was dating the daughter of Visalia's school superintendent. He got permission from him to go through the records of the minority students at Redwood and other schools in the district. (Of course, this would no longer be possible today because of confidentiality concerns, but that was a different era.) Once Noe got access to the minority students' records, his formula was simple. He simply checked the students' algebra grades and selected everyone who had received As or Bs. He then gave Roberto our names.

Destiny was on our side that day. If Noe hadn't made a favorable impression on the superintendent's daughter, he would never have called the principals in our area and told them to give him access to our records. Not to mention that if today's confidentiality policies had been in effect, Roberto and Noe would probably never have found out about us or have come to Redwood to talk with us. I would probably never have found out that I was qualified to go to college or ever heard of Santa Cruz. And the whole course of my life would have been different.

We were also fortunate because our principal, Mr. Reinhold Peterson, didn't hesitate to open our files to Noe. Not all principals were as open-minded. Noe told me he once tried to do some recruiting at a small school in the region but ran into resistance from the principal.

"What are you doing stirring up our Mexicans?" the principal asked him. "They have it pretty good. We (meaning the white ranchers and local business owners) take good care of our Mexicans, and they're better off than if they were still in Mexico. They're happy with how they're treated, and there's no reason to be putting ideas into their heads."

Noe told me he was so shocked by this "educator's" comment that all he could do was shake his head, pack away his recruitment materials, and resolve to try again in the future.

CHAPTER SEVENTEEN

Disneyland in the Redwoods

O VER THE NEXT COUPLE OF DAYS we're all so excited about Roberto's and Noe's visit that we talk of nothing else. That's especially true for me. My friends have never seen me so keyed up. "So, who's going to go to Santa Cruz?" I keep asking. Most of the guys say they'll apply, but they're also not sure whether they're ready to leave Visalia. COS is a place to transition before going on to a four-year college.

A few weeks later, Roberto and Noe come back to Redwood, this time with Linda. She tells us that Santa Cruz is setting up transportation for us so we can go on the trip to the campus, but we need written permission from our parents first. The problem is, I've never talked with Ama or Apa about college because I stopped telling them anything about myself or my desires and dreams years ago. I've never forgotten Ama's lack of interest when I got all As in fourth grade. All she's ever done is sign my report cards to prove that she's seen my grades. (However, she did take the time to write a nice, clear signature. That made it easy for the girls in the family to forge it so they could cut classes.)

Now I have no choice. I have to ask her to sign the form. When I do, she balks. "Why do you want to go there?" she asks. I hesitate. I'm eighteen years old and I've never set eyes on the Pacific Ocean, so I say, "It's a free trip to the ocean, and Santa Cruz is a beach town, and . . . I have a chance to go to college there someday."

To my surprise, she signs the slip without saying anything about how my going will interfere with my working and earning money for the family. Fortunately, autumn's a slow season for farmwork, so I won't be missing out on any chances to make money. Still, I know that the trip's going to cost me something and that I'm not going to get any help from her. I'm determined to do whatever I have to so I can go. I'm already on a tight budget—I don't buy albums, I don't go out to eat, I don't go to movies. Now I'm going to have to give up something else. Lunch. There's nothing else I can cut out.

The day of the trip, the bus leaves Redwood High School at four in the morning, but this is one time I don't mind getting up before dawn. I'm there early, along with Amparo, Ernie, Eddy, Pata, and Adolph, and some students from other high schools in the region. I know that Noe has visited Mount Whitney, the other high school in Visalia. Although our two schools are less than a half-mile apart, we're in two different worlds, and not just because the 198 Freeway separates us. We're so close that we walk to each other's campuses for athletic events, but Whitney is a more middle-class school, with very few Mexican or black students. I notice that there's not one student from Whitney on the bus today. When Linda greets us, she tells us that the trip is "all expenses paid"—our snacks coming and going, lunch, everything. We won't have to shell out a dime. I'm relieved because now I won't have to give up my lunches.

During the five-hour trip, Linda points out many places of interest. When we go through Hollister, she mentions that the San Andreas Fault runs nearby and points out some of the damage caused by past earthquakes. Farther west, we pass the Mission of San Juan Bautista. When we go through Pacheco Pass, on Highway 99 near Gilroy (a more direct route was built some years later), I realize that except for the summers when my family worked in the migrant camps north of Sacramento, I've never been this far from Visalia. When we reach Watsonville, I spot a sign that says Santa Cruz is only fifteen miles away.

And then we come to a stretch of highway that's higher than the hills surrounding us and I get my first glimpse of the Pacific Ocean. It's a short glimpse because we start heading away from the ocean and toward the city of Santa Cruz, which has about forty thousand residents. The campus is north of the city, off Highway 101, and the setting is more beautiful than anything I could have imagined— rolling green meadows on our left and the Monterey Peninsula jutting out into the ocean to our right and behind us. Although by now it's late morning, fog lingers over everything as far as our eyes can see. I've never seen anything so breathtaking. The road winds through a grove of giant redwoods so tall that they block out the sun. I'm hypnotized by the breathtaking sight of the ocean and Monterey Bay lying before me. I didn't expect any of this. I've fallen in love with this place already. If I don't get in here, I'll be devastated.

When we get off the bus, we're taken to what I later learn is Stevenson College. One of the first things I learn is that the campus is divided into a number of small-scale "residential colleges" that give students a sense of community by offering academic support, activities, and events. There are refreshments waiting for us, and tables are set up where administrators and students are available to answer our questions.

We split up into small groups and go on a walking tour led by some of the students. Our guide, a Mexican student, tells us about the classes and the campus in general. I try to pay attention but am distracted because we're walking across a wooden bridge at treetop level above a small canyon far below us. We also pass the bookstore and an outdoor amphitheater that's used for classes on sunny days and for guest speakers. When the guide tells us, "Santa Cruz is very casual. The women students are known to take off their tops at the outdoor classroom," I'm shocked. I didn't know girls would ever do that in public.

In no time at all, I lose my bearings because of all the trees. If it hadn't been for the guide, I probably would have gotten totally lost. (In fact, I spent a lot of my freshman year trying to find my way around the campus.)

We're led up a small but steep hill to Crown and Merrill Colleges. He tells us that Crown is more for science and premed students, and Merrill is for Third World studies. He takes us into his dorm at Crown. The dorms are situated around a quad with a central grass area where a number of students are sunbathing or studying. I can picture myself in their place. The dorm rooms house two students each. He shows us his room and describes it as small, with just enough room for two bunk beds, two desks, two small closets, and "not much else."

Some of the other students around me are nodding, agreeing with him about the size of the room, but I'm thinking the exact opposite. It's almost as big as the one I share with four of my brothers at home and has much more room than I need. And when he tells us that the university supplies sheets and pillows but that we have to bring our blankets, I'm not sure what to make of this because we don't use sheets at home. I guess I'll have to buy a blanket, too.

We return to Stevenson along a route that gives us a view of the ocean and the redwoods. A bus passes us, and he tells us it's a city bus that comes around every half-hour and goes straight to Santa Cruz's main street. It's free because student fees pay for the service. There's also a campus tram that crisscrosses the campus and a van that runs until midnight.

This place is like a Disneyland for students! I'm beginning to think there's no way I'll get in because it's too good to be true . . . for me.

We have lunch in the Stevenson cafeteria. Our guide says we can have anything we want and as much as we want. I fill up my tray. When I see that they have chocolate milk, I get two large glasses. The guide tells us that we will buy a meal plan for three meals a day and all we want to eat at any of the colleges. I decide I'll always eat here with the view of the ocean. If I get in, that is.

After lunch, we meet with representatives from the admissions office who show us how to fill out our applications. I start working on mine immediately, but one of the admissions people tells me I have plenty of time because the deadline isn't until December. "Make sure you take your time writing your essay," he advises me. "Your letters of recommendation and your essay are the most crucial parts of your application except for your transcripts."

I know exactly what I need to do now. I have to take the SATs again, get my letters of recommendation, fill out a family financial statement, write my essay, and get my grandparents to sign my application. Given UC's push for qualified minority students, I should be a shoo-in.

A few weeks later, I retake the SATs. I'm not about to rely on Ama again, and she says no when I ask to borrow her car, so I turn to Domingo and Mily. They've gone in together on a '67 Chevy that takes all their spare money to keep running, but they're very proud of it. Sometimes I've loaned them money, and because of that they let me borrow it that day. As I drive to Visalia, I listen to Neil Diamond singing "Red Red Wine" on the eight-track.

I'm fortunate that I have no desire to own a car because I know I can't afford one. I can't afford music either. The only record I've ever bought is one of Elvis Presley's greatest hits. I'm tight-fisted when it comes to my own needs. Despite the lack of aspirations in my family, I've somehow developed a vision of my future. I also understand the need for delayed gratification, even though I sometimes wonder why I don't go for immediate rewards like the rest of my family because the future is still cloudy for me.

Now that I know about Santa Cruz, I no longer feel as if the future holds nothing for me. Now I pray that I won't die before I can make a difference. I still get depressed, but now I can fight and resist it instead of giving in to it the way I used to. I keep reminding myself of what I want to accomplish.

I've also started thinking about my future kids. I want to be a good father who will always be there for them. I'll go to their games and plays and help them with their homework. I'll raise them completely opposite to the way I was brought up. I'll make it possible for them to live out their dreams without the struggle I've faced and am still facing.

I don't ace the SATs my second time around, either, but I do well enough. Now I need to get my recommendations. The first person I ask is Coach Pitman because he knows me so well. I'm stunned when he turns me down. "If it hadn't been for you," he says, "we would've won Valley last year. You let me down and cost me the Valley championship. I'm not going to write you a letter." He turns his back on me and walks away.

I never thought he considered me that vital to his dreams, or that he would hold such a grudge against me because of the problems I'd had during my junior year. But this year's team did very well without me, winning the league and coming in third in the Valley championships. Maybe he's holding my decision not to run in my senior year against me as well.

As I leave his office, I wonder whether my dream is going to die right here. Maybe I won't find anyone who'll be willing to write me a letter. I've never been very outspoken, and I haven't made much effort to get to know any of my teachers. I still don't feel comfortable speaking to adults or asking a teacher questions or for advice.

A few days later, though, when Mr. Inamine asks me about my plans after I graduate, I get the opening I need. "I'm applying to UC Santa Cruz, and I need three letters of recommendation," I tell him. "Will you write one?"

"Of course I will. I'll be delighted to."

His enthusiastic response gives me enough courage to approach Mr. Nagel. He also says he'll be happy to because I did well in his classes and as his assistant.

One more letter to go. The only other teacher I can think of is my French teacher, Ted Postelle. He tells me he'll be glad to write me a letter, too.

The next step is my essay. During one of Linda's visits, she and I sit down to review my financial statement. I describe my family situation in detail so she can advise me on how to write my essay. When I tell her that Ama and Apa haven't worked for the past three years and have been on Social Security, and that we've all been fending for ourselves and helping them out, she tells me, "You can get a free ride. Write what you've just told me," she tells me. "It'll show the admissions committee why you deserve to be admitted. Your grades are good. Your SATs are good. And you have such a compelling story that I'm sure they'll accept you and give you a Cal grant for all four years."

If that happens, all I'll have to do is earn my student contribution by working summers. I'm amazed! Is it really going to be this simple? Nothing in my life has ever gone this easily before, and I can't help feeling there's something fishy about it. I've been covering almost all my own expenses ever since I began working in the fields, so I don't see that earning enough money is going to be a problem. In fact, I'm glad I'll need to contribute because I promised myself a long time ago that I wouldn't take any money unless I earned it myself.

Still, I'm willing to swallow my pride and accept whatever help I can get because it's going to take many, many hours of hard work for me to make my vision come true. The more I can study instead of working, the better. I don't kid myself. I know I'm not that smart. I'm in the top ten percent of my class this year, but it's only because I'm putting in a lot of effort. My overwhelming hopelessness has disappeared. Santa Cruz is my escape from Goshen and my path to a better life. I hope I'm getting better emotionally and have turned the corner, that my despair is a thing of the past. But I also realize that if my improved mood is due to all these wonderful new possibilities that seem to lie ahead for me, I may retreat into depression again if I'm faced with setbacks.

And what will I do if my grandparents refuse to sign my application?

CHAPTER EIGHTEEN

Moving Out

I'S LATE FALL 1971, AND MY APPLICATION to Santa Cruz is almost complete. I have three strong recommendations. I've done my best with the financial statement. I'm almost finished with my essay, but it isn't as easy as I had expected. It's hard to give the admissions people an idea of who I really am in just a couple of pages.

I don't want anyone feeling sorry for me, so I don't write about everything. I write about my grandparents taking me in and about how I don't know my father, about how I know my mother only as an aunt. I describe having been a farmworker all my life and the adversities our family has endured. I also write about going off to the migrant camps in the summers and how those summers were among the happiest times in my childhood because we kids would all play until dark and then sleep outside under the trees.

The next time Linda visits, we go over my application and she says everything looks good. "Now take it home and get your guardians to sign it," she tells me.

That's the final hurdle I have to face. Will I be able to get Ama's permission? "Ungrateful" and "disloyal" are the mildest words she uses to talk about family members who have moved any distance from Goshen or Visalia. She often bad-mouths two of my aunts, Matilda—

we call her *la juera* (white girl) because of her light skin—for having moved to the Los Angeles area years ago, and Elsie, who moved to Perris, California, even though they didn't move away until after they got married, and Elsie still comes back to visit as often as she can. (Matilda doesn't anymore except for important family events.) All of Ama's other children except Bill live within ten miles of us, and he's only away because he's in the military. When he comes back, he'll come back to Goshen.

I'm sure to have trouble with Ama because she's been telling me ever since I can remember that I owe her my life. "I took you in out of the goodness of my heart," she always says. "You've been nothing but a constant pain for me! And now, in my old age, you want to abandon me and make me fend for myself!"

I was hoping I wouldn't have to say anything to her until I knew I had been admitted to Santa Cruz. But I have no choice. I've got to get her signature.

When I show her the form, she looks puzzled. "What's this?"

"My college application. It's for the University of California at Santa Cruz."

"What do you mean, college?"

"I have a chance to go to college. For free."

She explodes. "What about us? Who's going take care of us if you go away? You can't leave! After we raised you, this is how you reward us!" She starts sobbing so loudly you'd think someone had just died. I try to tell her I won't be leaving forever, but she interrupts me. "Ungrateful son! Thinking only of yourself! This is how you reward me after I took you in and cared for you when no one else wanted you!" I try to tell her I need to go so I can get a good job, but she won't listen.

"There are good factory jobs right here!" she shouts. "Look at Domingo! He's got a good factory job right in Visalia!" I happen to know that Domingo has had to take any job he can get because his girlfriend Laura is pregnant. He needs to marry her and support her and the coming baby. "I want something more," I tell her. "And for that I have to have a college degree."

"You should be happy with high school and COS! Why do you think you're so much better than everyone else?"

She doesn't understand that everything she's saying is proving my point, that without a college education, people are doomed to low-paying jobs and never getting a chance to advance. Everyone in my family except Bill and Al are working factory jobs. Lily, Elia, Rosa, and Delma all work in a clothes factory in Visalia. They make minimum wage and live week to week, but most of the people Ama knows still work as field hands, so she thinks the girls are doing well because they have indoor jobs instead of working outdoors in the hot summers and the cold winters.

She doesn't understand why I refuse to settle for a factory job. I may not yet know what I want to be, but it's not going to be anything that requires physical labor. Once I get my education, I'm going to leave all that behind me. "Throw this away!" She shoves the application back at me. "I'm not signing anything! Ungrateful son!" My only choices are to forge her signature and sign it myself, or to have one of the girls do it. I ask Elia. That way, if anyone asks me anything, I won't have to lie.

But over the next weeks, Ama doesn't let up. She goes on heaping so much scorn and bitterness on me that it's almost too much to bear. I walk around in a daze and am having trouble concentrating on my schoolwork. Mr. Nagel notices and asks me what's wrong. I tell him that my grandmother's upset because I won't be any help to the family if I leave and go to college.

"That's too bad," he tells me. "It's the best way for you to make something of yourself and help them down the road. You're smart, and I know you'll do well if you get to go." His words encourage me, but Ama keeps badgering me so much that I start to waver. I'm afraid I may cave in to her guilt trips. My brothers keep encouraging me to go, and even Joe tells me not to let her get me down.

Several weeks later, while Mr. Nagel and I are feeding his reptiles in his lab, he asks whether my grandmother is still giving me a hard time about college. "I'm not sure I can take it much longer," I tell him. "I'm afraid I may not be able to hold out if I have to go on being around her. I wish I could move out, but I don't have a place or a job that would pay enough for me to rent a place. I feel stuck."

He thinks for a moment. "I have a duplex just a couple of blocks from here. One of the units is empty. Why don't you move in there?"

"I don't have the money. Or an afterschool job to pay for it."

"Well, if you can find a roommate to share it, I can get you a job at the school. Plus, I'm an Amway distributor. You can make extra money that way, too." I know that Eddy is having problems with his parents because they want him to quit seeing his girlfriend, Cherry, and focus on his grades. But he wants to be with her, so he says he'll move in with me.

On a chilly winter day a few weeks later, I move out of Ama's and Apa's house. This doesn't take long because I don't have much except my clothes. Ama sobs and screams and tears her hair and even calls me names, but I ignore her. I'm not happy to be leaving the home I grew up in, but I don't have any choice. I know that if I stay there, she'll wear me down, and I'm determined that I'm going to survive on my own or go down in flames of failure.

The apartment is near downtown Visalia. It's easy for me to get around on my old bike, and I can go to games and school functions without having to look for rides home. I also ride it when I go out selling Amway products. I stumble through my presentation and often feel that the housewives only buy from me because they feel sorry for me. Still, the products are good enough that I get repeat business. Mr. Nagel gets Eddy into Amway, too, and between us we earn just enough to pay the rent.

Mr. Nagel also gets me a job on the school janitorial crew, cleaning up the school after hours. This is the best job I've ever had. It's indoors and it's warm. I consider myself fortunate. The only thing I don't like is having to sweep the gym floor on weekends when some of the students are practicing. I don't mind the work, but I hate it when my classmates see me working as a janitor.

Throughout my life, I've been lucky that people I've barely known have helped me when I needed it most. I don't know how my life would have turned out if Mr. Nagel hadn't let me rent his apartment and gotten me those jobs. I didn't have that close a relationship with him, and I rarely talked to him except in class, so why he went so far out of his way, I don't know. He was the right person at the right time. Without realizing it, he gave me my freedom.

✦

One day in early spring, Domingo stops by the apartment with my mail. In the months since I applied to Santa Cruz, a couple of other colleges have written to me, inviting me to apply and guaranteeing me full scholarships and financial aid based on my grades, SAT scores, and the fact that I'm a minority. All I have to do is fill out the application. I've tossed these letters away. I only want to go to Santa Cruz.

Domingo hands me a regular-sized business envelope. It's from Santa Cruz. My heart sinks. I've been thinking that if I were accepted, I would receive a thick, full-sized envelope full of forms, but that if they turned me down, all I'd get would be a one-page letter. Like the one I'm now holding.

I'm about to learn my fate. I slide my finger under the adhesive and open it. The letter's from Roberto, congratulating me on being accepted to Santa Cruz! "I know that you'll be receiving your official acceptance in the next couple of days," he writes. "But I couldn't wait to let you know because I know how anxious you are."

"Domingo," I say quietly. "I'm going to Santa Cruz."

"I knew you'd do it!" he exclaims. I'm glad that he's so excited for me.

Strangely enough, though, I feel like crying. I've waited for this moment all my life, but as usual for me, I keep my emotions bottled up because I'm afraid that maybe there's been a mistake. Maybe Roberto got it wrong. But a few days later, the acceptance letter arrives.

Within the week, Ernie and Eddy get their acceptances. This means all three of us will be going. So will Noe's younger brother, Eugene. He's never hung around with our group at Redwood, but we're happy that someone else we know will be going. Magda, Amparo, Pata, and Adolph all decided not to apply to Santa Cruz after all and to attend COS instead.

I didn't have the feeling that Pata or Magda were that interested in Santa Cruz, but I thought Amparo was. Adolph attends COS for two years and then transfers to Santa Cruz. And I learn that Eddy's aunt Rachel, my grade-school academic rival (along with Elaine), isn't accepted either. This surprises me because she's a better student than Eddy, Ernie, or Eugene.

I later find out, however, that she wasn't turned down. She wanted to go, but her dad forbade her to go and refused to supply any financial information, so she couldn't complete her application. This ends up happening to a lot of the women students. She wanted to go, and her brother helped her with her application, but they couldn't do anything about their dad's attitude. All she can do is stay in Goshen and attend COS until she can transfer.

Years later, I found out from Magda that she and Amparo didn't feel they were ready to leave home. Magda also told me she didn't feel confident that she could succeed in a university setting. That shocked me because I always considered her the smartest and most sophisticated student at Redwood. I'm glad I wasn't aware of her self-doubts. If I had been, I might not have been as bold as I was, and I might have ended up settling for Fresno State or Bakersfield State.

Now that I know I'm going to college, one thing I'm really looking forward to is dating. I've often thought about how nice it would be to have a girlfriend, especially when I was going through one of my depressed periods. I thought that if I did have someone, I'd feel happier and not so miserable. Magda, Amparo, Pata, and Elaine are friends who are girls, but I've never had a special "girlfriend." I've had crushes on girls since I was really young, and I've had one on Pata, but I don't dare risk sharing my feelings or my life with any girl I might care about. I'm too afraid that I would lose her once she got to know me. I want to be loved, but I don't think I could stand losing her love, so I avoid getting too close. I worry that I may never feel unconditional love. I don't even know if I'm capable of loving someone. I know I've experienced a lot of things that most people never have, and that somehow they account for my moods and self-doubts. I'm also aware that I'm too embarrassed and ashamed of my past to ever share it with anyone. (I never even opened up and shared my secrets with Debbie until we had been married for more than ten years and went into marriage counseling because she threatened to divorce me if I didn't.)

And are my crushes true love? Or am I just infatuated with someone who'll never be interested in me? I'm afraid of hurting them or myself, and when I realize how much I'm avoiding becoming attached to anyone, I'm surprised. All I know is that the thought of loving and being close to another person scares me. The thought of being loved back is even worse. I have no idea how I would handle it.

One cold winter morning, Pata forgets her sweater and I offer her my letter jacket. I love seeing her wearing it and am disappointed when she returns it to me after lunch. "Keep it," I tell her. "You can give it back in the morning." She returns it before she goes home that day, but for a few hours I get to feel what it's like to experience having a girlfriend, and it makes me feel happy.

Our group has always been unusual in that most of us have never gotten involved in going steady with anyone. Most of the time, we've done things as a crowd. For a while, Magda dated the student body president from Whitney. Like her, he was half-white and half-Mexican, and well off. But we couldn't believe she would date a Whitney student because they were always so smug and superior, so naturally we gave her a hard time. After a while, she broke up with him—I don't know if it was because of our pressure or whether they just drifted apart.

Once Eddy and Cherry got together, he was the only one of us with a steady girlfriend, and we stopped seeing much of him, although I saw them because we were sharing the apartment. He would include me in some of their outings, but Cherry didn't like me intruding on them.

The bottom line is, after I file my application to Santa Cruz and have nothing to do but wait, I start thinking about dating. I'm halfway through my senior year, and I've still never really had a date. Once in a while, I attend dances after our football or basketball games. Sometimes I borrow Domingo's and Mily's red Impala. I like to think it's a chick magnet, but I guess it depends on who's driving.

Before heading into the gym for the dance, I park on the street and reach into the glove compartment for the half-pint bottle of Southern Comfort that the guys keep there. Al says that if I want to lose my inhibitions, I should drink a little first. I take a swig. It's sweet and powerful, and I get a buzz on after just a couple of swallows. Now I'm ready to face the dance. The liquor makes me not care that I don't have any rhythm and have never been able to follow dance steps. I even feel bold enough to ask the prettiest girls to dance, and when they turn me down, I'm not devastated. I head for the freshmen and sophomore girls—surely they'll feel honored that a senior's asking them to dance. But they turn me down, too, and I hear them snicker behind my back as I walk away.

Magda, Pata, and Amparo don't attend these after-game dances, so I don't have any friends to dance with. After an hour or so, my mild buzz wears off. I can only sustain my bravado for so long before I get discouraged and head home. I feel lonely and sad, but I leave the rest of the Southern Comfort in the glove compartment. I know that drinking more isn't going to make me feel better.

Another problem is that I don't have a car or the money for real dates. I was old enough to get my license in my sophomore year, and Assistant Coach Padilla taught me to drive because he and Coach Pitman wanted to handle the scheduling of driving lessons so they wouldn't interfere with sports practices. When he got me behind the wheel and started explaining about the clutch and gas pedal, I said I already knew the basics because I had learned in the irrigation fields.

I told him how we used to drive and throw the siphon pipes out from the bed of the truck and that I used to drive my family to work on Highway 99 when I was twelve. I didn't tell him that it was nothing for me to get up to fifty miles an hour on the dirt roads with a canal on one side and a ditch full of water on the other when Mily and I were irrigating. Or about the time the highway patrol pulled me over but let me go. Even after I got my license, though, whenever I would ask Ama if I could borrow her car, she give would me excuses. "It needs work . . . the tires are bald . . . the oil's low, I need to go to town," and so on. I would get the car once in a while, but I have to put gas in it and wash it before I return it to her. Not only that, she wanted me to put in five gallons even though it takes less than a gallon to go to Visalia and back, and gas is only thirty-nine cents a gallon. I would almost tell her to forget it, but I knew that Pata was going to be studying at the library and maybe I could ask her to go with me to the local drive-in for a milkshake. So I would do what Ama wanted. But I never dared to cross the line with Pata by revealing my feelings, so she and I remained just buddy-buddy.

During my whole senior year, I have just two dates, both with the same girl. Suzy lives in one of the "rich" areas of Visalia, and we've been in classes together. One day she surprises me by inviting me to the Sadie Hawkins dance. I almost say no out of fear, but I'm so happy to be asked that I say yes. It's several weeks away, so I decide to ask her out on a trial-run date at the drive-in. She agrees to go, and I get Domingo and Mily to loan me the Impala.

I'm excited because this will be my first-ever date, and I know what teenagers do at drive-ins. I make sure there's a bottle of Southern Comfort in the glove compartment in case she wants to drink. She's pretty straitlaced, but so am I, so who knows? I drop by her house to pick her up, and as soon as I drive up she comes out the front door without inviting me in to meet her parents. This is a relief because I have no experience speaking to white adults. She's wearing a cute dress with a short skirt that stops above her knees. I get out and hold the car door open for her like a real gentleman.

"Thank you," she replies politely.

"Do you want to get something to eat first?" I ask.

"No, thank you. I had dinner already."

When we pull up to the ticket booth, she reaches for her purse, but I say, "I'm paying."

"Are you sure? I can pay my own way."

"No, no," I insist. I know from watching TV movies that the guy always goes and buys the popcorn, so that's what I do next. When I get back to the car, I say, "Do you want to get in the backseat where it's more comfortable?" I've also seen this in the movies.

"No, thank you," she replies. "I'm comfortable right here."

After the movie starts, I slide across the bench seat closer to her and unobtrusively rest my right arm along the top of the seat. Then I slowly let my hand creep down over her shoulder until my whole arm is around her. This is the first time I've held a girl so close. She doesn't seem to mind, or maybe she's pretending that nothing's happening. That makes me bolder. I let my right hand slide down the front of her chest. I feel something hard. The side of her breast! I've copped my first feel! But then I realize it's actually only the stiff fabric of her bra, and at that moment she pushes my hand away. I tilt her head and look her in the eye as I lean over to kiss her. For the first time in my life, I'm going to kiss a girl!

But it's nothing like I had imagined it would be. No bells go off. No spark. No emotion. My pulse doesn't start racing. My first kiss is a total dud. I move toward her again. This time I try what I think is a French kiss. Again, nothing. I put my hand on her thigh and feel the smoothness of her nylons. I let my hand wander higher, but she puts hers on top of mine and stops me. I back off. From then on, we hold hands, eat popcorn, and just watch the movie.

(Some years later, after Debbie and I got married, she told me that she was always having to fight off Mark, the high-school boyfriend she was still seeing when she and I met, almost every time they went out together. That made me feel good about Suzy because I had backed off and had let her know that I respected her. Of course, she didn't know that I had no idea what to do next.)

We do end up going to the Sadie Hawkins dance together, and that's it for my dating career in high school. When I get my class ring, I wish I had someone to give it to, but the chances of that are very remote. I give up and just try to enjoy myself with my friends, but I can't help thinking that if I've only been able to get one girl to go out with me in high school, I may as well forget about being able to attract any coeds once I get to college.

✦

As graduation approaches, we get more get excited about starting the next chapter of our lives. But Eddy's facing a problem. Cherry got pregnant a short time after he and I moved into the apartment. Her parents were upset and kept him from seeing her for a while, but it takes me almost until graduation before I realize what's going on.

The prom comes and goes. I don't invite anyone, and I don't go. All I do is clean up the gym afterwards. The prom would have cost too much anyway. Next on the agenda is the traditional senior all-night trip to Disneyland. Everyone else in our group is going, and I've wanted to go for years, but again it's too much for my budget. I spend the night finishing my janitorial chores and telling myself that I will go to Disneyland one day. In the meantime, Santa Cruz will be my own "Disneyland" starting in the fall.

During our graduation rehearsals, I notice that something's changing for many of us Mexican students. When the woman teacher who's coordinating the name list asks us how our names are pronounced, I realize that we're becoming more aware of our culture—and that we're rejecting our anglicized names. When she calls out "Ernie Moreno," he replies, "My name is Ernesto Moreno." This catches her by surprise but she changes it on her sheet. And when she calls out "Raymond Resa" and I tell her "Ramon Resa," she nods again and corrects it.

From then on, she seems to assume that we all want to use our Spanish given names. (Although it so happens that there's another Raymond Resa in my class, and when she calls out his name as "Ramon," he answers, "My name is Raymond," which leaves her totally confused.) I wonder whether those of us who are going to college are also somehow becoming aware, after all this time, that we need to be proud of who we are and that we should be representing our people with just as much pride. It's also at around this time that we start calling ourselves "Chicano," which started to come into use about a year ago and is cropping up more and more often.

Graduation day is just as hot as it was when I left eighth grade four years ago. Ama and Apa don't show up this time either. I don't really expect them to, but I do look around for them just in case. When it's my turn to go up and receive my diploma, they call out, "Ramon Resa." It's the first time I've ever been called by my real first name in school. I do win the Goshen Mounted Police scholarship, and the principal announces that I've been awarded a Cal grant for all four years at Santa Cruz.

That night, Eddy and I get a lot of beer and invite our friends to a party at our apartment. I get drunk for the first time in my life, but I don't realize it until I find myself outside on the lawn with no idea how I got there. The next day, Mr. Nagel stops by. When he sees all the beer cans, he asks, "So, did you have a good party?" Then he asks us not to do it again.

Partway through the summer, I move back to Ama's. I don't see much of my friends except for Eddy. Magda gets a job at J. C. Penney, and I see her there occasionally. A month or so before classes were over, I went there hoping to get an indoor job. I thought that surely I was capable of working as a stock boy, and I had seen some of the white kids working there the previous year. So I went in and asked for an application. I had never filled one out before because you don't need applications for field work. The lady looked at me funny and told me she didn't think they had any openings.

"Can I fill one out anyway, just in case an opening comes up?" I asked.

"Sure, we can keep it on file," she replied. I was sure I would not get a call back. I also tried Montgomery Ward and Kmart, and in both instances I got the same response. This made me wonder what it would take to get an indoor job. It would obviously help if I were white. Work experience would also help. Farmwork doesn't count. I found that out when I wrote down what kind of work I had done in the past and one of the nicer ladies kindly told me that farmwork was not considered a "real" job. (I doubt she had ever done hard labor, or she wouldn't have said that.) Later on, when I saw some white guys working as stock boys, I asked them how they had gotten their jobs. One said, "My dad's in the same club as the store's general manager." Another said, "My dad told him I needed a job for experience, and Mr. Jones said, 'No problem, we need stock boys for the summer.'"

I don't have contacts for those kinds of jobs, but I do for fieldwork. That's how I've gotten my jobs irrigating. This summer, I work at the school and wait for the magic day when I'll start college at last. I'm tired of working outdoors in all kinds of weather, and I never want to do it again.

PART FOUR

College Boy
(1972–1976)

Santa Cruz classmates: back row (left to right) Gloria,
Delia, Maria, Jerry; front row (left to right), Tony
(Maria's brother), me, and Debbie, 1975

CHAPTER NINETEEN

New World

F INALLY! THIS IS THE DAY I'VE been looking forward to ever since my elementary-school teachers first started encouraging me to think about college. I've just turned nineteen, and I'm about to head off to Santa Cruz. Ernie and I have been assigned to room together, and I think that should work out fine because we come from similar backgrounds and get along.

Mrs. Tobin and the others must have seen something in me that I wasn't aware of. Little did they know that someday I would actually make their dreams for me a reality. I don't know how I feel right now. Proud? Scared? I realize that if I succeed, my children will have a chance for success too. The pressure of knowing that I can make such a difference for a generation yet to be born is almost too much for me to think about.

Now we have to figure out how we're going to get to Santa Cruz. The solution comes from a totally unexpected source—Mercy offers to drive us in his van. By now he's married and has a couple of kids. He also has a new girlfriend on the side. She's Anglo with dyed blonde hair, and he's very proud of her. He wants to show her off to us and also give her a pleasant day in Santa Cruz. We think nothing of the fact that he's cheating on his wife. Nobody in the family raises an eyebrow, not even Ama. I suppose that given her behavior, going to dances and picking up men, it doesn't seem as if he's doing anything out of the ordinary.

I guess that Mercy's behavior is par for the course in our family. They do so many things that society would consider inappropriate, such as our aunts getting beaten by our uncles and the sexual behaviors we witnessed. For example, when we were kids, we learned to mimic what we saw when our adult aunts and uncles would have sex in the same room with us after they thought we were asleep.

Ernie's brother Rob drops him off at our house before five in the morning and loads up Mercy's van with clothes, a stereo, a TV, and several other cartons. All I have is my clothes and one box of odds and ends. Ama seems to have finally accepted that I'm going to college no matter what and has stopped accusing me of abandoning her. When I climb into the backseat of Mercy's van, she's so sad to see me leave that she weeps and carries on as if I'm dying and she'll never see me again.

As usually happens whenever our family goes on a trip in a vehicle, something breaks down. This time the van gets a flat near Pacheco Pass, but Mercy is carrying some spare retreads, so we're not stopped for long.

Ernie and I have been assigned to Crown, the science-oriented college where we had lunch the day of our tour. As Mercy drives up, I can't believe this is really happening. I'm half-expecting someone to come over and tell me there's been a mistake—that I haven't been admitted and that I have to go home.

A student volunteer comes over, asks our names, and tells us, "Resa and Moreno, right. Your dorm's Galileo, room 215." And with that simple comment, I'm a real college student.

After Mercy and his girlfriend take off, Ernie and I check out our room, unpack, and go to sign up for our meal cards and classes. Eugene and Eddy have their brothers to guide them, but this is all new to Ernie and me. We don't even know how to find our way around the campus at this point. After the registrar's office, we locate the financial aid office. We can't buy books or pay our tuition until we get our aid, but we find out that we'll have to come back tomorrow. We thought that the university would deduct the tuition and fees automatically and then give us the rest to live on, but that isn't how it works. We'll get a check, and it'll be our responsibility to manage our money. Since neither of us has parents to help us take care of these things, we're on our own.

The bookstore is full of students—and parents who are picking up shirts and sweatshirts and paying for everything. Obviously, I want to buy a UCSC sweatshirt, but I won't be able to until I get my aid checks, and then I'll have to buy my books and pay my tuition before anything else. I wonder how it feels to have parents who come with you and help you move and settle in. And I vow that when I have kids, I'll be right there with them when they start college. And I'll pay for everything, even sweatshirts.

We have a couple of days to settle in before classes start. We've been given temporary meal tickets. Dinner at Crown the night we arrive is our first opportunity to sample college food. It includes lots of pasta, various drinks, and fruit. I've never seen so much food. I can eat as much as I want, and even have seconds. At home, I always felt hungry and was concerned about taking too much and not leaving enough for the others. Here, I don't have to think about that anymore. I feel I look skinny and undernourished because although I'm five-foot-seven, I only weigh about a hundred and twenty. The dorm food will soon remedy that situation. As we're eating, some other Mexican students join us. They tell us that Merrill has more minorities, and we decide to check that out. We can eat at any college we want, so if we see more Mexican students there, we'll make that our dining hall.

The next day, when we go back to the financial aid office, I'm astonished to see a lot of white students in line. I had no idea that there were so many poor white students who needed aid too. I had taken it for granted that every white student had money. Obviously, I was mistaken, but there are still a lot of black and Mexican students waiting too.

I get my first check, which covers the fall quarter. Then I learn that I need to open a checking account because I'm supposed to pay for everything with checks. I've never been inside a bank before and have no idea what to do, so I take the bus into town and walk into the nearest Bank of America office. In no time, a clerk helps me open a checking account. Now all I have to do is get someone to show me how to write a check. I start thinking that getting into college was easy compared to what I'm facing in terms of having to figure out how to handle managing my money and time now that I'm finally here.

(For the first couple of months, my checks kept bouncing, which I didn't understand because I knew I had enough in my account to cover them. I went to the bank and called them thieves. The clerk went over my account with me and told me I wasn't taking the various fees into account. I didn't know they charged fees, late charges, or bounced-check charges. When Debbie and I started seeing each other, she helped me learn to handle my checking account.)

My first few days on campus, I get lost every time I try to go anywhere, even though we got a map in our registration packets. As I had noticed on the tour, the redwood trees make everything look the same. Often I can't even see any buildings, just paths through groves of trees so tall that I can't see their tops.

A couple of days after I arrive, I find myself at College Five with no idea how I got there. I figure I might as well visit Eddy. Like the other colleges, this one has dorms built around a courtyard. The students who are hanging out there look flaky to me. Some are painting abstract images on canvases, others are dancing in circles, apparently in worlds of their own. A lot of them are wearing T-shirts and loose pants that are spattered all over with colorful circular and wavy designs. I later learn that this style is called "tie-dye." And I can't help noticing that most of the girls aren't wearing bras. I feel glad that I didn't end up in this college. It's all too weird for me. Well, I don't mind the girls too much, but I wouldn't approach them anyway. I'm not comfortable around pretty girls.

I find Eddy in his room, sitting at his desk with a pipe in his mouth and looking very much like what we all used to imagine college students looked like. Then he puts down the pipe and starts rolling a joint. When we were in the apartment, he and Cherry used to smoke dope occasionally. I know that he never got hooked, and they always offered me some, but I've never done drugs of any kind. No matter how lousy or down in the dumps I felt, I've never been tempted to use drugs as an escape. I suspect that most of the students at Santa Cruz probably smoke grass, but I still feel it isn't something I want to do. We have a nice visit, but when I leave, it's with the feeling that he and I will be going our separate ways. Not to mention that he and Cherry will have to decide what to do with their lives once the baby comes.

When I take a look at my course schedule—before classes start—I think how lucky I am because I'll have so much free time to study. This is nothing like high school with classes from eight in the morning to three-thirty in the afternoon Monday through Friday. This first quarter, I have only three courses of five units each. One class meets on Tuesdays and Thursdays for two hours, and the other two are on Mondays, Wednesdays, and Fridays for an hour each. Great!

Mistake.

At every one of my first classes, I find out that we also have to attend at least one extra section each week. These are led by graduate student teaching assistants who are assigned to help the professors. All of a sudden I don't have as many free hours as I thought. I'm thinking of majoring in psychology, so I've enrolled in physical anthropology because it'll meet one of my science requirements and I don't think it'll be as hard as chemistry or biology. Also, I'm interested in evolution. The female instructor's good, and she makes the lectures interesting, but I start wondering whether I made a mistake signing up for this class because I don't see any other minority students.

Then I happen to look slightly behind me and my heart stops. The most beautiful girl I've ever seen is sitting a couple of rows behind me. She's wearing a loose white Mexican blouse with colorful embroidery around the neckline, and her dark-brown hair cascades all the way to her waist. I stare at her mesmerized, then glance away. I know I don't have a chance with her. She's too gorgeous.

CHAPTER TWENTY

Debbie

A COUPLE OF DAYS LATER, AS I'm on my way to the anthro lecture hall, I turn a corner—and there she is, sitting on a bench. I stop and stare, captivated. She glances at me and her eyes lock with mine.

"Hi," I stammer.

"Hi."

"Uh . . . are you Chicana?" I ask, then kick myself for saying something so stupid.

"No," she smiles.

"That's okay," I blurt out. What an idiot I am! I'm so terrible at speaking to girls, and here she is. I haven't been able to stop thinking about her since I saw her in class two days ago.

I gather up my courage and sit down next to her. "I saw you in anthro. What college are you in?"

"Five."

"What's your name?"

"Debbie Binger. What's yours?" I'm struck by how soft and gentle her voice is.

"Ramon . . . I'm at Crown. I'm a psych major because my family's crazy and maybe I can help them." She laughs at my corny joke

Debbie at 16, just before leaving high school
early to start at Santa Cruz

and tells me she doesn't have a major but she's interested in art. We talk for a while. She laughs easily, and I love listening to her. I do my best to hold her attention, but she finally says she needs to get going. As she walks away, I can't believe she talked to me for so long. A girl that gorgeous, and I had the courage to approach her.

The next time I see her in class, I can't concentrate on the lecture because I can't take my eyes off her. When she notices me looking at her, she smiles at me. The minute the class is over, I make my way over to her before she can escape.

"Hi," she says with a teasing smile.

I think I fall in love with her right there.

From that day on, we get into the habit of sitting and talking for a while after class, and I'm the happiest I've ever been. I don't want to ask her to do anything with me yet—not even coffee, much less a date, because I'm afraid to go too fast. Also, for some reason I'm not getting the feeling that she wants to go out with me. I don't know how to tell whether a girl is interested or not, but this is the sense I get. I'm also finding out that she's very shy, and I don't want to botch things up by being too forward. I also notice that when I do ask her a casual question about her plans for the weekend, she's a bit evasive. She seems to like my company, but at the same time I feel she's not letting me really get to know her.

So, although I can't stop thinking about her, I try to make the best of the weekends and to enjoy being in college. Before many weeks go by, I make an amazing discovery. Although my dismal dating record in high school led me to expect more of the same in college, I have no problem attracting girls! One day, a cute girl in my psych class starts a conversation with me before the lecture and continues talking with me afterward. Then she asks me if I'm doing anything later. I beg off and give her an excuse, probably because I'm hoping I may see Debbie later if I'm lucky.

I start going to the dances in the Crown cafeteria and meet all kinds of girls. I dance with one girl who suggests that we go outside and make out. We lie on the knoll in the darkness and things proceed to get hotter and heavier than I've ever experienced. But when she asks me whether I'll respect her afterward and whether I'll see her again, I have Debbie on my mind. I tell her the truth, and she tells me she appreciates my honesty. Then we go back inside.

I also meet Maggie, a cute, bubbly redhead. She makes it very clear that she likes me, so we spend some time together. It isn't that Debbie's giving me the cold shoulder, but I have no idea what's going on in her head about us. She's very quiet, and I do most of the talking. She also lives on the other side of the campus, and the only time I see her is after class.

One day a few weeks after we've met, I talk her into meeting me at my dorm room later in the day so we can walk over to our class together. As I'm heading back to the dorm on the campus tram, I meet a beautiful blonde girl. We start talking, and when I tell her which dorm I'm in, she asks, "Oh, can I come and see your room?"

I hedge and tell her I don't have time, but she follows me there anyway. When I walk into my room with her behind me, I see Debbie sitting on my bed talking with Ernie. Ernie knows I'm interested in Debbie, mainly because she's all I talk about. I hurriedly introduce the girl to Ernie and tell him she wanted to see our room. Then I tell her "Bye!" and turn to Debbie. "Come on," I say, and she and I leave together.

As the weeks go on, I find myself getting depressed again, but now I have a good reason. I want to see and be with Debbie all the time, and I can't. So I take it very hard when Ernie and Eugene tell me one day that they saw Debbie holding hands with a "big black guy." Now I know why I haven't sensed that she wants to go out with me. She already has a boyfriend. She had mentioned that her high school boyfriend was also at Santa Cruz, but I had gotten the impression that they had broken up. I've been misinterpreting her kindness. I should have known she was just being nice.

I resolve to put her out of my mind. I start going to mixers and dorm parties and dating other girls. I can't resist talking with Debbie every chance I get, but I don't let on that I know about her boyfriend, and she never volunteers anything about him. Then one day she calls me and invites me to drop by her dorm room. I'm excited because this is the first time I'll be spending some time with her outside of class. I hurry over to College Five as fast as I can. When I get there, she offers to bake me some banana bread. I don't know what it is, and frankly it doesn't sound appealing because the only bread I've ever eaten is sliced white bakery bread.

"Sure," I say. I'll try anything to impress her. She gives me a warm slice fresh from the small dorm oven. I take a couple of bites and promptly throw up. For some reason, warm, sweet foods make me gag. "Oh, my God!" she exclaims, and runs to get me a towel. Then, a couple of weeks later she makes guacamole for me, but she uses too much lemon juice and I throw up again. At that point, she swears she'll never try to cook for me again!

I kept feeling confused because I wanted to spend all my time with her, but I couldn't read the signals she was giving me. Or maybe she wasn't giving me any except that she wanted to be friends.

The first quarter speeds by. It turns out that Ernie's kind of a mama's boy and goes home to see her almost every weekend, so I have our room to myself. Debbie stops by after class and sometimes on weekends. We watch his small black-and-white TV and play his stereo and sit and talk for hours. Over time, I find out a little about her family—her father's a psychiatrist in San Francisco, her mom's a homemaker who has a college degree, she has two younger brothers, Steve and Tom, and her uncles are all doctors or other professionals.

But I still don't know where I stand with her.

I also find out that there's a two-year age difference between us. She turned seventeen a month after classes started, so I assumed she must be very smart to have begun college so young. I didn't believe her until I made her show me her driver's license. I'm still embarrassed because I'm almost a year older than most of the other freshmen, and I wonder if she thinks I'm stupid. When we talk about our classwork, I defer to her automatically. After all, she's the smart one, so she must be right. Is she aware of my feelings of inferiority? Does she realize that they're due not only to our age difference but also to the fact that she's white and I'm not? I still take it for granted that white people are more intelligent than I am and that I'm always the least knowledgeable person in any group I'm in.

My feelings of inferiority are so strongly ingrained in me that no matter who I'm with I think I'm the least knowledgeable person there. It's hard enough for me to prove myself equal to other minority students, but impossible to think I could ever feel superior to the white students. It takes Debbie's constant reassurance in our class to convince me that I belong. I have a difficult time in the smaller discussion sections because we're expected to contribute. I wish she was in my group, but her section is on another day. I would feel more empowered with her by my side. I'm sure that even though she's quiet and shy, she dominates her group because she has to be a genius to have started college so young.

We never talk about how we've done on exams. I'm sure she's blowing me away. After our midterm exams, I tell her I did okay, she tells me the same, and I know she's only being modest so I won't feel bad. The mid-terms are hard for me, but I'm passing our class. I need to do well on my finals to get decent evaluations.

I'm scared of grades, so Santa Cruz's pass/no pass and evaluations system is great for me.

In the meantime, I go on seeing Maggie, who drops by as often as she can. One day, she knocks on my door when a group of us, including Debbie, are watching TV. "Come on in!" I say, like an idiot. But when she sees me sitting next to Debbie, she says, "No, I'll see you another time," and leaves.

I think Maggie's wonderful. We like so many of the same things, such as watching sports, which Debbie doesn't. She also likes to play sports like baseball, which Debbie doesn't. Maggie talks and kids around easily and is always up for anything. She also keeps telling me she likes me a lot. No one's ever told me that before. I can't tell her I feel the same, but I let her know I like her, too, and I mean it. I'm attracted to her and we do spend a lot of our free time together. But I still have deep feelings for Debbie. I know she's the girl for me, but I can't forget that she already has a boyfriend. So I go out with Maggie because she likes me. And if someone tells you they care about you, what can you do but try to care for them back?

Then, one night when she and I are outside her dorm kissing, she suddenly says, "I love you." I don't say anything. I just hug and kiss her again. . . . I do love her red hair. "Did you hear me?" she asks.

"Yes."

"I want to know where we stand. I want to know how you feel about me."

"I like you a lot," I tell her, "and I want to go on seeing you."

"What about that other girl?" I know she means Debbie. I know I have to tell her the truth, even though I have no idea how Debbie really feels about me. So that's what I do. "Maggie, you're beautiful and wonderful," I say. "But I think I've met the girl I want to marry, and it's Debbie."

"But how does she feel about you?"

"I don't know. She talks to me a lot and seems to enjoy being with me, but she has a boyfriend."

"You love her but she has a boyfriend? What if she doesn't love you back? . . . I love you and I want to be with you. Why don't we keep seeing each other and see what happens?"

"That wouldn't be fair to you," I tell her. "I can't pretend I don't care for Debbie. I know she's the only one for me. And if I can't win her love, I'll just have to live with that. But I don't want to lose you, and I hope we can still be friends."

"Sure," she says. But I can see that she's heartbroken. She gives me a long, tender kiss, and walks away into her dorm. We go on seeing each other casually, but this is the last time we kiss. (Many years later, when I first started working on this book, I looked Maggie up on the Internet. We exchanged a couple of e-mails and she told me she had ended up back in San Diego, where she went to nursing school and married a pathologist. She also told me that the moment she came into my dorm room that day and saw me with Debbie, she knew I had made my choice.)

Gradually, Debbie and I start seeing more of each other. She comes to my room or I go over to hers, but I still don't know where I stand with her or how she feels about Mark, her boyfriend. Maybe she thinks we're just friends and nothing more. I guess I would rather be friends with her, if I have to, than not see her at all. When I'm with her, I forget Mark's existence, but I'm cautious with her because I'm afraid I'll drive her away if she realizes I'm getting too serious.

As finals approach, I start spending more time with Maggie because I want to try to forget Debbie. I don't want to use Maggie, and I try to make her understand that our "relationship" is doomed, but she doesn't realize how it makes me feel when she tells me she loves me. I'm not used to hearing anyone say "I love you" to me. I'm tempted to say, "I love you, too," and I know that's what she wants to hear, but I just can't. I keep thinking about trying to forget Debbie and being happy with Maggie. I know she would be devoted to me and that I could make it work and make myself fall in love with her eventually. But I also know I would never forget that Debbie was the love of my life and that this would always be an issue between Maggie and me because she would know.

Still she and I make plans for the holidays. Before I "broke up" with her, I told her that Mily was attending San Diego State University and that I hoped to visit him there. Maggie's family lives in San Diego and she's going home for Christmas, so she offered to arrange for us to fly there together. Even though we've broken up, she says I can still go with her and stay at her house and that her parents will drive me to San Diego State.

A week or so before the quarter ends, though, things change between us. One evening, Maggie invites me to her dorm room. Debbie is off somewhere, probably with "him." When Maggie opens her door, I'm stunned to see that all she's wearing is a filmy baby-doll teddy. The room is dimly lit and soft music is playing. She gestures for me to come in. I can't stop staring at her. I've never seen a girl wearing almost nothing before.

She sits on the bed. "Come on," she says. "Sit by me." Before long, we're lying down and I'm on top of her. We're kissing passionately and I know I'm about to make love to a wonderful girl for the first time in my life. Then I stop and roll away from her.

"What's wrong?" she asks. "It's okay."

But it isn't okay. I can't stop thinking about Debbie. I want my first time to be with her.

"I'm sorry," I tell Maggie. "I can't do this. I have to leave."

I kiss her goodnight and leave before I change my mind.

As I trudge back to my room, I keep asking myself the same questions. Why did I have to meet Debbie so soon? How do I know she's really the one for me? Why am I throwing away Maggie's love for a girl I can only dream about?

The same questions keep haunting me as we all gear up for our final exams. I'm miserable. I wander around in a mental and physical fog. Winter in Santa Cruz is cold and damp, and I feel as gloomy as the weather. I'm nineteen years old and I'm in love for the first time. The puppy-love crushes I've had in the past are nothing compared to this.

Ernie now has a girlfriend who spends a lot of time in our room. "Forget Debbie," he advises me. "Go look for a nice Mexican girl. You're never going to reconcile all the racial and economic differences between you."

"No," I insist. "If I can win her over, together we'll make everything work out." For me, the die is cast. It's Debbie or no one. But how can I hope to win her away from Mark?

During finals week, the campus empties out as students finish their exams and leave for the Christmas holidays. Ernie finishes early, and he and Eugene leave to go home. I haven't been keeping up with Eddy much, but he and his brother Rudy have headed back to Visalia. Cherry is about to have their baby, so Eddy's going to be a teenage father. I don't know how this will affect his college plans. He hasn't said anything about dropping out. He's had tons of girlfriends in his eighteen years, and although he's never given me any details, I'm sure that Cherry wasn't his first or only girlfriend. Compared to him, I'm totally naïve.

I spend the night before my last exam alone in my room studying. I got good grades on my midterms, so I'm feeling fairly confident about my finals. Maggie and I are still planning to fly to San Diego in the morning. Even though we're not dating anymore, she says it would be silly for me to cancel.

I haven't seen much of Debbie because we've both been busy studying. When I told her I hoped to see her one more time before Christmas break, she said only, "We'll see." As soon as I stop having to focus on my exams, my sadness and loneliness wash over me again. We've never talked about calling each other during the break, and the thought of not seeing her again for weeks is like a physical pain.

I call the hall phone at her dorm, but she's not there. I know that her parents are supposed to pick her up tomorrow, and I'm glad of that because I thought she might have driven home with Mark. I mope around my room all evening and finally crawl into bed telling myself there's no use torturing myself. I need to stop thinking about her. Then I hear a noise outside. When I look out, I see her huddled on a bench.

"Can I come up?" she asks.

CHAPTER TWENTY-ONE

Christmas Miracle

S SHE KIDDING? I'VE BEEN HOPING to see her and here she is!
"Sure!" I try not to sound too eager. When I open the door and she
comes in, I see that she's shivering with cold and sniffing back tears.
"What's wrong?"

"I went over to Mark's and told him I didn't want to see him anymore."

"Why'd you tell him that?"

"I told him I thought I liked you."

"What did he say?"

"He got really upset."

"Are you okay?" I ask, but inside I'm thinking, "Thank you, Mark!"

"I am now . . . I mean, if you don't mind my being here."

She tells me she's been trying to break up with Mark since their
last year in high school, but he was so persistent that he even followed
her to Santa Cruz by persuading the admissions people to admit him
even though he had been turned down earlier. She also says that he's
one of the reasons she left high school a year early but that she also
wanted to be more independent. This makes me realize again how
different our lives have been. I grew up having to make all my decisions on my own because I didn't have parents, while hers have always

211

discussed and reviewed everything she wanted to do, to the point where she couldn't decide anything on her own without them second-guessing her. I realize that this is the first time she's ever opened up to me and told me so much about herself.

I finally tell her how happy I am to see her because I was afraid we wouldn't see each other for a long time. And then I can't help asking, "So . . . you really like me . . . ?"

"Yes."

When I reach for her and put my arms around her, she wraps her arms around my waist and we look into each other's eyes. Her eyes are still misty. I wipe her tears away with my finger and lean forward to kiss her for the very first time. And it's exactly what I've always hoped a kiss should be—heaven! The moment is right, the girl is right. . . . I can't stop kissing her face and lips and eyes. Finally she laughs "I can't breathe!" and tries to pull away from me. I laugh, too, but I don't stop kissing her. I never want this moment to end. She protests that her lips are getting sore, but I don't care. I want to go on kissing her all night.

She tells me that her mother's sister and her husband live in Sanger and that most of her family will be there for the holidays. Sanger is only about thirty miles from Goshen. I've picked grapes there. I tell her, "You can come see me at Christmas and meet my family." I want to show her off to them. I've never shown any interest in any girl before, and of course I've never brought anyone home. I can't wait to have everyone meet the girl I'm going to marry.

"Aren't you rushing this?" she asks.

"No," I say, and kiss her again. After a while, when I ask her why she didn't say anything about liking me before, she says, "You were with Maggie and I was with Mark. I've been trying to break up with him all quarter. But I thought you liked her, so I didn't break up with him until he became more and more demanding." I find out later that she meant that Mark kept trying to have sex with her, but she didn't want to.

"I didn't think you really thought that much about me."

"I did!" she protests. "I even brought my friend Elizabeth over here one day so she could see what you looked like, but you weren't around." It seems as if we've both been suffering in silence for weeks.

I can't help asking again, "Why didn't you tell me?"

"I was afraid you didn't really like me," she replies, and starts crying again. I kiss her again because she's so adorable. I hate seeing her cry, but I know now that it's because she's happy.

We sit on my bed in each other's arms and talk until after two in the morning. I'm exhausted. Between my exams and my despair, I haven't been sleeping. But now I don't care. When she finally tells me she should be getting back to her dorm, I try to talk her into staying because it isn't safe for her to be out this late.

This is the year that Santa Cruz has come to be dubbed "The Murder Capital of the World" because several female students have recently been murdered and a number of other killings have taken place in the area. Two men, Edmund Kemper and Herbert Mullin, will eventually be arrested and convicted of the murders, but right now the whole area is on edge. The campus has increased its security measures and set up extra vans, but they stopped running hours ago.

I tell her I'll walk her back, but she's concerned about my having to walk back alone. Finally I say, "Then you'll just have to stay. I won't bug you or try anything."

"Okay," she finally agrees. "But I'm keeping my clothes on."

I don't care if she sleeps in her jacket and on top of the blanket as long as she stays. "You can use Ernie's bed," I tell her, but I don't mean it. I want to lie next to her all night. She looks at me and smiles, and I know she knows I don't mean it either. My mattress is on the floor next to the window. I hold the blankets up. She slides in next to me and we lie there holding each other. She's in her tank top and panties, and I'm in my boxers. We cuddle until she falls asleep in my arms. I fight my sleepiness as long as I can because I want to stare at her all night. What if this is all a dream?

After a while she half-awakens. "What're you doing?"

"Looking at you."

"Go to sleep, Ramon." I love the way she says my name. "I'll still be here in the morning, don't worry."

I finally let myself fall into a deep, pleasurable sleep. When I open my eyes, she's awake and looking at me. "What're you looking at?" I ask.

"You," she smiles.

What a feeling to wake up next to the one you love! Then I start to wonder, what if she decides she's made a mistake? I get out of bed and pull the covers off her. She looks so cute in just her panties and tank top. When I help her get up, she hugs me tightly and my doubts dissolve. We decide that she'll come to Goshen for Christmas and that I'll meet her parents another time.

After I reluctantly let her go back to her room, I pack and Maggie and I fly to San Diego. Debbie's not happy about this, and I find her jealousy endearing because this means she really cares. I enjoy my first plane flight, but it's a bittersweet couple of days because Maggie's trying to keep her distance from me, and I don't know how to act around her.

When her dad picks us up at the airport, I think they're going to drop me off at San Diego State right away so I can see Mily. Instead, we drive to their home in Escondido, and I spend two days with her family. She introduces me as a friend, but I can tell that she's talked about us with her sister, who's cool to me from the start. The next day, she takes Maggie out shopping, and I'm left by myself in the biggest house I've ever seen. The living room seems as big as a football field and has multiple sitting areas. I'm staying in a guest cottage that adjoins the house, and when I walk out into a hillside avocado orchard, one of the neighbors mistakes me for the gardener. In fact, her parents offered me a job as a gardener.

The whole visit is awkward, and I'm relieved when Maggie drives me to see Mily, who is very taken with her. After she leaves, he asks about our relationship. I tell him that we're basically friends and I explain what's happened between us, but I really want to tell him about Debbie. I get my chance the next day when we're driving his old VW Bug to Goshen. I talk about her the whole way, even when he's trying to sleep. I can't wait to have my family meet her. I'm surprised that she wants to come to my house instead of my going to meet her parents in Sanger, but I want her to see how I live and to get to know me better. I also want her to know what she'll be getting into if she decides to marry me.

As it turns out, she doesn't get to meet my family at Christmas after all.

CHAPTER TWENTY-TWO

Meeting Debbie's Parents

ALMOST EVERYONE IN OUR family makes it home for Christmas, and Ama stops lamenting about all her boys not being home. Two days before Christmas, during a lull in the visiting and talking and holiday preparations, I announce, "Debbie's coming to visit on Christmas Day."

The room goes silent. "Who's Debbie?" Lily asks.

"My girlfriend."

Delma looks amazed. "You have a girlfriend? Really?"

"And she's coming here for Christmas?" Elia asks.

They know how serious this is. In our family, guys only bring a girl home if they're intending to marry her.

It's been only a few days since Debbie and I said goodbye. I can't believe how much I miss her. It's as if she's been in my life forever instead of just three months. I write her letters every day telling her how much I miss her and that I can't wait for my brothers and sisters to meet her. I also work at a nursery for a few days and earn eighty dollars. I write to her about how happy I am that I can buy her a gift as well as some gifts for my family. (When she writes back asking me what I want, I tell her, "New shoelaces, because mine keep breaking. That would be a very useful gift."

"That's not enough," she replies—but she gets them for me anyway.)

But on Christmas Eve, tragedy strikes. Several weeks ago, Cruz, my mother's husband, fell and struck his head against a tractor at the farm where he was working. When he went to the ER, the staff told him he was fine and could go back to work. He complained of headaches but went on working. On Christmas Eve he comes home from work, collapses in the driveway, and dies of a brain hemorrhage. My half-brothers and half-sisters are devastated. He was a good father to them. I ache for them and console them as best I can. They're too young to lose their father.

But I also feel distant from them because the only sadness I feel is what I would feel on losing an aunt or uncle. How could I? After all, he was nothing to me. I never received a moment of fatherly love or tenderness from him. He was kind to me and never mistreated me, but he never acknowledged me as a stepson. As far as I could tell, I was just a kid who would come over and hang around every once in a while. I could never feel an emotional attachment to him, but I feel guilty that I don't have more grief in me.

That night, I call Debbie and tell her the news and that it's best if she doesn't come. We go to church on Christmas morning and then come home and sit around somberly. The mood reminds me of our Christmases long ago when the freezes used to keep the holiday away. But this is much worse. No one feels like opening presents.

Early in the afternoon, I call Debbie and ask her if I can come up to Sanger to see her.

"I think it'll be fine with everyone," she tells me. But then she drops a bombshell. Apparently Mark went looking for her after she left his room but couldn't find her, so he called her parents and told them he thought she might be with this "Latin lover, who's not to be trusted." The next day, when her parents arrived, she had to tell them about me.

So I'm going to be meeting her parents under anything but ideal circumstances. Not to mention that I've changed my appearance quite a bit over the past few months. With my wire-rimmed glasses, hair down to my shoulders, a moustache, and a red bandanna tied around my head, I now look like a militant Chicano.

Domingo loans me his and Mily's Impala, and I leave for Sanger in the late afternoon. I'm glad I'm driving to see Debbie rather than her coming to me because there's a dense tule fog and I can't see more than a dozen feet in front of me. I'm used to the fogs but she isn't. It's like being inside a cotton boll. You feel as if you're the only person on the road. Eventually I pull up in front of a two-story white house. When I ring the doorbell, not knowing what kind of reception I'll get, Debbie's uncle, Don, greets me at the door with a hearty "Merry Christmas! You must be Raymond!" Debbie's right behind him. She gives me a hug as I walk in and face all her cousins, aunts and uncles, and her parents.

Her mom, Barbara, hugs me and her dad, Charles, shakes my hand. Debbie's brother, Tom, and her cousin, Dave, both almost teenagers, immediately latch on to me. The dining room table is huge and decorated with a Christmas theme. At home, we have a tree and the typical lights strung up on our porch, but I've never seen anything like this. I feel as if I've walked into a Norman Rockwell *Saturday Evening Post* cover. The variety of foods and the delicious smells are overpowering.

At my house, Debbie and I would have served ourselves turkey and tamales on chipped or plastic plates and eaten on the couch with our plates on our laps because there wouldn't be any other place to eat. The house would have been full, with everyone interested in seeing the girl I've brought home.

At dinner, I sit between Debbie and Tom. I feel intimidated and don't know how to act. Everyone keeps asking me questions left and right, about my family, my career goals, my interests, and on and on. This makes me antsy. My family never asks anyone anything. They just take whatever you say and rarely ask follow-up questions. In Debbie's family, they listen to my answers and use them to ask more questions. Finally, she sees how uncomfortable I am being the center of attention and takes some of the heat off me by asking about my family and how everyone is coping with Cruz's death. I tell her they're doing okay.

I'm looking forward to exchanging presents because this is the first Christmas that I have a special person to give a gift to. I hope Debbie likes my gift, a pair of orange earrings she was admiring one day when we were window shopping in Santa Cruz, but she's a bit upset because I spent so much money. She gives me a jacket she spent her holiday making for me. Her parents surprise me by giving me several presents. I appreciate the gesture because in our family we draw names, and we each get only one gift. I don't know how her parents pulled this off because I had called only a few hours earlier to ask Debbie if I could come and see her. Besides the earrings, I've brought along some freshly picked oranges. Debbie has never liked grocery-store oranges, but she says that the ones I've brought are delicious, like nothing she's ever eaten before.

At dinner, I learn that Don is the superintendent of the area school district. He has a doctorate in education and is originally from Alabama. He's very friendly and seems to go out of his way to try to make me feel comfortable by telling me about the smart Mexicans in his schools and saying things that he thinks will show me that he understands Mexicans. "We have a really nice couple who are friends of ours," he tells me. "They bring us Mexican food all the time. I love chiles rellenos and tamales."

I nod and say something like, "That's good." I feel overwhelmed, not only because he's the head of the school district but also because he's Anglo. But although I appreciate that he's talking to me, a nobody, and asking me about my life and my future goals, and that he means well and isn't a racist, I don't enjoy hearing about how they have "smart Mexicans" in Sanger.

I notice that Debbie's dad keeps glancing at me and nodding. He asks an occasional question, but mostly he seems to be studying me. I don't know if this is because of what Mark told them or whether this is how all psychiatrists behave. Debbie's mom is the complete opposite. She's chatty and bustles around. I sense that she's reserving judgment about me and doesn't want to jump to conclusions.

Just about everyone in Debbie's family is there, including her grandparents and her great-aunts and great-uncles. The grandparents dominate the gathering, with everyone waiting on them and treating them with a lot of respect. I'm the lone outsider, and if it weren't for Debbie I would be out of there like a shot. I talk to her alone as much as Tom will let me, but he's constantly underfoot. He doesn't seem to realize that she and I haven't seen each other for a while and that we'd like some time alone.

I leave after a couple of hours because the fog will only get worse the later it gets. As I drive home, I wonder what I'm getting myself into. Debbie's family is so different from anything I've encountered. I think how lucky she is to have such a stable, intact, and successful family. She has both her parents, her dad's a doctor, his dad was a doctor before him, her uncle's in charge of a whole school district, and her grandfather's a retired manager of J. C. Penney, where I couldn't even get a job as a stock boy. Her aunts and uncles are all educated and well off. It's obvious that college is a given for everyone in her family. In fact, Debbie tells me at some point that none of the kids even think about not going to college. The only question for them is, which one?

I also think about Don telling me how impressed he was that I'm the first one in my family to attend college. He tells me that in his district he's starting to see a lot of Mexican students who are becoming the first ones in their families to go to college. But I'm not sure he understands how hard it is to make it to college when you come from a background like mine. I don't know how to tell him that hard work and studying may not always be enough to get you there, and that if you don't go, it isn't because you haven't tried hard enough.

Maybe it's that way for white kids, but I wonder if there are any school superintendants or top administrators who come from our background and who have experienced the poverty and racial prejudice we've known. School boards all seem to be made up of white business owners, and all the school principals are white, too. But if you haven't lived the life, how can you truly comprehend the dynamics involved?

The day after Christmas, I go back to work at the tree nursery along with Lily, Delma, and Mily. The girls have been working there for several years, and they got us our holiday jobs. As I'm working outside in the miserable cold alongside a number of Mexican guys, one of them asks me, "How come a college boy like you is out here working in the fields?"

"I couldn't find anything else."

He shakes his head. "I always thought college people only work indoors."

That same day, Debbie and her family go to Yosemite for five days of skiing. And I tell Bill's wife, Kitty, that I'm going to marry Debbie someday.

CHAPTER TWENTY-THREE

My New Goal

CAN'T WAIT FOR THE WINTER QUARTER to start. I feel so energized! This is the first time in my life that I have someone waiting for me, and it makes the world so different for me. When Debbie and I parted on Christmas night, we knew we wouldn't see each other for several weeks, and it has felt like forever. Because her dorm and mine are at opposite ends of campus, trying to get hold of each other the first day we get back is maddening. I keep trying to call her at the dorm, but no one ever picks up because then they'll have to track down the person being called. Whenever the phone in my hallway rings, I run to answer it because I hope it's Debbie. Finally I can't take it anymore. I walk over to her dorm intending to wait for her. But when I knock on her door, she's there.

"My parents just dropped me off," she tells me. "I was just going to call you."

"I couldn't wait to see you! I was worried that you'd forgotten all about me."

"I'm not going to forget you!"

I reach for her and she comes into my arms. Our warm, tender kisses make all my doubts fade away.

After that, we're inseparable. We find classes that we can take together. It's nice to spend afternoons and evenings in my room studying the same subjects. I also study and keep her company while she has night art classes. I know nothing about art, but watching her doing etchings, dry-point, woodcuts on linoleum, and lithography, I can see how talented she is.

We spend as much time as we can getting to know each other, but with the pressure of cramming for midterms and finals in the winter and spring quarters, we take to riding the city bus on its hour-long loop from the campus down to the beach and back. It's a quiet interlude when we can sit, hold hands, and talk. When the driver stops at the beach for his break, we watch the waves crashing against the rocks. I can't afford to take Debbie out to dinner or to the movies, but she understands this and seems satisfied with these "dates."

I continue dabbling in psychology because I don't have any other specific field that interests me, and I'm curious to learn how the human mind works. Debbie and I enroll in a child development course because I want to understand how to be a good father when that time comes. I also want to understand some of the patterns in my family, like why a woman would give her children away as my mother did, why my aunts all pick destructive and abusive men, why no one leaves the family circle, and why, if someone does, they're considered deserters.

Late that winter, a family crisis occurs that changes the course of my life. At some point in the fall, my favorite aunt, Helen, had gone to see a doctor about a mass in her breast. He told her had breast cancer and would die without treatment. She drove home all alone with this news. Although she started radiation treatment, the doctor treated her with such contempt that she decided she would rather die than be subjected to more of his callous behavior. He made it obvious that he resented having to care for "her kind," and that because she was poor and Mexican, she didn't deserve decent medical care. She stopped going to treatments and died several months later.

Helen was the nicest aunt I could have had. I always felt welcome in her house. I take her death much harder than Cruz's, and it makes me come to a decision about my major. I never want anyone to go through what she went through. I'm going to become a doctor.

＜-ｋ＜

A few weeks later, Debbie and I go to an outdoor reception on campus. Tables are set up with wine and cheese, but she and I go to eat because we haven't reached drinking age. She finds the array of cheeses interesting. I stick to the yellow cheese I'm used to eating on my enchiladas. A lot of the professors and advisers are present, and many students are taking advantage of the opportunity to seek career guidance.

When I see that my adviser's free, I approach him with Debbie at my side. "I've decided to change to pre-med and try for medical school," I tell him. "How do I go about doing this?"

"I think you should stay with being a psych major," he replies. "Pre-med's too difficult. Besides, your people need psychologists as much as they need doctors."

I can tell immediately that he doesn't remember who I am from the few meetings we've had. Nor does he have my records with him, so why is he making a snap judgment that I'm not qualified? Debbie's equally shocked because we just overheard him encouraging a couple of Anglo students to think about going into medicine. He even told them that Santa Cruz had a great record of getting students into medical school. When we leave, I'm feeling dejected and Debbie's extremely upset. I think she's just realized that racism still exists, although she did tell me once that the police had stopped Mark on her parents' street when he was on his way to see her. Mark's dad was a doctor, but he still got stopped for being black in a white area. Debbie's parents are very liberal, so this didn't sit well with them or her. Now she's just seen that while Santa Cruz is supposed to be such a liberal university, students like me still have to fight for equal treatment.

My adviser's reaction really affects me because it's the spring of 1973 and the Chicano movement is getting stronger. I find a group of radical Chicanos, and I and my old and new friends start identifying more and more with La Causa, Chicano rights, and César Chávez's farmworker movement. My long hair and red bandanna symbolize my emerging involvement. César makes frequent visits to Santa Cruz to recruit and to encourage us to fight for equal rights for farmworkers. El Teatro Campesino comes, too, and their fiery performances stoke our commitment to the cause.

During the grape boycott, a number of us students walk the picket lines outside Safeway, and Debbie joins us. Though other white students also take part, I think some of them are there because it's fashionable to support the downtrodden. I know that Debbie believes in our cause. I tell her about how poorly we were paid and about the chemicals we were constantly exposed to. She's learning firsthand what it was like for me to grow up as a farmworker starting when I was barely old enough to walk.

I try to talk with Apa about the movement, but he says that César is only stirring up trouble for the common worker and that the ranchers will get mad and pay less. He doesn't believe in fighting for rights. People of his generation are happy to survive.

At one point, we march with César and even go all the way to Los Angeles for a rally. One weekend he comes to Visalia for a march to Porterville. The night before the march, Ernie and I stay up and guard the house where he's staying because some growers have put out a contract on his life. In the morning, we march with him all the way to Porterville. We get a lot of hate-filled looks and racist epithets thrown at us, but we obey César's directives and don't respond. I'm full of admiration for his desire to find just and peaceful solutions to the farmworker issue.

Now that I've decided to become a doctor, I take stock and realize that I'm a year behind the other pre-med students because I made the decision so late. In high school, I took only the basic science classes— no physics, chemistry, or other sciences except for biology. And because of my inferiority complex, I've taken "soft" classes during this first year because I had so many doubts that I could survive. Still, it was reassuring taking the child development class with Debbie because both of us struggled with the material and with writing our papers, so that made me feel a bit more confident.

Starting in the fall, I'm going to have to take most of the science courses in sequence. This will mean a heavy course load. Still, the EOP has tutors for all the courses I'll be taking, so I can take advantage of everything they offer. I forget about getting any help from my adviser because I don't think he has my best interests at heart, but through my political involvement, I link up with a group of dynamic Mexican pre-med students I can turn to for advice. They become my main source of support throughout my remaining three years at Santa Cruz, just as my high school friends were for me. And I rely on Debbie for love and comfort. Without her or them, I doubt that I'll be able to make it. I feel totally unprepared for this journey. But I keep thinking about Aunt Helen and why she died, and I know I must try.

CHAPTER TWENTY-FOUR

Two Families, Two Worlds

DURING OUR SPRING QUARTER, Debbie and I visit each other's families. Her parents live in Marin County, and the only thing I know about that area is that the people who live there are rich and weird. Of course, I find people in Santa Cruz weird, too.

Their house isn't as big as I expected. In fact, it's smaller than her aunt and uncle's in Sanger. I feel ill at ease from the moment I get there. Maybe I didn't feel that way in Sanger because so many people were there, but Debbie's house feels empty. She and her brothers all have their own rooms, and there are two rooms just for sitting and reading. There's a TV in one of those rooms, but I soon learn that there's also a TV in a room that used to be a garage. Debbie and I end up out there in the evenings. We get into a sleeping bag because that room's colder than the rest of the house. It's a great makeout spot except her brother Tom coming in and out, and for some reason her mom needs to keep coming in to ask her a question every so often.

I see that there's a towel set out for me and that everyone in Debbie's family has their own towels—and I remember that in my family we used to share one towel among all of us.

Her mom goes all out to impress me by making a cheese soufflé for breakfast, but I don't like melted cheese and runny eggs. In fact, I can barely tolerate the food they eat, which consists of lots of vegetables and fish, very little meat, and small portions. When I tell Debbie I want to go to McDonald's because I'm still hungry, she says I wouldn't be if I ate the food her mom makes. I do try, but not very hard. (Debbie tells me later that her mom said I'd be hard to live with unless I changed. I thought she meant that I was generally difficult, but it turned out that her mom was referring to my picky eating habits.)

I make it difficult for her parents to like me, and in fact I have been changing, but not in ways that make it easy for the people around me, especially Anglos. I've started standing up for myself and I no longer let myself be pushed around. But I'm also starting to take it out on all the white people I'm around except for Debbie. In the past, I would have been meek and would never have spoken back, but now I don't hesitate to say what I think. I'm always astonished by all the things they take for granted—their own rooms, all the clothes they want, trips and vacations.

It seems to me that the students at Santa Cruz are divided into two groups, the ones whose parents can pay their full tuition and expenses, and the ones like me who depend on financial aid. Sometimes I find it hard not to resent Debbie because her parents pay her fees and give her an allowance. I feel she gets as much money as she needs whenever she needs it, while I have to wait for my allotment checks after I've spent all the money I earned working during holidays and breaks. Her parents do deposit money in her checking account for her, but to her credit she's frugal and spends very little compared to most of the more affluent students. Her mom's always writing to her and telling her to buy some new clothes or some things just for fun.

Debbie's parents are very liberal, so when I tell them about my adviser discouraging me from thinking about medical school, they're as shocked as Debbie and I were. One important thing happens during our visit—Debbie and I talk her mom into supporting the farmworkers union and she agrees to boycott Safeway. (Actually, we learned only a year or two ago that she went on supporting the UFW for years after the boycott ended.)

A few weeks after my visit to Debbie's home, she comes to Goshen with me during spring break. The family has been curious about her since I first told them about her at Christmas. I know they're going to love her. She doesn't wear makeup or spend a lot of time on her hair. I don't think she needs to because to me she's beautiful no matter how she looks or what she wears. (But I do wonder whether they'll notice that she doesn't wear a bra because I've never seen anyone in Goshen go braless.)

She and I take the Greyhound bus from Santa Cruz to Goshen, a ten-hour trip. When we arrive, no one's there to pick us up. We have to walk the mile to my house, but that isn't too bad because Debbie packs lightly and has brought only her backpack.

I realize immediately that she's having a much easier time adapting to my family and home than I have to hers. She's not put off by anything—not the smell of the dogs, or the messiness, or having so many people all crowded into our small kitchen. The girls are taken by her willingness to fit in and not act superior. Kitty always seemed comfortable in our house, but her background was closer to ours. Debbie's totally different from the other more middle-class white girlfriends that my brothers have brought home in the past. Those girls obviously had trouble hiding their discomfort and would always leave as soon as they could.

At one point, the girls start talking about her in Spanish. One of them comments, "Ramon must be serious about her since he brought her home," and one of the others laughs. Debbie doesn't realize that in our culture bringing a girl home is serious, so she asks me in English what they mean—at which point, they realize that she understood what they were saying. They're astonished, then embarrassed. But they're relieved when she starts laughing, too, and pleased because she hasn't taken their joke personally.

Apa and Ama also like it when she speaks to them in Spanish. Still, Ama has seen both Bill and Al marry Anglo girls, and she keeps telling me that I should marry a nice Mexican girl. But after meeting Debbie, she never says anything like that again. She seems to accept our relationship. In fact, our first evening there, she tells us, "You can sleep in our bed." It's the only double bed in the house.

Debbie and I look at each other in shock. "We're not sleeping together," I tell Ama. "Debbie will sleep on the sofa, and I'll sleep in Joe's room." But when we go to bed, it's hard for me not to lie down next to her. I go to Joe's room but leave the door open.

A few hours after we fall asleep, her voice wakes me up. "Ramon!"

"What is it?" I hurry into the living room. "Are you okay?"

"Something's scraping on the floor! What is it?"

"Just the mice."

"Mice!" She jerks upright and pulls her knees up to her chest.

I go over and sit down next to her. "There's nothing to be afraid of."

"I know," she says hesitantly. "I'll be okay."

I take advantage of the situation to lie down next to her for a while, and I marvel that she doesn't let anything faze her, not even mice scurrying across the kitchen floor in the middle of the night when she's trying to sleep in a strange house. The next morning, she tells me, "I think I heard a snapping sound in the middle of the night. What was it?" When I look around and find a dead mouse in a trap, she's more upset that it got killed than about the ones she heard scurrying around while she was trying to sleep.

On our second morning at home, I go on sleeping when Ama wakes Debbie up at dawn with her *norteño* music, When I finally get up, the two of them are sitting at the kitchen table drinking coffee and chatting half in English and half in Spanish. I tell Debbie I'll cook breakfast for her. I've been telling her for months that she'll love how I cook eggs in lard because they're so much better than the water-cooked eggs they serve at school. I add about an inch of lard to Ama's cast-iron frying pan. Once it's hot, I throw in two eggs, cook them over medium, and set the plate in front of her. I can't wait for her reaction!

"They look good!" she says. Then she takes one bite and chokes. She's never eaten anything cooked in lard. Her family uses only butter or vegetable oil. I guess it's an acquired taste and that she'll get used to it in time.

At the end of our stay, just before we leave to catch the bus back to Santa Cruz, Ama motions me into her room. "*Mijo*," she says (she only calls me that when she needs something), "can you lend me some money for the phone bill? If you could give me twenty, I'll pay you back." She never pays me back, but every time she "borrows" money, she always says she will. All I have is twenty-five dollars. Later on, when Debbie and I are on the bus, she asks, "What did your grandmother want right before we left?"

"Money."

"But you don't have any!"

I shrug. What am I going to do? I give Ama what I can out of duty, even though I'm pretty sure she'll use the money to buy shoes to go out dancing in. Sure, I have only five dollars to last me the rest of the month, but my food is taken care of. I won't starve. And giving her the money is less hassle than putting up with her weeping and feeling sorry for herself.

⊱ ⊰

The rest of the spring turns into a difficult time for me because, after our trips to each other's families, my Chicano friends start pressuring me to drop Debbie and go out with Chicana girls—but I'm seeking an identity and trying to learn about my culture at the same time that I've fallen in love with a white girl. When I was younger, I never thought too much about my Mexican upbringing. I started assimilating into white society because I knew I needed to. My family situation became embarrassing to me, so I've distanced myself, but I still feel as if I'm in limbo between two worlds and I don't know if I'll ever really be part of either.

Now that I'm in college, I'm finding out who I want to be. But now I'm also getting told that I'm not being "Chicano" enough. So I do what I've always done. I go my own way.

I have a hard time with white society in general, but not with white people who treat me fairly. Unfortunately, I encounter too many who are like some of the Chicano friends I'm now hanging around with. I hate my friends' reverse discrimination because they're no better than the whites they're condemning. I continue attending meetings about issues affecting Chicanos, and I bring Debbie with me. After a while, they forget she's white and treat her as one of us.

I end my first year in college on a real high. Not only have I met the girlfriend of my dreams, but a well-known and respected professor likes my work. One day in my Chicano studies class, which is made up of about a hundred students from all levels from freshmen to seniors, our professor, Ralph Guzman, says he wants to read us a student paper about picking grapes in the San Joaquin Valley. I'm astonished when I recognize it as a ten-page analysis I had done of a book called *Los Californios*. He reads the whole thing and then mentions my name and says I captured exactly what he wanted, that he likes how I added personal anecdotes, and that I should keep up the good work. Later on, he tells me privately that I should consider taking up writing.

Before I realize it, my freshman year is almost over. I'm looking forward to a break from the pressures of studying and feel lucky to have made it through. I took my general requirements, and classes I thought I could handle, and I muddled through. Debbie and I promise that we'll find ways to see each other over the summer, but as it turns out, we see each other only once.

When I go home, the only job I'm offered is as a night janitor at one of the manufacturing plants, so I go back to irrigating. This time I'm given some parcels that are close together and that I can handle on my own. It's a relief not having to deal with anyone. I use my spare time writing to Debbie and studying. My area doesn't have any trees, so I carry a small umbrella that gives me a little shade. At first, I revel in the freedom from the pressures of the academic year, but the physical labor is backbreaking, the hours are long, and it's a seven-day-a-week job, so I can't take even a weekend off to go see her.

Debbie's summer is completely different from mine. She writes to me about the trip to the mountains that she and her family just took and about the one to the coast that's coming up, and about the classes she's taking for fun, either by herself or with her mom or dad. As I work twelve hours a day, seven days a week, week after week, I start wondering whether the differences in our economic backgrounds will turn into a problem. I love her and she's all I think about, but I'm having trouble controlling my growing resentment of the advantages she takes for granted.

I finally beg her to come and see me. I probably sound desperate, and I even joke that spending so much time out in the fields under the hot sun must be addling my brain, but the truth is that I'm afraid she'll realize she made a mistake and that she'll go back to Mark. I can't stand the thought of losing her. Finally, she does come to Goshen, the only time we see each other. One day, she brings me lunch out in the fields. She wants to spend the afternoon there, but I won't let her. It's too hot and there's no reason for her to suffer through that.

By the end of summer, I'm so exhausted that all I want is for classes to start again. I miss the mental stimulation of classes and studying and am sick of all this hard work. I resolve to study harder so I'll never have to irrigate again. Sometimes I wonder whether I would have had it in me to work so hard to escape the life that was handed to me as a child if farmworker life hadn't been so difficult and exhausting.

A lot of my Chicano fellow students spent their first year taking it easy, as if college is a time for partying. Now some of them are in danger of flunking out, while others have already gone home and won't be coming back because, even though Santa Cruz uses evaluations instead of grades, students can still be expelled.

I can't afford to get kicked out. I've put too much into this to let myself fail. The last thing I want is to be seen as a quitter or as not having what it takes to succeed. I never want to give someone like Mr. Moss the satisfaction of knowing that he was right about me. When I was accepted at Santa Cruz, I felt like going and telling him about my accomplishments and then reminding him of how he had tried to discourage me. But I haven't done much yet except make it through my first year of college. Getting accepted was a great accomplishment, but graduating is a totally different thing. I'll wait until I've achieved that goal, and then I'll go and tell him that I made it in spite of his attempts to shunt me off into wood shop.

As I finish my last days of work, I think to myself that next year, with two years of college behind me, I'll surely be able to get a better-paying job, or an indoor one. There's nothing like working in the fields to make you look forward to studying all the time and to appreciate how easy college life is. My brothers and sisters—Mercy, Elia, Lily, and the others—are already feeling stuck for life, but I've been given a gift that few of my generation of Mexicans will ever have. Yet I seldom stop to remember how lucky I've been in getting exactly what I wanted at exactly the time I needed it most.

CHAPTER TWENTY-FIVE

Pre-Med Pressures

START MY SOPHOMORE YEAR AT Santa Cruz as a biology major. The minute I arrive, I hurry over to Debbie's dorm. We haven't seen each other for five weeks. It seems like forever . . . but as I near her dorm, I'm almost afraid to see her again. Has our relationship survived the summer? Maybe it's all over.

No, it isn't. . . . When I knock on her door, she opens it with a big, loving smile, throws her arms around me, gives me a deep kiss, and exclaims, "I missed you so much!" I feel immediately reassured.

After a few minutes, I tell her I have a big surprise for her. During her visit to Goshen, she begged me to see a dentist because she was afraid that if I didn't do something about my teeth, I would start losing them. I hadn't been to a dentist since I had that rotten tooth pulled when I was eight.

When I told Debbie I couldn't afford dental work, she said her parents could help, but I refused. I'm not about to take money from her or them. I'm not part of their family, and I'm not her parents' charity case, either. During the summer, though, I made enough money to see a dentist. I show her my new fillings, and she's shocked to see a couple of empty sockets. I have to tell her that a couple of my molars were too far gone and I didn't have the money to save them. She kisses me again. "I don't care about the holes. I care about you."

I know she cares about me and that everything's fine between us, but I soon learn that there are problems with her family. Debbie's mother's been trying to discourage her from getting too involved with me, or with anyone. Debbie has mentioned this when we've talked and in her letters. She even shows me her mom's letters, and I'm dismayed by her comments, although I have to laugh when she urges Debbie to think about "experiencing other guys"—and then, obviously realizing the sexual implications, immediately adds, "But not the way Mark wanted you to!" Debbie reassures me that she doesn't want to be with anyone but me, which makes me feel secure enough that I can start focusing on my pre-med studies again.

This is going to be my make-or-break year, and I soon find that the pre-med curriculum is as hard as I thought it would be. I have to take chemistry, physics, and calculus in the fall quarter and more chemistry, as well as other courses, in the winter and spring. Of course, there was no way I could have known in high school that I would need them, since that was long before I decided to become a doctor.

This course load is almost guaranteed to make me fail, but Debbie's love and support keep me from going insane. I see less of her than I want to, and the time we spend together isn't ideal because I always have my books on my lap when I'd rather have her perched there instead so I can hold her. She draws or paints while I cram.

Our major break during the fall quarter is spending Thanksgiving weekend with her parents, who pick us up and drive us to Marin. That drive gives me insight into why she left home when she was so young. They pepper her with questions the whole way home, and when she answers they tell her what they think she should have done or said. I can see her getting quieter and quieter until she finally refuses to answer any more questions—at which point her mom asks what's wrong because they're only interested in what she's been up to.

When we get to their house, I'm expecting a turkey dinner with all the trimmings, including dessert, but instead we have a small roasted duck. There are lots of green vegetables but no mashed potatoes or dressing.

In my family, we would have had turkey, tamales, beans, rice, and tortillas. I like simple food and Debbie's family likes foods that are exotic or have sauces. I still can't get used to how they eat. The next morning, we have eggs with mushrooms, which again I have trouble eating.

At one point, her mom tries to accommodate me by buying tortillas. When she sees me folding one up and using it to scoop up my food, she wants me to show Debbie's brothers how to eat the Mexican way I do. I don't know if other Mexicans eat with tortillas this way, but we often do because we don't always have clean forks or spoons.

By the end of the weekend, I tell Debbie I need to stop at McDonald's to get a hamburger. She tells me that her mom said I need to be "more open."

⤺ ⤺

When it comes to my studies, Debbie totally understands why I'm choosing to put myself under so much academic pressure. It's because for most of my life I've been told I'll never succeed and that I shouldn't bother trying to achieve goals that are beyond my reach. I have a chip on my shoulder from having been told over and over that I'm not qualified. I'm determined to prove wrong everyone who ever told me that.

Sometimes I feel like chucking the whole thing, but I'm not a quitter. Whenever I fall into the depths of despair, I always bounce back eventually, but I usually need a push. When I get discouraged, Debbie lies next to me on my bed and we cozy up for a while. This always recharges me.

Fortunately, I also have the Chicano pre-med students to turn to for inspiration and information. Antonio Velasco and Jeff Salinas are juniors and the leaders of our group, while Max Cuevas and Jeff's younger sister, Lisa, are sophomores like me. When Antonio and

Jeff apply to medical school next year, they'll be among the first Mexican students in the country to take advantage of affirmative action.

But we're already hearing mutterings from the white male premed students about the "unfair advantage" that minority students are being given. We try to ignore them and focus on our studies, but when I hear all the complaining, most of it from students whose fathers are doctors, I think about the fact that my ancestors were never given a chance to prove themselves. That's why there are so few minority doctors. We have no foundation to build on. Male Anglos have had generations to get where they are today, but it's only now, thanks to affirmative action, that we're getting a chance to create those first stepping-stones for ourselves.

I'm amazed that these privileged white males are oblivious to the "unfair advantage" they've had over us for generations. One of my classmates has a dad who's a doctor, went to a respected private school, and has traveled all over the United States and Europe. I tell him that while he was vacationing in France, I was working in the fields to earn my own living. His parents even hired a private adviser to prepare him for college, while I went to a public school where the counselor tried to place me in wood shop based on my race. I have almost no preparation for my pre-med courses, but this classmate's gotten summer research positions thanks to his father's connections. My family didn't even want me to go to college, but his father is paving the way for him.

Is that fair? Although he's a nice guy, what has he had to do to get where he is? Just do well in his classes. That's it. How easy would my life be now if I'd had the same upbringing? But arguing is fruitless because he and people from backgrounds like his have no inkling of what we've had to overcome. No matter what I might tell him, he'll still think it's "unfair" that he has to compete against us.

Another problem is that, however much I want to argue with these classmates and shut them up, I'm not doing well enough in my classes to be a convincing example. In fact, I come close to flunking almost all my fall and winter courses. I survive thanks to our group because we study together and explain the information to each other. Lisa's the one who gets things most easily and tutors us. Thank goodness for Santa Cruz's system of pass/fail and substantive evaluations, because my performance is only marginal but still passing.

That is, until the spring quarter, when I take Chemistry 1-C. It's my only difficult class of the term, and I'll be happy to squeak by. But no matter how hard I study, I fail both the class and the lab. The other students don't seem to have any problems, and I wonder whether I've made a big mistake by getting into pre-med. Was my adviser right after all in telling me it would be too hard for me? It takes me a while to realize that most of my classmates have taken summer courses to prepare them for pre-med, a chance that I, of course, never had. So here I am struggling along with no background while they're bored with the material because they already know it. I feel shame because I've failed, but my teaching assistant tells me I can repeat the class during the six-week summer quarter. I know it's my last chance. If I don't make it through, my dream of becoming a doctor is dead.

The EOP gives me a small summer stipend to tide me over while I retake the chemistry course. Eddy and Cherry, who got married in the spring, are now living in married students' housing on campus. Debbie and I were at their wedding and held little Eddy, now already a year old, during the ceremony. I stay with them for the six weeks to save money.

Actually, taking the summer class has its rewards. At least I'm not out in the fields. I'm also much closer to Debbie, even though she goes back to her parents' house for the summer. We get to see each other several times. Meanwhile, I know I need to get a job and earn money as soon as my class ends. Life isn't fair. I resent having to work constantly but still ending up with barely enough money for essentials, while Debbie gets to do volunteer work with children for her dad, who's on the faculty of the Langley Porter Psychiatric Hospital at UC San Francisco. She also gets to take interesting summer classes and go on family vacations. I know this is my problem and not hers, but my bitterness is affecting our relationship. I can't help comparing her family to the rich tennis kids back at Redwood. I know I need to let go of this resentment or I'll lose her. I also vow that when I have children, I'll give them every advantage I never had.

Debbie and I have our first real fight one weekend when she comes to see me at Eddy's. It's about the economic differences between us. When I tell her how I feel about her parents' money, she retorts, "I can't help it if they have money and you don't!" The visit turns out badly and she finally leaves in tears. I wonder if I've ruined everything. Why do I have to be so bitter? She's right—it isn't her fault. I'm going to have to learn to let go of my bitterness, or we may as well break up now. As soon as I calm down, I write to her and apologize. I add, "I love you and I want to marry you one day." She writes back and says she's sorry, too. She also says it's too soon for us to be talking about marriage.

The only bright spot is that I squeak by the chemistry class with a pass, so I'm back on track for the start of my junior year. I go back to Goshen, but again the only work I can get is irrigating. This time, I work with Adolph. I have to train him because he's never worked in the fields before and knows nothing about irrigating. For a while it's a disaster, but we manage to do all right.

He's going to Santa Cruz in the fall, also in pre-med. His counselor gave him bum advice, so he had to complete his requirements at COS before he could transfer. We decide to room together and get an apartment in town for our junior year.

CHAPTER TWENTY-SIX

Junior Year

THE TRANSITION FROM SOPHOMORE to junior year is a lot smoother than the freshman-sophomore shift. We're halfway through and have more confidence in ourselves and our abilities. I find the year unremarkable except that my courses, which include biochemistry and anatomy, are harder than ever. I continue to struggle, but I pass.

Like a lot of students, starting in our sophomore year, we had started moving around a lot in shifting groupings of students in different apartments off campus. In my junior year, I end up sharing an apartment with a couple of other pre-med guys, including Max Cuevas, and Debbie moves in upstairs with four Mexican girl students. We arrange that the girls will do the cooking and we'll clean up. Our group dinners create a homelike atmosphere and give us all a chance to talk and hang out.

We hang around exclusively with other Mexican students. Debbie's accepted as one of us and goes with us wherever we go. She doesn't have any other friends, and my friends are hers. Although she's shy and quiet, if someone says something about whites that she finds wrong or offensive, she pipes right up and gives that person a piece of her mind. This happens one evening when Max makes a racist remark to her that she probably likes "white cats." Nobody's ever said anything like that to her before, and she lets him have it. This amuses the rest of the group, and Max is afraid to speak to her after that. I've seen more than one person back down and apologize to her.

Ernie lives across the way with some guys from Merrill who share his interest in partying. We go over there every once in a while, but for the most part the noise they make is an annoyance. One Anglo neighbor gets upset about the Mexican music and tells us to go back where we came from. I guess he doesn't know Americans when he sees them unless they're white.

✦

I experience a stroke of luck when my invertebrate anatomy professor takes an interest in me and does something very few people have done. He tells me that when I apply to medical school, he wants to write a recommendation for me. Just as I did in high school, I've failed to really get acquainted with any of my professors, so I don't have any idea who might be willing to write the three letters I'll need. I'll have to work on that during my senior year.

I thank him for his confidence in me, but I realize that whenever someone does something kind for me, I see it less as an opportunity than as one more person I can't disappoint. The number of people who have helped me keeps growing, and I'm constantly fighting my feelings of unworthiness. I still feel, no matter what group I'm with or what course I might be taking, that everyone else is smarter and more deserving than I am. This is such a deep part of me that it follows me throughout all my years of school and for decades later. It wasn't until the early 1990s, when I became involved with Rotary and ended up being elected president, that my confidence level seemed to shift once and for all. That seemed to be the validation I needed to turn that emotional corner in my life, and I've never been the same since.

Christmas break turns into a reminder of where I came from and what I've come out of. When I go home, I find out that Frances and my stepbrothers and stepsisters are having problems. I write to Debbie about my concerns:

> I've been hearing all these crazy stories about Frances again. She's beyond help. I feel so sorry for her kids. I don't think I'll tell you all the details, but it involves Frances bringing men home after dances but telling Candy and Annette not to do things like that. And they say, "Why not? You do." Also, Danny's been getting into fights and Angel's been picked up by the cops a couple of times. Terrible stuff, and Frances doesn't seem to care. My "mother" is pulling her usual dysfunctional stuff, and the rest of the family is suffering for it.

There's nothing I can do to help. I wish I could stop letting my messed-up family intrude into my life. I've tried to disassociate myself from them in the past, but it isn't that simple. On the one hand, if I distance myself I won't be able to serve as a role model for my younger relatives, so I feel guilty about shirking my duty to them. But if I let the family entrap me, I may end up back where I started, and I can't let that happen, either. I have to think of my future and of my dreams for the kids that Debbie and I will have someday.

In the spring of 1975, the last quarter of my junior year, my classmates and I are right on the scene when Antonio and Jeff break through the Anglo male medical school monopoly. Antonio is accepted to UC Davis and Jeff to USC. This gives the rest of us hope. Then the male Anglo pre-med students really start fighting back. The uproar over affirmative action, especially the Allan Bakke case, colors the rest of our time at Santa Cruz, and beyond. Bakke, an Anglo male, files suit against the regents of the UC system for reverse discrimination after twice being rejected by the UC Davis medical school. Eventually, the case will make it all the way to the US Supreme Court, which in June 1978 will issue a complex set of rulings having to do with affirmative action that still reverberate today, more than thirty years later.

I can't help being angry about the controversy. After all, we've been denied entrance into the exclusively white male domain of medicine for generations. But at the first signs of progress, the white males start crying foul. Why weren't they concerned when we were knocking at the door and asking for a chance?

The pressure mounts on us to prove that if we're given the chance, we'll be productive, worthwhile, successful doctors—doctors like Antonio, who ends up graduating from Davis in 1979 and twelve years later receives the medical school's first "Humanitarian Physician of the Year Award" for his efforts to protect farmworkers from pesticide poisoning by cofounding the Natividad Medical Center's Farmworker Pesticide Treatment Clinic in Salinas. In 1992, he's named Family Physician of the Year by the California Academy of Family Physicians, and his other work includes cofounding the Salvadoran Medical Relief Fund.

But in the fall of 1975, when he enters Davis and I'm starting my senior year, he and the rest of the minority students will be hounded at every step by the media because of the storm of controversy around affirmative action that's pitting minorities and women against the entrenched white male establishment.

≮·≮

During the summer between my junior and senior year, I finally get a job that isn't farmwork, at least for part of the time. Jeff and Antonio, having graduating from Santa Cruz and now preparing to head off to medical school, get a month-long grant to provide medical information to the farmworkers at the Woodville migrant camp near Porterville and at several other camps in the Valley. This means we'll be able to list community service on our medical school applications, which is priceless. Also, being able to go back to the Central Valley makes it even better.

About ten of us pre-med students move to Visalia for the length of the grant. We each have a stipend and a car allowance. I borrow Lily's and Delma's little Toyota. They're in danger of having it repossessed because they aren't earning enough to pay all their bills. They let me have it for the summer as long as I make the payments. I feel good because I like to help them out if I can.

Before going into the camps, we go through a mini-training camp of our own where we learn elementary dental hygiene, basic medical care, how to dispense medical information, and a number of other topics. When we get to the camps, we're shocked to see so much poverty right in our own backyards. The camps are crowded and run-down.

One of Debbie's roommates, Maria, grew up in a camp, and her parents and younger brother and sisters are still there. I gain a lot of respect for her because she's never mentioned this, much less complained, unlike many other Chicano students who grew up with more and often badger their parents for even more.

Unfortunately, we aren't able to accomplish much for the migrants. We have a hard time breaking through the medical bureaucracy, and we're threatened with legal action when we try to get them decent medical care. The people at the county clinic insist that they're not their problem and refuse to see them. One day, Christina, another pre-med student who's also one of Debbie's housemates, and I take an elderly man to the Tulare clinic when we discover that he has severe high blood pressure. They turn us away, so we have to drive him all the way to the Porterville clinic, where we find a doctor willing to treat his condition. The next day, I drive a mother with four kids there for their immunizations.

At every step of the way, we're blocked by one bureaucratic medical agency or another. Their job is supposed to be to help the people we're working with get decent care, but all they seem to care about is their own job security. I question whether we're doing any good, since the workers won't have anyone to help them after our grant runs out.

(I have no way of knowing it at the time, of course, but the Porterville clinic is only two blocks from the medical office I end up opening ten years later. My plan during this summer, as clearly as I've thought it through at this point, is to practice in Visalia after medical school, assuming I get in. All I know about Porterville is that I've picked oranges there.)

My experience on the grant strengthens my resolve to become a doctor because, during that whole time, we encounter not a single Mexican doctor in any of the town clinics we go to. All the doctors we meet are white, male, and arrogant. They look at us with disdain, and when we try to get a meeting with the president of the Tulare County Medical Society to discuss valley fever, which can sometimes be fatal, he blows us off.

I do manage one triumph, though—a a three-thousand-dollar grant from an organization in Fresno to take a hundred of the migrant kids somewhere special. Some of the other students on the grant want to take them to a museum, but I know firsthand what their lives are like and I want them to do something that's fun and only fun. Nothing "educational." When I was a kid, my biggest dream was to go to Disneyland, but I never got the opportunity. The grant isn't big enough to pay for that, but Magic Mountain is only three hours away.

After a lot of planning and haggling, the camp director gives us permission for the outing. The adult chaperones and I stock up on plenty of food and drink. I don't want any kids left behind because their parents can't give them spending money for food. The looks on the kids' faces when the buses pull up at Magic Mountain, their exuberant joy throughout the day, and their smiles and laughter on the way home make me realize that we've given them a day they'll never forget. I even finagle it so we manage to give them some money to buy a little souvenir.

Taking the kids to Magic Mountain is the high point of a summer that turns difficult when Debbie and I start having serious problems. We've always been poles apart in terms of our backgrounds, but now the gap between us is growing wider than ever. It's my fault because I can't stop resenting the economic advantages she takes for granted.

I love her because she's so generous and caring. I know she can't help how she grew up, but she has no idea what it's like to have been raised in grinding poverty. She tells me we're too different, that I'm inflexible and have constant money issues. I try not to bitch about my money problems, but I finally admit how hard it is for me to see her going off on vacations and taking expensive summer classes "just for fun," and doing pretty much whatever she wants.

I thought our love could overcome these differences and that nothing could drive a wedge between us, but it seems I'm wrong. My expectations about rich white people make it almost impossible for me to understand and accept her family. I get another rude awakening about how different we are when she tells me that her dad's been invited to give a series of speeches in South America some months later and wants to take her with him. I'm excited because it's a great opportunity for her. It also gives me an idea. I suggest that maybe I can go too, if I earn enough money working the rest of the summer after the grant ends.

She says she'll talk with her dad, but a few days later she tells me that he doesn't think I'll be able to earn enough for such an expensive trip. This sets off our most serious discussion yet about the economic barrier between us. I can't believe that even if I work twelve hours a day, seven days a week, for the next two months, I won't earn anywhere near the cost of the trip. When she says she won't go if I can't, I tell her, "Go!" but I don't mean it and she knows it. I'm angry at how unjust life can be.

Ultimately, she decides not to go. I know that her parents think I'm being selfish for making her feel guilty and depriving her of a once-in-a-lifetime trip. Not only that, she tells me her mother feels that if I can't learn to live with the fact that our lifestyles will always be different, we might as well consider separating now. Debbie insists to her parents that we can work it out. I'm so upset about this incident that in the weeks that follow I start rereading her letters. And I finally decide that she doesn't love me anymore. Maybe all my talk of marriage and our being together is too much for her given everything that divides us.

One night as we're talking on the phone about a month before classes start again, we agree that the money issue has been a barrier between us so far and it probably always will be. We break up on that call. I spend the next several weeks in the fields while Debbie goes on vacation with her family. We don't speak again.

But the minute she and I return to Santa Cruz for the start of our senior year, we seek each other out. We've been miserable without each other, and we promise we'll try to understand and support each other better.

"If you don't marry me," she tells me, "I'll follow you wherever you go." So, just like that, we're more or less engaged, even though we don't tell anyone.

I'm so glad to have her back after coming so close to losing her. I promise myself that I'll try to be more tolerant of her family. After all, they may be my family soon. We spend most of that first day back on campus talking about our differences, how we can best overcome them, and what will happen if I get into medical school.

CHAPTER TWENTY-SEVEN

Applying to Medical School

'M A PROCRASTINATOR BY NATURE—not a good thing if you're in your last year of college and want to go to medical school. I'm constantly scrambling to keep up and get my papers in on time. I study all the time, but things don't seem to stick. It's as if my brain is wrapped in cellophane. Sometimes I worry that I don't have what it takes to achieve my goal, but then I take a step back and decide that the problem still boils down to my having missed so many basic courses in high school.

In addition to our senior-year coursework in the fall and winter quarters, all of us in our pre-med group have to take the Medical College Admission Test (MCAT) and start filling out our applications to schools. We're all under the same pressures and we know we're all competing for the same scarce slots, but we don't think of it that way. We feel that if one of us succeeds, we'll all feel like winners. Some of us will get in and some of us won't, but the bottom line is that we need to get as many of us in as we can. We're not doing this for ourselves. We're doing this for our people. We need to break into the ranks of white male doctors and blaze a trail for our children.

When I sum up my reasons for wanting to be a doctor in the essay I have to submit with my application, I mention my background and that I had no father or mother, and I talk about the "work my butt off" work ethic I developed from being a farmworker starting when I could barely walk. I also tear into the medical establishment and write about how racist and uncaring it is toward minorities and the poor. I write about my Aunt Helen's death and that there are no Mexican doctors to treat us and serve as role models. I promise that after I finish my medical training I'll return to my home area so I can serve the poor and mentor others of my race. In effect, I write a tirade in which I basically put down the medical establishment—not to mention doctors like Debbie's dad, who attended the University of Minnesota in Minneapolis.

Actually, he offers to look over my essay and give me some feedback. Although he isn't on the admissions committee at UCSF, where he works, he does review some of the applications and has some influence.

A few days after I send it to him, he calls me and tells me he isn't impressed. In fact, he's upset by my tirade. "I have to tell you that I find it very offensive," he says. "You aren't going to do yourself any good by submitting this. I think you should rewrite it."

"I believe in what I've written," I tell him. "And I stand by it, because these are things I've witnessed time and time again." He then warns me that he can guarantee I wouldn't get into UCSF or any other school with that attitude.

Over the past two years, I've become more militant. What I've learned from my reading only confirms that the life I've lived has been one of oppression and racism. Although Debbie and I and our group have been active in César Chávez's farmworker movement for a couple of years now, I become even more of an activist.

In the fall quarter I join a sit-in when the vice chancellor tries to fire Roberto Rubalcava, who by now has gone from EOP director to the assistant vice chancellor of enrollment and admissions. The administration wants to decentralize the EOP and place its responsibilities within each of the seven Santa Cruz colleges. The students argue that the colleges lack the staff and expertise to deal with minority student needs. We're joined by Brown Berets in our demands for more admissions of underrepresented minorities and more faculty of color.

Debbie is there with me, and we have support from Anglo students. But when the administration threatens to expel us, some of the protesters cave in and leave. So, much to my disgust, do several pre-med students who have been involved in leading the sit-in. When they're told that we could be arrested and that this would show up on our records and keep us from being accepted into medical school, those leaders and a number of other pre-med students walk off—leaving the rest of us to take the heat. Eventually, the rest of us leave in disgust.

This year, I've moved back to campus again and have a single room. Debbie's still living in town with the same housemates, but she comes to my room to rest between classes and sometimes stays overnight. We love sleeping together, and we have heavy petting sessions, but we don't have sex because we still feel it's the right thing to draw the line. I know that Mark used to put a lot of pressure on her, and it's important to me that she know I respect her and the act of making love. So we wait, but we still enjoy lots of hugging, kissing, and cuddling.

The three major schools I apply to are the University of Minnesota, the University of California at Irvine, and the University of Washington in Seattle. On the day the applications are due, Adolph and I scramble to get everything finished so they'll be postmarked and in the mail by the deadline. We look over them to make sure we haven't missed anything. We have all our recommendations, and my packet includes strong recommendations from my anatomy professor and from Ralph Guzman, who had read my freshman Chicano studies paper in front of the whole class.

But as we're putting everything into the envelopes, we realize we've forgotten our photos! We jump into Adolph's car and speed into town. It's almost six in the evening, and the photo store's about to close. But when we explain our plight, the clerk does a super job of taking a couple of quick shots and developing one for each of us. Now all we have to do is find the nearest mailbox. It's only a block or so away—but just as we're about to deposit our futures into the slot, we see that we've missed the last mail pickup for this box by more than an hour.

I've failed. I can't believe I've just ruined my hopes for medical school by an hour. It's all my own fault for being lazy. Adolph and I are both cussing ourselves out when we spot a mailman emptying out another mailbox a few blocks away. We jump back into the car and pull up behind him right as he's leaving.

"Is there any way you can take our applications so they'll be postmarked today?" we ask.

"Sure!" he replies. "Not a problem. I guarantee it."

Now all I can do is wait.

The first school that invites me to interview is the University of Minnesota. The letter arrives halfway through the spring quarter. As I board a plane for only the second time in my life, I can't help thinking how ironic it would be if I'm accepted at Debbie's dad's school. My classmate Christina has also been asked to interview there. While the medical students are showing us the campus, they tell us about the shortage of minority doctors in the state. During my interview, the committee seems impressed with my responses and with what I tell them about my need to serve my people. "If you're accepted here, would you consider staying on and living here?" one committee member asks me.

I can tell by their manner that they want me to say yes. "No," I finally answer. "I want to go back to my people in California because they need us just as much. Also, I want to be near my family so I can be a role model for the next generation. I can't lie to you about this because it's too important to me. Not even if it means you're going to reject me."

I fly back to Santa Cruz knowing I've blown a great opportunity. When Debbie asks how it went, I tell her the truth, that I couldn't lie to them and commit to staying in Minnesota. I add that Christina said she told the committee she would do anything to get into med school, even stay in Minnesota. (As it turned out, she didn't end up getting into medical school. She eventually became a physician's assistant and is still working today in the Central Valley.)

"I'm glad you didn't lie," Debbie reassures me. Then she calls her parents and tells them I don't feel I'll get into Minnesota. Sure enough, I get a rejection letter from Minnesota, but they invite me to apply again in the future. I'm not disappointed. I don't want to leave California, and I have a feeling I won't have to. It seems logical to me to pretty much limit myself to schools in California. I don't have the money for plane trips, and I can't afford to skip many classes. I still have to pass all my courses, and I'm also supposed to write a senior thesis that I haven't started yet.

I'm working in a cancer research lab under a well-known researcher who's gotten a matching grant to encourage minority students to get into advanced degree programs and professional careers. He pays half of my earnings, and the grant picks up the other half. I'm supposed to write a research-based thesis to meet my graduation requirements. The researcher also has a couple of graduate students working under him. One of them has applied to medical school several times but been rejected, and I know he's planning to apply again. When I tell him that Minnesota turned me down, he says he's sorry I didn't make it. And even though he's a white male who I'm sure is being affected by affirmative action, I know he's sincere.

He's the only person in the lab who shows any interest in me. Everyone else, including the researcher, seems to pretend I don't exist. Anyway, the only time I'm in his presence is during our weekly meetings, and I rarely say anything because I'm too intimidated by him and the graduate students.

I never actually get a chance to do any research. All I do is milk mice by hand for the project, so for me, this job is just a way for me to pay my fees. Ultimately, I never do my senior thesis at all because I don't need to after I'm accepted at Irvine.

Although I'm sincere when I say I want to stay near my family, I'm becoming more and more distanced from them. Joe calls me "College Boy," not in a mocking way but simply because that's how it is. When I started college, I crossed a bridge they'll never attempt. Medical school will effectively sever another of the links between us.

Some of my relatives are amazed that I'm not satisfied with what I've accomplished already. I tell them that to become a doctor, I need to spend four more years in medical school. I don't bother trying to explain to them about applying and being interviewed and that I'll be lucky if I get accepted, or that I know that the only thing I have going for me is my poverty-stricken background and my stubborn unwillingness to admit how much the cards are stacked against me. Nor do I tell them that all I need is to get my foot in the door because I know I can show everyone I'm capable if I'm just given the chance.

When I tell Ama about my plans, she says, "*Bueno* . . . but when are you going to get a job?" I know she thinks that four more years of school will be as much a waste of time as my first four. "Most of the guys have good cars and nice houses because they didn't waste time away at some fancy college," she reproaches me. "They worked for what they have."

Yes, they've worked, but the difference is that I've learned about delayed gratification, a concept that's lost on her and most of the others in the family. I try to talk with them about thinking beyond today, but it's useless because everybody's after money. The more material goods and the newer your car, the higher your standing with the rest of the family. Whenever I go home, I hear about who has a new car or a new baby. No one talks about how well their kids are doing in school except to brag about their exploits in baseball or football. When

I try to encourage the children to do their homework so they can get good grades and go to college, the parents always step in with comments like, "Don't bother with him. He's not very smart, and he's lazy to boot."

I know they're only mimicking what was said to them years ago. When the parents tell me, "You're an exception. We could never compete," I protest that the only difference between us is that I'm willing to go after a dream. "If I fail," I say, "at least I can say I went for it!" On one visit, I try to persuade one of my cousins to go after something better if he isn't happy with the life he has now. He just shakes his head. "It's too late for me," he says. "I'm stuck in my job at the plant, and it'd be too hard to go back to school." He's only twenty years old.

CHAPTER TWENTY-EIGHT

Interviewing at Irvine

BY THE MIDDLE OF THE SPRING QUARTER, I'm down to two schools, the University of Washington in Seattle and UC Irvine in Orange County, south of Los Angeles. Then I get a letter from Irvine inviting me to interview. Debbie's as excited as I am. Like Santa Cruz, Irvine is one of the newest UC campuses and the site of the system's newest medical school. In fact, it's so new that some of the classrooms are still under construction.

As I'm flying down to Irvine, I realize I've been on two plane trips this year. Except for Bill and Al flying because of their military service, I've flown more than anyone else in my family. This makes me think about how unadventurous my relatives are. In fact, they're reluctant to take any chances in life. Domingo's been doing so well at the plant in Goshen that they want to promote him to floor manager, but he turned it down because he doesn't want the responsibility. Lily and Delma are offered a chance to take a course so they can become receptionists, but they say no because they don't feel confident that they could handle such an important job.

What makes the rest of my family afraid to venture out of their comfort zone, while I'm going after dreams that seem totally out of reach? I don't know, but I refuse to settle for their lot in life. I want to show them that we can do anything we want to if we try. But if I fail, I'll prove them right. They'll tell me, "See? Don't reach for the stars. You'll only get burned." I know that even though they want me to succeed, they expect me to fall short.

My first interview is with a Mr. Escobedo, an attorney in the local community, who tells me he was asked to come in and interview minority candidates because Irvine has no Mexican medical faculty or staff members yet. He starts out very conversationally by commenting, "You picked a great day to visit. The air's so clear today."

"You call this clear?" I think he's joking. The view through his window is veiled in hazy, brownish smog. Then I realize he's serious. He gives a good-natured laugh. "I guess that coming from Santa Cruz like you do, it does look smoggy to you."

We hit it off right away. During the interview, I describe my background and tell him my hopes for my future. I get emotional when I tell him I'm committed to returning to my community and serving my people, and especially to being a role model for my family and showing other Mexican young people that we can succeed. Or, as César Chávez said, "*Sí se puede.*" Mr. Escobedo tells me he's moved and impressed by my responses because I've given him information about myself that wasn't in my folder. "I'm going to do whatever I can for you, because you deserve a chance," he says.

I believe him, and I feel lucky to have been able to meet with him. I said what I believed in—even some of the things that Debbie's dad had found offensive—and he was receptive. Sometimes I still wonder what direction my life would have taken if Mr. Escobedo hadn't been asked to interview me.

The rest of my interviews don't go as well because the only things that seem to interest everyone else are my evaluations and my MCAT. I'm not concerned. I surprise myself by showing more confidence than I ever have before. I'm more forceful in my responses, not like myself at all. But I feel I need to really sell myself because I'm having the same sense I did when I first saw Santa Cruz—that I need to be here, that this is the only school where I have a chance. Neither my MCAT nor my evaluations are all that impressive, but maybe having evaluations is an advantage because the interviewers will have to read them instead of just scanning a transcript with letter grades. I will myself to impress the committee because I know that these meetings are the only card I hold, the only way I can show my capabilities and potential.

On the flight home, I feel a sense of relief and peace. As soon as I get back to my dorm, I call Debbie and ask her to meet me for dinner. "How do you think it went? How did you feel?" she asks eagerly. "Tell me now! I can't wait!"

"Just come over right away. I want to see you." It's so nice to share your news with someone you love and to want to see them as soon as possible. Within minutes, she flings open my door and plants herself there without even giving me a hug or a kiss. "Well?" she demands.

I give her a big hug and an even bigger kiss. "I think I might get into Irvine!"

"How do you know?"

"I just feel it. I can't explain it, but I have such a strong feeling of everything pointing to Irvine that I'm going to cancel my Seattle interview." She thinks I'm crazy to be putting all my hopes on Irvine and not keep the University of Washington open because it's my last option.

A few weeks later, Debbie's mom and dad come to Santa Cruz for the opening of her senior project, a week-long exhibition of her art that will fulfill her degree requirements. She's spent the whole year painting and drawing to prepare for it, in addition to doing a joint major in biology. After the reception, they take us out to dinner.

Whenever they visit her, I'm automatically included in their dinner outings, and I have been ever since she and I started dating. The first few times they invited me, I didn't want to go. I was ashamed to show my ignorance and poor table manners, but Debbie insisted. "You have to get over your hang-ups," she used to tell me. "And what better way than with my family?"

When she and I are on our own, we go out to inexpensive Mexican places, which are the only ones where I feel comfortable. When I was growing up, money was always such a problem that we thought "eating out" meant stopping at a drive-in and ordering a fried burrito. I always got a charge from eating something that wasn't homemade.

(The only time I remember really "eating out" was a day that Joe and I were in Visalia with Ama. We were walking through Woolworth's when she suddenly announced, "Let's stop and eat!" We went to the long counter that extended all along the wall near the accessories section and climbed onto the soft, red-cushioned leatherette stools. I was excited and nervous because I had never eaten out before. When the waitress asked us for our order, Ama told me in Spanish, "Tell her we want hamburgers." I ordered three hamburgers, and when the waitress asked, "Do you want fries with that?" I knew what fries were from watching TV. So I asked Ama if we could have fries, and she said okay. But as we waited for our food to arrive, we were all nervous and uncomfortable. Were people staring at us? Did they know that we didn't know what we were doing or how to act? As soon as the food arrived, we ate quickly and left. I don't remember going out to eat again.)

Debbie's parents always take us out to more upscale restaurants, often ones that specialize in fish and have heavy white tablecloths and fancy silverware. I get confused with all the forks and spoons, and I hate it when the waiters hover around us. They make me nervous. I always think they want me to hurry up so they can clear the table for the next customers. I have a hard enough time eating at McDonald's. In these expensive places I have to remember to keep my elbows off the table. I order the easiest item on the menu, or a hamburger and fries if they have it. Her parents tell me I should try something different, but I'm concerned about the prices, and even though it's always their treat, I can't stand the idea of ordering something I might not like and having it go to waste. One time I did order swordfish, and they were pleasantly surprised that I ventured out of my comfort zone.

This evening, they take us to a Chinese place. As soon as we order, her dad starts peppering me about the Irvine interview. "Why are you so sure you'll get in there? And why did you cancel the Washington interview before you know for sure? You should call and reschedule." As I try to explain my reasoning, I get another glimpse of what Debbie's been up against all these years. Even after knowing them for three years now, I'm still not used to their endless questions, comments, and advice.

They're so different from Ama and Apa. I haven't even told my family about my trip, but I know that if I did, Ama and Apa wouldn't ask any questions or offer any comments.

One of my favorite things about Chinese restaurants is opening our fortune cookies and sharing our fate. That night, mine reads, "Rest easy. Your future is secure." I show it to Debbie. I believe with all my heart that it's telling me the truth.

And the following week, I receive a letter from the financial aid office at Irvine:

Dear Ramon:

We would like to congratulate you on your acceptance to UC Irvine Medical School. You will be receiving your official letter soon, but because Irvine starts at the end of June, we feel we must get working on your financial aid. Please fill out the enclosed financial aid application and return it to us as soon as possible. Sincerely . . .

I grab the next bus into town, tear over to Debbie's apartment, throw open the door, and hand her the letter. She looks at it, then leaps into my arms. "I knew all the time you could do it!" she tells me. I'm glad she did, because in spite of the fortune cookie, I still had my doubts.

However, I receive my acceptance during the ongoing furor about the Bakke case, which is still winding its way through the courts. We all realize that whichever way things go, there are going to be serious implications for the jobs and careers of our generation.

My own success creates some fallout among some of Debbie's parents' friends and some of my classmates' parents. One couple who are liberal Marin County friends of Debbie's parents get very upset when they learn that I've been accepted by Irvine. They feel I've taken their son's place. (I didn't learn about their reaction until years later, maybe because Debbie's parents were afraid to tell me how their friends really felt about affirmative action, which was that they were all for it as long as it didn't affect their son. What this couple failed to acknowledge was that every school their son applied to turned him down. Instead, they said that affirmative action was unfairly favoring minorities or women, when in fact he wasn't good enough.) If well-to-do "liberals" can feel this way, what could we expect of the rest of the country?

Irvine also rejects the wealthy classmate I kept comparing myself to—the one who had benefited from private school, private tutors, summers in France, and all the other advantages of being the privileged son of a well-connected doctor. I learn that his father, like Debbie's parents' friends, is furious. Even though the incoming class is still eighty-five percent white and sixty percent white male, I "took his spot." What it comes down to is that white males hate it when the shoe of discrimination ends up on the other foot. I'm determined that my kids will have a level playing field.

Until now, Debbie and I have avoided talking about our future because we realize everything hinges on what happens to me. I've been asking her to marry me ever since our first Christmas, when she was only seventeen, but back then she would only laugh and tell me she was too young. "Still, I'm going to marry you someday," I always replied.

Over the last year, our discussions have gotten more serious, and there hasn't been any question that we're going to get married. The only holdup has been what my future would be and when to marry. Whenever I express doubts about my opportunities, she tells me, "I don't care if you get into medical school or not. Wherever you go, I'll go." She's adamant about this, although her parents keep telling her it's ridiculous for her to promise to follow me no matter what. In their family, the man's future has to be secure before marriage can even be considered. In mine, as I know only too well, we wing it. Rarely does anyone plan more than a few weeks ahead, and planning to achieve lifetime goals is unheard of.

Now it's Debbie's and my turn to wing it, except that we don't have a clue as to how to go about getting married!

PART FIVE

Medical Student
(1976–1981)

Medical school commencement,
UC Irvine, June 1981

CHAPTER TWENTY-NINE

Getting Married

WE'RE IN A REAL TIME BIND. It's already the middle of the spring quarter, commencement's the second week of June, and Irvine starts just a week later. We have less than three months to make all our arrangements and move. Because Irvine accepted me so late, all the married medical student housing is full and we're placed on a waiting list. Debbie and I will have to go to Irvine and look for a place on our own.

First, though, we Chicano students hold a separate graduation ceremony a couple of weeks before the official commencement. We want to do this because we know our families have never experienced a commencement, and we feel they'll be more comfortable at an event where they'll be with other families like them.

Of course, I invite my whole family. Ama and Apa can't come, but I'm touched when Bill, Al, and Joe tell me that they'll be there with their wives. Bill and Kitty and Joe and his wife, Anita, will fly to San Francisco from Fresno, while Al and his wife, Kris, will drive up from Visalia. Kris is Anglo like Kitty, and Anita is Mexican.

Al and Kris arrive as expected, but we don't hear from Joe and Bill until about ten at night, when they call and tell us they're stuck in San Francisco. They were going to rent a Cadillac at the airport and drive down to Santa Cruz in style, but that was as far ahead as they had gotten in their planning. They have plenty of cash, but they didn't realize that car rental agencies don't accept cash. None of them have a credit card. They ended up taking a taxi to Ghirardelli Square and then calling Al for a ride. None of this is a real surprise to me because, in my family, things almost always go wrong somehow.

"*Pendejos!*" Al yells at them. "You're always messing me up!"

But we have no choice. We drive Al's car into San Francisco and arrive at the Square after midnight to find them huddled up against the wind looking scared and cold. As soon as they jump into the car, they start recounting their adventures and telling us they were acting like hotshots and waving all their cash around but no one would take it. When they finally decided to take a cab downtown, they had no idea where to go and the driver had dumped them where we found them. They think it's all very funny, but Al's still pissed off at them.

He's even more pissed off when we find out that, of course, they didn't think to make hotel reservations either, so they impose on him even more by bunking with him and Kris. When I tell Debbie about their adventure, I call them "country pumpkins." (She doesn't tell me for a long time that it's actually "bumpkins.")

Still, I'm glad they get in a day early and make it to my ceremony, and I enjoy the proud looks on their faces as they share in my achievement. For me, this special Chicano commencement is my entrance into the ranks of the college educated as I become the first member of my family to receive a four-year degree. Debbie's parents are there as well, and her mom comments on how nice the ceremony is. In the end, neither Debbie nor I go to the big, all-campus commencement ceremony. She attends a smaller ceremony at College Five, which was renamed Porter College about six years after we graduated.

The next people in my family to attend college will be the new generation—Bill and Kitty's daughters, Cindy and Jana, and Marina, twenty years down the road. Mily drops out of San Diego State with one semester to go.

A few days later, Debbie and I make a hurried trip to Irvine to look for an apartment. We fly down to Orange County and head for the nearest car-rental desk feeling very sophisticated and self-assured because Debbie has a credit card that her parents gave her. But when she hands it over along with her driver's license, the agent tells us they don't rent to anyone under twenty-one, and she's only twenty at this point.

I call Mily, who makes the hour-long drive from San Diego, picks us up, takes us around apartment hunting until we find something adequate, and then drops us off at a chain motel. We know that when Mily tells Bill and Joe about having to come and get us, we won't be able to live it down for a long time. That's what we get for thinking we were so smart and had all the angles covered.

Now we have exactly one week before our wedding and the move to Irvine. Because everything's been last minute and Debbie doesn't care about having the "ultimate wedding," we've been letting her mom and her Aunt Beth handle the arrangements. The date is set for the afternoon of Saturday, June 19, 1976, at the house in Sanger where I first met Debbie's family on Christmas Day three-and-a-half years ago. Beth never had any daughters, only boys, so she's been thrilled to help Debbie's mom with the details. I'm glad that Sanger is so close to Goshen because Apa and Ama won't have any excuse not to show up. Still, Apa, who's now seventy-six, has already told me he might not feel up to it.

A couple of days before the wedding, Debbie's mom and dad come to Goshen and finally meet my family. I can tell that Apa's not comfortable around her father, "the Doctor." He and Debbie's mom are insisting on paying for the wedding because they say that's the tradition. I'm not sure. I feel that the man should pay. I swallow my pride and give in, but I keep telling them to spend as little as possible.

Debbie on our wedding day, June 19, 1976

A few months ago, when Debbie and I and her parents were all in San Francisco together and we were starting to plan the wedding, I saw a ring I wanted to buy for her. I didn't have the money that day, so I borrowed it from her mom (and paid her back as soon as I could). It only cost twenty dollars, but when I give it to Debbie, she's so happy that you would think it was a huge diamond.

Our wedding day is early-summer hot but not unbearable. Apa does come with Ama. Many of my relatives are there, as are my high-school friends and Noe and his wife, Elvira. Eddy and Cherry are there, too. He dropped out of Santa Cruz in his junior year and returned to Visalia. Now they're expecting their second child. Debbie's family is much smaller. Her dad has two brothers and a sister, and her mom has two sisters. But with the grandparents and great-aunts and great-uncles, we each have about the same number of family members there. I've

The ceremony

asked Mily to be my best man. Unfortunately, I almost ruin everything when I ask him to cut my hair that morning. Why I do this I'll never know, because Bill's always been the family barber. Maybe it's because he and Kitty haven't arrived yet. Mily convinces me that he knows how to cut hair. Like a dummy, I believe him. He proceeds to butcher it, and all his attempts to fix it only make it worse. In a panic, I head to the local Kmart barber, who does his best to make me look presentable. When Debbie sees my hair, she flips out. "You idiot! You've ruined it!" she exclaims. It was nice and long until Mily messed with it. Now it's shorter than she's ever seen it. All during the brief wedding ceremony, she keeps staring at my mangled hair, and I can see that she's barely able to keep a straight face. Mily stands next to me and avoids her eyes.

After the ceremony, we have an outdoor buffet dinner that's been prepared by family friends who own a small catering business. It's

Debbie and me with Noe Lozano and his wife Elvira

so enjoyable visiting with everyone that we linger for hours chatting and accepting congratulations from all our well-wishers. Finally Debbie's mom whispers to us that our guests are waiting for us to be on our way, and reluctantly we climb into her parents' green VW Bug, which they've given us as a wedding present. They had promised it to us so we would have a car in Irvine.

Everyone waves good-bye as we drive off into the sunset. Literally, because it's one of the longest days of the year and we're heading west toward the ocean. But a few blocks later, I pull over. "Where are we going?"

"I don't know," Debbie says. "Didn't you make reservations somewhere?"

"Was I supposed to? I thought your parents were handling everything."

"No, not that part, but they've given us five hundred dollars for our honeymoon." She then teases me, asking me how I could have put so little thought into the night when we're finally going to consummate our four-year relationship. "Maybe we should wait until we get to the coast tomorrow night," she jokes.

As if screwing up my hair wasn't enough, I've also messed up our wedding night. I stop at a pay phone and call hotels along the coast, but they're all either booked up or too expensive. We settle for a hotel in Fresno. There, we sleep together for the first time as husband and wife. As we tenderly learn to make love to each other that night, we have to laugh at our inexperience and ineptness. We vow to practice a lot. And forever afterward, when we're asked where we spent our wedding night, we have to confess, "Romantic downtown Fresno."

The next day, I find a modestly priced hotel on the coast for the second night of our short honeymoon. We can spend only one day there because we don't have the time or money for more. I have to be in Irvine by Monday. On Sunday, we continue down the coast, then inland to Irvine. We thought we would be able to move into our apartment that day, but we arrive after the office has closed. We need to find a hotel for the night. Debbie wants to go back to the chain motel we stayed at on our apartment-hunting trip, but I feel it's too expensive, especially because we have an apartment already waiting for us.

I find a cheap hotel in a seedy-looking area. The room has a hole in the wall. The mattress sags in the middle and smells of . . . well, I don't want to guess. We have to leave our car sitting outside with all our possessions in it. Debbie's so upset with me that she won't speak to me, so needless to say our third night as a married couple is a disaster. The next morning, when we check out, I learn that this place usually rents out rooms by the hour. Also, if the TV had been working, which it didn't, we could have paid to watch some "interesting" movies. I check the car and sheepishly tell Debbie, "It's okay—nothing's missing," but the only response I get is a glare.

CHAPTER THIRTY

Zombie Years—
Classes

T HE NEXT DAY, WE MOVE OUR things into our apartment, and I head off to orientation. I take the car, which leaves Debbie feeling a bit trapped in this unfamiliar city. She needs to buy groceries, but neither of us knows when I'll get home. When I arrive at the orientation, I get my first look at my classmates. Most of the 150 or so incoming students are white males, but I'm surprised to see a number of brown and black males, and more women, especially minority women, than I expected. In fact, there are as many minority women as white female students. We find out later that most schools try to increase their minority enrollment statistics this way, by admitting students who fill two minority categories at once—female plus ethnic group or racial background.

But my first thought as I look around is, as always, "They're all smarter than me." Just like that, I'm back into my inferiority mode. And as I start talking with some of the other students, I feel even more out of place. The Anglo males are older, and most appear to have graduate degrees in chemistry, organic chemistry, or pharmacy. The Mexican students all are cocky and self-assured.

The med-school campus is small, and all the classrooms are clustered together. I learn that our class is the smallest of any of the medical schools in the UC system. How I was admitted is still a shock to me. When I think about all the top students from all over the country who applied, I consider myself extremely lucky.

Actually, our Santa Cruz class has done very well. I got into Irvine. Max and Lisa are at UC San Francisco. Ernie's been admitted to Hastings, the prestigious UC law school in San Francisco. So has his new girlfriend, Graciela, whom he later ends up marrying. What's more, Javier Elizondo, who was one of my roommates during our sophomore year, shows up at Irvine two days after classes start. One of the black female students received a last-minute admission to her first choice, UC San Diego, and Javier was fortunate to be the first alternate at Irvine, so he got the spot. Adolph didn't make it into medical school right after graduating from Santa Cruz, but he ends up spending another year there doing graduate work and is then accepted to the University of Michigan Medical School at Ann Arbor.

Our first day also includes the first sessions of some of our classes, including gross anatomy and meeting the cadavers we'll spend the next months dissecting. I dissected a cat in my anatomy class at Santa Cruz, but having a dead person lying on the table in front of you is totally different. I can't help thinking about them as they might have been when they were alive.

It takes me weeks to get used to being in their presence. I lose my appetite, and when I come home smelling of formaldehyde, Debbie won't let me touch her until I shower. Even then she makes a face. Over time, though, and the closer exams get, the less queasy we feel. Eventually we start bringing our lunches into the lab with us, but we never forget which hand is holding our sandwich and which one is holding a piece of the cadaver. Still, Thanksgiving is hard for me because the white meat resembles the muscles we are studying at the time.

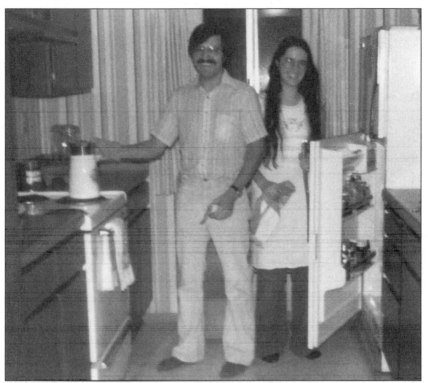

Debbie and me in the kitchen of one of our
student housing apartments, Irvine

At one point later in my first year, Bill, Al, and Joe and their wives make a trip to Disneyland and stop by to visit us. I can't resist taking them down to the cadaver lab. We all have keys so we can study late at night if we want to. It's evening and the lab is deserted. I don't tell them where we're going because I want to see their reactions. As I lead them down a corridor lined with specimen-filled bottles, Anita asks uneasily, "Is that an unborn baby in that jar?"

"Yes," I reply. "And all the other bottles have human organs in them. Like this heart, here."

Joe looks around apprehensively. "Where are you taking us?"

"Oh, I just want to show you where I spend most of my time," I reply casually.

I unlock the door and that terrible smell assails us. I've gotten used to it. I go over to my table, which is covered with a white drape like all the others. With one swift motion, I pull off the sheet, revealing my cadaver. Joe, Al, and Bill bolt out the door. The girls are frightened and back off but don't run off like their macho husbands. When we leave the lab, I get an earful of cussing from the guys. This is one of the few times I remember having fun in med school.

When I finally get home that first day, Debbie tells me she kept getting lost while trying to use the public bus system. The day was smoggy, and she was disappointed when the bus driver told her this was one of the clearer days—the same reaction I had during my interview with Mr. Escobedo. Welcome to Southern California. We didn't realize how nice we had it in Santa Cruz.

My anatomy homework is simple enough that I finish it in less than thirty minutes. I don't realize that this first day as a medical student is also the last day I'll be caught up with my work until I graduate, five years down the road.

The next thing I know, my first two years of medical school turn into what I still think of as the Zombie Years. Anatomy, microbiology, and neurology . . . now I understand why med school's so hard. We're told it's like learning a new language in an impossibly short time, and that's how it feels. But my whole future, and Debbie's, and our future family's, is riding on it.

I'm constantly on the edge of despair. I walk around in a daze, afraid I'll flunk out at any moment. I'm passing my courses, but barely, and I'm on the edge of quitting. I must have been crazy to think I could pull this off. Every day I feel like giving in to my anguish because I'm so far behind. No matter what I do, I can't catch up. I study and sweat over every subject, but I don't seem to understand the material. Every time I go in to take an exam, I know I have a very good chance of flunking it. I don't let Debbie know how desperate I'm feeling because I don't want to upset her. That would only make me feel worse. She enrolls in a nursing course at Saddleback Junior College in Mission Viejo so she'll be able to assist me once I have my own practice. Fortunately, after our first month we move into student housing, so I can walk to my classes and to the library and she can have the car.

She's doing great. I wish I could say the same for myself. When I show her my exam results, she just tells me I have to study more. I think I'm already studying hard enough, but I keep getting answers wrong because I misread or misunderstand the questions. When we go over them, she points out that I have to pay attention to what they're asking for. I'm trying my best, but why do I miss things like the "all of the above" choice and circle only one answer, or fail to see the "but" that tells me what the answer should be? I'm so frustrated by my apparent inability to read the questions right that I wonder if I'm dyslexic. I've always had trouble visualizing letters and adding numbers in my head. When people spell out loud, I have to ask them to repeat themselves over and over before I can get the letters in the right sequence. I decide not to get tested for dyslexia or learning problems because I'm afraid of what I might find out. So I just go on struggling.

Quitting med school is obviously an option. I can always try nursing or, at the very least, settle for becoming an orderly. There are plenty of other areas in medicine that I can go into, but anything other than becoming a doctor would mean I'm a failure. In any case, quitting isn't an alternative because I wouldn't just be letting myself down. I would be letting down all the other minority students here and all the ones who will follow us. But at the rate I'm going, I may fail anyway.

One day late in my first quarter, I hit bottom. I'm on the verge of giving up and going home a loser when out of the blue I receive a letter from Aunt Lucinda. I'm surprised to hear from her because I don't keep in touch with her except on visits home. She writes:

> I knew you were smart and you would make something of yourself someday. I thought you would grow up to work in a store like J. C. Penney and wear a shirt and tie. But for you to be a doctor, I never imagined that. I can't believe my "little brother" is going to be a doctor. I am so proud of you.
>
> Love, Lucinda

Her letter makes me resolve to stick around. I can't disappoint her. If she has that much confidence in me, I can't let her down. I forge ahead with more determination.

Given how hard school is, I'm glad I decided not to take the standard four-year curriculum but to take the five-year track instead—three years of coursework and two years of clinical rotations—as many of the other minority students are doing. I try to keep in mind that I've had only the basic undergraduate pre-med courses but am competing with top students and graduate students who find the material repetitious at the beginning because they have so much more background than I do. However, I feel a little better when I find out that even they start having trouble keeping up before long.

On the other hand, I soon learn that however much lip service is paid to the idea of equal opportunity, prejudice lurks just under the surface. A few weeks into the fall quarter, one of the white women students comes over to a couple of us minority students. She tells us that while she and a group of white students were talking informally with one professor, he informed them that minority students didn't belong at Irvine and that he was going to make it hard for us to pass our exams.

Our class has more nonwhite students than any class before us, but all the professors are white. The only black administrator is the financial aid director. There's only one Mexican administrator, an assistant dean whose main role is to advise us and try to keep us on track. He's aware of the prejudice we're facing and urges us not to succumb to it.

Before long, we pick up on other indications of what we're up against. I do poorly on my first exam. This shakes my already precarious confidence. I thought I had the material down cold, but the exam is very different from what I studied. Most of the other minority students do badly, too, but the Anglo students do well for the most part. We later find out that some of the instructors have been holding study sessions with small groups of them. Were we ever told about these groups or invited to join them? No.

We form our own group and get together as often as we can to coach each other. Even so, my basic feeling about myself remains the same, that I'm always two steps behind everyone else, not just academically but also culturally and economically.

One day, while a group of us, white and Chicano students, happen to be sitting outside, we get into a discussion about our situation as minorities. I know that a lot of the Anglo students have parents who are doctors or other professionals, and when they seem to be making an effort to understand us and how we're fitting in and being treated, I start sharing a little about myself.

I tell them why I feel I'm starting out two steps behind them and why this gap is so hard to overcome. Some of the students don't understand what I'm saying, so I ask them to imagine what it would be like for them if their parents were new to this country and had no education, and if the only jobs their parents could get paid minimum wage. "Where do you think you might be right now?" I ask. "You'd be lucky to finish high school and get a job in a factory. But that's the situation I grew up in, so I have a hard time relating to you because I don't have the financial or educational advantages you've had all your life. I had to really fight to get where I am right now." Some of them get it.

I'm under so much academic pressure that I don't slack off during the breaks between quarters the way some of the other students do. As the year goes on, I find that no matter how hard I try, I have to keep reviewing my courses over and over and taking makeup exams. I study constantly and never feel I can afford to rest or let down for a moment. I envy my classmates who feel they can take time to unwind, go to beach parties, or take off on weekends. And time pressure isn't the only problem. Money's scarce, too. Debbie and I spend the five hundred dollars her parents gave us as a wedding gift on a used microscope because we can't afford one on our financial aid.

The only high point of this hellish first year is Debbie's twenty-first birthday in October. To celebrate, we get dressed up and go out to El Torito, which to me is one of the more expensive Mexican restaurants in Irvine. We share a margarita because we only have so much to spend, but we have a good time. When we get home, we find a birthday card from her mother in the mail, along with a twenty-dollar bill bill and a note telling us to go out and celebrate on them. We kick ourselves for not checking the mail before heading out to dinner.

When the first quarter ends, Debbie and I take just a couple of days to spend Christmas with my family. Even so, I go back to work at the tree nursery to earn a little money so I can buy her something nice because she's fantastic about stretching our financial aid as far as it'll go. (Of course, she gets upset and thinks I should have used the money to pay some of our bills.)

The other workers at the nursery don't understand why a medical student like me is out working in the fields with them. They bombard me with questions and comments, but mostly they can't believe that someday I'll actually be a doctor, and a Mexican doctor to boot. None of them has ever met a Mexican doctor. "You're pulling our leg," they keep saying.

They also ask me medical questions I can't answer because I'm not far enough into my training, and I can see them wondering if I'm for real. I finally get the bright idea of reciting all the names of the muscles and bones in the body, along with their functions. That impresses them, and I realize I have learned something during my first quarter after all.

Then I go back to Irvine, where I and a number of the other minority students study and retake our exams. I pass this second time around, but by now the break is over and the new quarter is beginning. This becomes an unending cycle.

By our second year, several of my minority classmates have dropped out. The only Native American student flunks out because he spent too much time socializing. Debbie and I rarely do anything with any of the other students, Mexican or not. It's my fault. She'd like to go out and see people, but I feel I don't deserve to take the time off. I also don't want anyone to know how much I have to struggle to survive each day. I cling to the hope that I can make it through to the end of the first two years. If I can make it through to my clinical rotations, where we'll actually be working with patients at the UC Irvine Medical Center teaching hospital near Anaheim and rotating through the various departments to gain experience in all the medical specialties, things will get easier. I know they will.

Unfortunately, Irvine hits us with a big surprise in our second year. They choose my entering class to change the rotations policy. We're informed that starting with our class, we will have to pass the first part of our "boards" before we can start hospital rotations. These boards are the first of several sets of examinations given by the National Board of Medical Examiners to test the competence of medical students. Until now, students at Irvine usually took their first boards after their second year. Ideally, but not always, they were supposed to pass their boards before starting their internships, but at the latest they had to pass them before starting their residencies.

This change comes out of nowhere. No one said anything about this when we arrived. I and many of the other minority students took the boards a couple of times in our first year but failed. This hasn't been a concern because we knew we could take them as many times as we wanted to, and we all thought we had plenty of time. Now all of a sudden we're under the gun to pass our boards, or we won't be allowed to start the actual hands-on medicine we've all been looking forward to.

In the midst of this crisis, someone apparently alerts the administration to the possibility that this policy change, and its timing, could be discriminatory because it might be seen as unfairly targeting minority students. Perhaps the possibility of unwanted publicity makes the administration back down, but in any case the policy changes back. We'll be able start our clinical rotations before passing our first boards, just as all the classes before us have.

No matter how I try, I can't shake the feeling that I'm in two worlds but don't belong to either. All around me I see a sense of belonging that emanates from the Anglos and even from some of the minority students. They don't seem to be having any trouble adjusting. But I'm like a lost boy in a strange and foreign country. Even though everyone around me is speaking English, it's as if I don't understand their language. However, it's really that I don't comprehend their ways. Our cultures are too different. I can't get into theirs, and I never will. I am what I am. I can change my future, but I'll never be able to alter my past. I can never go back in time and have the financial or social status they grew up with. My history is messing with my present. I know I'm the one with the problem here, and I don't know how to cope with it.

To recharge my batteries, I try to get away by going home whenever possible, and I persuade Debbie to come with me although she sometimes feels concerned about losing time from her studies. But I'm finding that even home is no longer a haven. Not that it was ever easy to be with my family, but there was still a certain sense of belonging. Now I'm feeling a change in the way everyone looks at me. My going to college was beyond anyone's expectations, but it was something they could accept because they all know teachers or other people who have attended college.

But they don't know anyone who's gone to medical school. Of course, they go to medical clinics for their health care, but the doctors they see there are demigods who deign to see them only by appointment. No one in our family knows anything about doctors personally. All they know is what they experience in the clinics. We're intimidated by anyone wearing a white coat and tie.

Now I'm going to be one of those demigods. I see the looks on their faces. They're intimidated, but sometimes I wonder if they also feel resentful because they think I'm looking down on them. Whenever I go home, I try to act the same as I always have, but I can't. I've gone too far beyond the aspirations I had for myself, not to mention anything they might have expected me to achieve. They don't realize how much pressure they put on me every time they introduce me as "The Doctor," because then I have to explain that I'm still in training. It doesn't matter. Everyone keeps asking me for medical advice. I do the best I can.

Over time, going back to Goshen becomes so uncomfortable for me that I can't even look forward to that as an escape from my personal hell. Debbie tries to tell me that the problem's more with me than with them because I've changed so much but they haven't. In a way, I see her point. They have no way of understanding my experience. Also, I'm struggling so hard to survive that none of the mundane, everyday topics that are so important to them—kids, sports, soap operas, TV shows—matter to me. I'm in limbo, trapped between my old life and an unknown future.

Also, I haven't made any friends with the other students. I don't have the time or energy for friends. And I have to give whatever free time I have to Debbie. Unfortunately, she and I aren't getting along very well. Although she's now in her second year of her nursing courses and doing very well, she hates how the male doctors treat the nursing staff, and she isn't finding the work as rewarding as she expected. At home, I'm too wrapped up in my worries to pay attention to her. This makes her feel lonely.

Even though she knows how hard I'm struggling and keeps urging me to study more, I never tell her about my constant terror that I'm going to flunk out. She has no idea why my self-esteem is so low. She begs me to open up to her, but I turn a deaf ear and bottle everything up. She doesn't know how much shame I carry because I grew up the way I did. How can I tell her how unworthy I feel, how much I feel I don't belong and never will? How can I tell her I feel like giving up and running away? I'm so close to falling apart that I'm not strong enough to give her the love and emotional support she should be getting from me. After all, she's suffering as much as I am, and she doesn't have any family or friends to turn to. I'm the only one she has, and I'm not there for her. We're failing to live up to what we promised each other on our wedding day, that we would always be there for each other "for better or for worse." And we're both too young to realize that neither of us is perfect and that we're bound to disappoint each other.

CHAPTER THIRTY-ONE

Zombie Years— Rotations

’M EXCITED TO BE STARTING CLINICAL ROTATIONS, because to me this is what medicine's all about—seeing and helping people with their ailments (even though we're still students, so we don't know what we're doing and still have a lot to learn).

Our mind-numbingly difficult coursework is behind us. We can finally buy our short white lab coats, which signify that we're still students. The long coats are reserved for the doctors and professors. This doesn't lessen our enthusiasm. Once we don our lab coats and stethoscopes, we're dressed for the part of young doctors in training. We leave the Irvine campus to the first- and second-year students and join the fourth-year students, interns, and residents. Over the next two years or three years, we'll spend six weeks in each of the hospital's departments getting experience in the various specialties. It's about twelve miles away from the campus, which should be a fifteen-minute drive, but it can take almost an hour if we get caught in traffic.

Our coursework has taught us about the human body from the inside out and from microscopic structures to gross human anatomy, but this has all been in isolation, without seeing the overall picture.

I'm eager to start meeting real individual patients and to get a sense of who they are, and then try to identify and understand their particular illness, disease, or condition.

However, before we can go to our first rotation, we have to learn two skills: how to draw blood samples, and how to do a complete "H&P"—taking down a patient's medical history, followed by a complete physical examination.

I'm dreading the blood-drawing because as far as I know, I've never gotten over my fear of needles. How can I be a doctor if I can't handle a little poke in the arm? Of course I don't tell the classmate I'm partnered with how apprehensive I am. When the moment of truth arrives, I offer to be the first "victim" because I figure that if I pass out, he can just leave me lying humiliated on the floor and get another student to practice on. He approaches me with the needle and syringe. So far, so good. He follows all the steps to keep the injection site sterile. I cringe and my arm tenses up.

"You having a problem?" he asks me.

"I'm kind of afraid of needles."

I can tell he's annoyed as he feels for the vein, but I hardly feel it when the needle punctures my skin. As the syringe fills with my blood, I'm elated! I don't feel one bit faint! The world isn't spinning! I'm not seeing stars! Maybe I'm over my needle phobia! As soon as he finishes, I get out my kit and prepare to return the favor.

But the moment my needle enters his skin and I see it dangling from his arm, blackness overtakes me. I wake up flat on my back on the floor with him and several other classmates hovering over me. Obviously, I'm not over my problem with needles after all, though I somehow do manage to get through our mini-course in drawing blood eventually.

Now we have to prove that we can do a thorough H&P. A professor who acts as our proctor puts us together in teams of threes and assigns a patient to each of us. Our job is to get as much information as possible and carry out as thorough an examination as the patient will allow. It's a bit like playing detective. You ask questions to solve a mystery that the patient's hiding from you and sometimes from himself or herself. The better you get at eliciting and identifying clues, the easier your job is.

Unfortunately, learning to do H&Ps is hard. For one thing, most of the patients in teaching hospitals are elderly, so they have long medical histories. We're supposed to get everything, basically back to when they were born, including all their illnesses and hospital stays as well as information about their lifestyle and so on. This can take as long as an hour, and that's before we even get to the physical examination.

Another problem is that between the fourth-year medical students, the interns, and the residents, the patients have already been through multiple H&Ps. By the time we show up, the last thing they want is to repeat their story to a bunch of wet-behind-the-ears third-year students who want to poke and prod and look at every orifice. Male patients almost always balk at the rectal exam, which is understandable because they've already been through the ordeal with a half-dozen other people. Since we students have had to practice on one another, I fully understand the patients' reluctance. We're not very skilled at probing, so sometimes we hurt our "victims," and we're also so new to this aspect of the physical exam that we're embarrassed. So rectals are "uncomfortable" in a couple of ways.

We meet individually with a total of three practice patients and do our best to carry out the H&P procedure. After we write up our individual reports, the three of us meet with our proctor and present our findings orally one at a time. The proctor critiques each presentation so the other two students can learn. After we finish our three H&Ps, the proctor tells us whether we've passed or not.

I and my teammates feel we did a good job on the two presentations we've already given and that we're ready to move on to our first rotations. I feel confident about the one more practice patient I have

left because I already have the first two under my belt. For some reason, though, my two partners don't show up for our last patient
encounter. I carry out the H&P on my own, trying to remember everything I've learned in the last several weeks. It's amazing how much
detail we're supposed to elicit, and how much we miss. After I finish, I write my conclusions as precisely as I can. At the end of my
summation, I have ten pages of notes. There's no way I missed anything of importance.

At the appointed time, I present myself to our proctor.

"Where are the other two?" he asks.

"I don't know, sir."

He sighs. "All right. Proceed."

After I finish, he says nothing one way or another. I have no clue
as to how I performed, but I'm sure I did fine, even if I did stammer
and stutter more than usual. Several days later, he calls me in for my
evaluation and proceeds to tell me what I did wrong in each area of
my report. He wraps up by saying, "You did a poor job. You failed to
prove that you've mastered the art of taking a history. I don't believe
you're ready to advance to your rotations."

I'm speechless. After surviving the last three years, I've flunked
the easiest course I've taken so far? As I leave his office, my two partners, who have finally shown up and are waiting to go in after me, ask
me how I did. When I tell them, they're as confused as I am. They say
that when we've presented together in the past, I did my summations
as well as they did. Their words mean a lot to me because they're both
white, but they seem really upset that this has happened to me. What
happens is, he passes them—even though they didn't show up for all
of our patient appointments—and he fails me.

This means that they get to start their rotations but I have to wait
to be assigned another proctor to review my H&Ps. I'll have to wait to
start my rotations until the next round begins in six weeks, provided
my new proctor passes me.

The worst of it is that I have to go home and tell Debbie. I hate the thought of disappointing her again. When I do tell her, she's outraged and tells me I should file a complaint. I don't have the energy. I'm tired of this shit, of getting undermined all the time. I feel dejected, humiliated, and sorry for myself. Why do I have to repeat my H&Ps while my classmates get to start their rotations?

Then, as has been true so often in my life, the unexpected happens. A few days later, Jonathan Tobis, a young white cardiology resident, tells me he's been assigned to evaluate my H&Ps. I wonder how much I can trust him because it seems that every time I'm close to getting my life in order, I get kicked in the gut. This has been the pattern ever since my experience with Mr. Moss in eighth grade.

He has me do an H&P on one of his heart patients. Great, I think to myself. Heart patients' cases are usually very complicated and require extensive histories. I do the most comprehensive H&P I can. But what if I'm missing something? What if I fail again? I take a lot of time with the patient and cover every base I can think of. I review my notes over and over again, but I can't think of anything to add that would give me a better chance of passing.

Tobis and I meet alone in his office. He asks no questions as I do my recitation. After I finish, he makes a few notes, then looks up and says, "I see nothing at all wrong with your H&P. It's complete and accurate and very well presented. I don't know why you were failed initially, but you don't have to do any more for me. I'm passing you as of now." He adds that although it's unfortunately too late for me to start a rotation at this point, I can hang around his office or study in the library until the next rotations start. He also seems upset about something, and when he asks me who my previous proctor was, I get the feeling that he doesn't understand why I was failed. But he can't do anything about it because he's only a resident.

Finally, I can advance to what I've been waiting for ever since I decided to become a doctor. I can't afford to take my waiting time as a break—I spend it studying in the library—but I do regain some of my confidence. I'm so happy that I drive home right away to tell Debbie I'm back on track, or almost back on track. And I have no further problems with any other doctors or with the clinical rotations.

Clinical rotations are hard and exhausting because they take up almost every waking hour. We're on call for thirty-six hours at a time, and we get saddled with most of the scut work, like doing the two A.M. blood draws and preparing all the lab reports for morning rounds, which start at seven A.M. in most of the departments. We also have to be ready to be called upon at any moment to recite information about the patients.

Morning rounds, which include the staff doctor, the residents, the medical students, and the nurses who are charged with the particular patients being seen, are stressful for everyone. I don't know how the patients put up with the intrusions of these flocks of people, most of whom come across as very self-important. To me, the worst part is the way we discuss them right in front of them as if they're only bodies or "cases" instead of human beings with feelings. Not to mention that because this is a teaching hospital, we turn them inside out and discuss the most intimate details about them without any regard for their privacy.

But we're stressed, too. The staff doctor uses rounds to pepper us with questions, and we're expected to know every detail plus all the facts of the patients' illnesses. I still lack confidence and feel very unsure of myself, so I don't volunteer to answer even when I know the material. I try to stay under the radar. But eventually, after everyone else responds to questions, the staff doctor invariably notices me and asks me a question, for example, to name three causes of the patient's disease.

I always feel everyone staring at me as I stammer out any answer. After I finish, I'm sometimes told to look up the material and present to the group at tomorrow morning's rounds. I end up feeling I've made a fool of myself, and I know it's my own fault for not trying to answer some of the earlier questions, which tend to be easier. Answering questions in rounds is a game that the smart students know how to play, but I don't have the nerve to jump in.

For us minority students, rotations are difficult in other ways because the patients, and even the staff, sometimes mistake us for janitors or orderlies instead of doctors in training. Even though we're wearing hospital scrubs just like the Anglo students, we'll be asked to clean up patients' room or to get hold of the doctor. I notice that no one asks the white students to do these things. It seems obvious that after years of being seen only by Anglo male doctors, neither the patients nor the staff are used to seeing black, Mexican, or female medical students. They see us as they always have—the subservient class. Sometimes the doctors even ask me to act as an interpreter, which only puts me further behind with my other work.

When I walk into patients' rooms to conduct exams, they always ask who I am. When I tell them I'm a medical student, some of them say, "I want a real doctor." Sometimes what they mean is "a white male MD," but I know that sometimes they mean they want an MD and not a student of any kind because they assume we're not competent. If patients are insistent about wanting to see a "real doctor," I always accommodate them rather than making a big deal about it. I don't see the point, because if I force the issue, I'll end up with an unhappy patient, and that'll only make my job harder.

My first three rotations include surgery, the emergency room, and internal medicine. I don't feel much excitement about any of them. They're just hard work, especially surgery, where rounds start at five-thirty in the morning and can last for hours. After that, we spend the rest of the day standing around in the operating room, which kills my feet and back. We're never allowed to touch the patients or do anything at all except try to observe the "kings of the OR" in action. Every once in a while, they deign to look at us or ask us a question. I know right away that surgery isn't my field.

I feel the same way about the ER. The medical staff seem to burn out really fast, and I quickly start feeling numb, too. It's as if the patients are basically objects that we can practice learning procedures on. For example, one day an alcoholic man who's known to everyone for his many ER visits comes in again to be treated for one of the consequences of his drinking. The resident assigned to supervise me tells me to draw an arterial blood gas, a very painful "stick" that I know hurts the old man when I do it. After I finish, I ask my resident what I should do with it. He shrugs. "Dump it. We don't need to know his blood gases."

I don't react much to his callousness because I don't have much empathy for the ER patients either. I feel that many of them are abusing the system and wasting everyone's time coming in with minor problems, or for treatment of their self-induced problems, like drugs and alcohol. The rape and molestation cases are different—we see a lot of these cases, and they're so painful. I don't consider a career in the ER for one moment.

When I start my obstetric-gynecological rotation, I'm not sure how I'll feel, but I do know I've always wanted to help bring a new baby into the world. My first delivery is a Mexican woman in her twenties. She has a couple of other kids and is used to working with medical students throughout her pregnancies. This means she's actually more experienced than I am, and she does her best to help me along, including letting me know when I fumble as her baby's about to be born.

The baby's head appears, and I feel the joy of seeing a new life come into the world. I may think I'm guiding the delivery, but I'm really not doing anything because nature is taking care of most of the work. Thanks to the mom's helpful hints and her experience, and in spite of my getting in her way, we manage to bring a baby girl into the world. She pops out and I turn to the dad and tell him that they have a little girl just as she gives a loud yowl as if to let him know herself. What a beautiful sound, I think as I dry her off. I hate handing her over to the nurse, but I do. Then I turn back to the mom. And notice that her stomach is bulging out on one side. I turn to my resident, who's standing on the sidelines looking bored.

"Something doesn't look right," I tell him. He feels her abdomen and gets a perplexed look on his face. Then he shoves me out of the way, takes a position between the mom's spread legs, and reaches in with a gloved hand. "We've got another baby in here, positioned feet first!!" he yells. "Call for a C-section—stat!" The dad and I are relegated to a corner as people rush in to prepare her for the operation.

A few weeks later, after I have twenty or so deliveries under my belt, I get a sixteen-year-old girl with her first pregnancy. She's very scared, so I sit by her side for hours trying to reassure her. A couple of months earlier, I did a hypnosis elective and learned how a soothing voice and touch could hypnotize people, even including babies in the burn unit. I decide to try with her even though hypnosis isn't accepted medically and using it has never been mentioned in any of our lectures or classes.

What the heck, I decide, she's in so much distress that I may as well see if I can help her get through this by getting her to relax, even if it isn't standard medical practice. I try to put her under by rubbing her scalp and speaking to her in a soft, rhythmic cadence, and before I realize it, she's under. I suggest that she relax and listen to my voice as I guide her through her labor. In no time at all, she's ready and, without any more discomfort, delivers a baby boy. She tells me afterward that she thought it was going to be a lot harder. I don't tell her I hypnotized her. I'm concerned about getting in trouble because the head of ob-gyn is very strict and by the book.

But helping her that day teaches me an important lesson that I've kept in mind ever since—to trust my own judgment, to do things my way when it comes to treating people, and to put their comfort first.

CHAPTER THIRTY-TWO

My True Calling

IT TURNS OUT THAT OB-GYN IS PREPARATION for my finding my true
calling. I always feel a strong pull to the babies I deliver, and I hate
handing them over to the nurses or pediatric medical students.
Because I delivered them, I somehow consider them mine. The moment
I begin my pediatrics rotation, I know I've found my calling.

I grew up surrounded by infants and children in my family and
am totally comfortable holding them and caring for them. In fact,
it's common for us to have two or three babies a few months apart in
age climbing into our laps or crawling on the floor or wanting attention. I'm amazed that so many of my fellow students find being around
newborns difficult or uncomfortable. On the other hand, most of
them come from very small families and have little or no experience
with newborns or toddlers. I'm so comfortable in pediatrics that the
time flies.

I'm also happy that most infants are normal and require very little in the way of medical interventions. Inevitably, though, some
patients die. I find I'm able to deal with deaths better than I thought
I would. I sometimes wonder whether one reason underlying our
medical training in working with cadavers may be to desensitize us
as well as to teach us anatomy.

I think I've learned this lesson well—until I experience my first infant death. During one delivery, we're called in "stat" because the OB resident stops detecting the fetus's heart tone in the very last minutes of labor. The mom and dad quickly realize that something's gone very wrong. The dad is told to leave the delivery room while the mom tries to push the baby out as quickly as possible. When we hurry in, the pediatrics resident and the intern don't seem particularly tense, so I assume that the situation is routine and that there's still a good chance to save the infant, who is full term and appeared normal until a few minutes ago. But the baby—a little boy—is in worse shape than they realize. When the resident hands him over to us, he's unresponsive and turning blue. We rush him to the nursery, but in spite of all our efforts he doesn't respond. We have to pronounce him dead.

This little boy isn't my baby, but, even in those few minutes with him, I bonded with him. I leave the nursery with tears in my eyes and can barely hold back my sobs. I can only imagine the grief that his mother and father are feeling. I don't know what I would do if a baby of mine were to die at birth. I think I would probably die, too. I start to wonder if I want to run the risk of experiencing this kind of grief.

We're always being taught to not let emotions get in the way of our work. We're supposed to show cool, professional detachment at all times. If we have a bad outcome and lose a patient, we're supposed to just put it behind us and go on to the next case. I wonder whether keeping us so busy, continuously on the go and so sleep-deprived that we become numb, isn't actually a calculated part of our training like our work with cadavers. In any case, there's so much to do after a baby dies, and so many other kids to treat and so many ER calls to make, that we don't have time to grieve.

Still, sometimes it's impossible for me to stay detached. One of my pediatric rotations is at St. Joseph's Children's Hospital in Orange, where I meet Sheana, a bubbly eleven-year-old redhead with an irrepressible sense of humor—and cystic fibrosis. I enjoy sitting with her during my nights on call. Between bouts of coughing, she laughs at all my corny jokes.

I know that the disease is going to kill her within a year or two at most, but she either isn't aware of how serious her condition is, or she pretends not to be. She carries on in her hospital bed as if she's at home in her own room. I think to myself that if I ever have a daughter, I want her to be just like Sheana. A few weeks later, when my rotation ends and I have to go back to the UCI Medical Center, I say good-bye to her and tell her I'll come back and visit her soon. A couple of months later, when I finally go back to St. Joe's to see her, she's not in her bed.

"Where's Sheana?" I ask a nurse who's walking down the corridor.

"She's gone."

"Gone where?" I ask, even though my heart sinks because I already know the answer.

"She died last week."

In a daze, I walk outside to the central garden area. I used to bring her out here so she could get some fresh air. I sit on the bench we used to sit on, and I cry. Sheana's the first child patient I've felt such an attachment to. I vow never to let myself get so attached again. It hurts too much.

But it's hard to keep my emotional armor on. Manuel, an adorable little Mexican toddler only eighteen months old, has a severe type of pancreatic cancer. His odds of survival are less than three percent. His parents are wonderful with him, and I can't help spending all my spare time with him. I know he's going to die and that I'm going to suffer tremendously for getting so involved, but I can't help it. No matter how often we're warned to keep our emotional distance with patients, sometimes one little patient won't let you.

One day he goes in for another CT scan, and it shows that the tumor is gone. It's simply disappeared. He's cured. Everyone's baffled. His parents are overwhelmed with joy and thank us for all our care. We know that they think we pulled off a miracle, but we have no idea why his tumor disappeared. All we had been able to do was remove as much of the tumor as possible. The cancer had spread so far that the surgery was really pointless, but it was all we could do. When I learn that Manuel is cured, I cry again, but this time out of relief.

His remarkable recovery is the catalyst I need to stay in pediatrics, even though I know I may lose patients I care about. I can't see myself retreating to a specialty like radiology or dermatology where there's less risk of getting attached to patients and then losing them.

During our pediatrics rotation, we have to spend time in the clinics, which treat outpatients, as well as "on the floor" with patients who have been admitted to the wards for treatment. We've been told that pediatrics is mainly clinic work and that it can be boring because most of the children we'll see are just there for well-baby checks and immunizations. It's rare to see a complicated case or even a child who's very sick, but the ward work is necessary so we can be sure we know how to identify more serious cases.

The day I see my first clinic patient, I know I'm never going to be bored. When I walk in, the mom is holding a cute four-month-old baby girl in her lap. Baby Millie gives me the biggest smile I've seen in a long time. I lay her down, and she coos and laughs during the whole exam as I find her tickle spots. This doesn't feel at all like work, and I wish my time with her would never end.

My enjoyment of working with babies is a complete contrast to my classmate Rob's experience. He has already decided on cardiology as his specialty and is doing the pediatrics rotation because it's required. One day, I see him go into an examining room, only to emerge a few minutes later with his tie askew, his shirttails pulled out of his pants, and his hair disheveled. I can't help it—I have to check out what kind of monster kid would make a grown man look like an escapee from a battlefield.

So I go in, introduce myself, and tell the mom that Rob had to leave but that I'll take over. It turns out that Rob's tormentor is seven-month-old Baby Tate. In minutes, I have him laughing and babbling. One more proof that this is my calling. I can handle taking care of babies like this for the rest of my life—including maybe our own, because ever since Debbie and I got married, I've been trying to talk her into our having a baby.

She feels it's too soon, but I don't want to wait. I want to be a father now. Eventually she promises that we'll start trying once I'm in my last year of medical school. I tell her I want a small family, unlike the large one I grew up in, but when I say "small," I mean five or six kids. She has a different definition. "I don't think five is 'small,'" she tells me. "And you're crazy if you think I'm going to get pregnant that many times."

"Okay, then," I capitulate. "Four will be fine."

CHAPTER THIRTY-THREE

Survival Mode

Y THE FALL OF 1980, I'M WELL on my way to graduating, with only one year to go in my five-year track. A few electives are the only barriers standing in my way. Sometimes I can't believe I've made it this far. I've survived, but am I intact? I don't think so. I've suffered more than I ever thought I could, and I'm not the only one. Debbie's suffered tremendously, too.

Our marriage isn't what we envisioned. Medical school has taken so much out of me that I've become a different person. When we met, I was loving, attentive, caring, and basically nice—but from the moment I started at Irvine, I changed into a frightened, selfish man totally obsessed with this thing called "medical school." It took over my life completely, and I became lost to Debbie and to myself.

Has it been worth it? Getting married only a week before I started medical school didn't give us any time to get to know each other as husband and wife. Besides, Debbie was only twenty and I was twenty-three. Maybe we should have waited. What was I thinking, putting someone so young through the torture of coping with me and what I've had to endure—a situation in which there was no escape for her? I guess she could have left me and gone back to her parents, but that's not her nature. She told me she would follow me wherever I went, and she's kept her word. But what about my promises to cherish her?

Although we tried to be honest with each other while we were dating, we each kept a lot locked up inside that we've never shared. I didn't know that she felt her parents had abandoned her—her father for his work and her mom to pursue her masters degree. When she needed them to intervene with Mark, they discouraged her from breaking up with him for fear that people might think them prejudiced. So she stayed with him for four years, until she met me. She had no idea that I was flawed to the bone—that the charm I exuded was false and that inside I was a scared little boy just waiting for something to go wrong like always.

And I didn't tell her how much I resented that she had two parents and what I envisioned as a wonderful childhood, while I had neither. How was I know that her life before I met her wasn't as great as I imagined?

I've let Debbie down countless times, but there's nothing I can do to make her feel better or to express my love enough. I keep my emotions reined in because I'm afraid that if I let anything out, I'll fall apart completely. When she begs me to open up and talk with her or spend time with her, just a few minutes, I turn away. She must see me as someone who's never available to her—someone just like her dad.

We each bring the terrible baggage of our childhoods into our married life, but it will be years before we start to understand this is haunting our marriage. I have expectations of her and she has similar ones of me, but we don't know how to make each other's dreams come true. All we can do in the meantime is try to survive until the ordeal of medical school is over—while all around us we see the marriages of young couples like ourselves collapse under the intolerable pressures and stresses of medical school.

When we got married, I vowed to myself that I would be the perfect husband. But I haven't been much of a spouse for the last four years, and I feel that Debbie hasn't been a supportive wife to me, either.

So we're both holding resentments against each other. Although we can't talk about what's going on between us, I think we're both hoping that our problems aren't too serious to overcome. But for now we just go on.

✦

In the fall of my final year, we decide it's time to have a baby. We enjoy trying, and at first we aren't concerned, but as the months go by we start feeling frustrated. Debbie starts keeping a chart to track the best time to conceive. It's hard to let go of our disappointment as we wait each month. Then, in January 1981, she's late. We buy a pregnancy test kit and see a small ring at the bottom of the tube. A positive? We run out and buy another test to make sure. This one comes out positive, too. We're going to be parents! It's finally happened!

But before long we start to feel the fear that every prospective parent feels. Will we be good parents? My fears center around my lack of a father figure while I was growing up. Except for the sketchy information I've received in medical school lectures, I don't know what "normal parents" are. When I see people with their children, they seem to know what to do by instinct, but I also see that they're repeating the mistakes their parents made—spanking, failing to value education, and so forth. I want to be the perfect daddy.

In my pediatric rotations, I've cared for a lot of babies who are born too early and too small to live, and others who are born with severe genetic disorders and will require full-time care for their entire lives. For the past two years, Debbie's been working in the Irvine Medical Center genetics lab, so both of us are only too aware of the multiple challenges of a child with birth defects. We don't actually talk about it, but Debbie knows that the odds of our having a normal baby are in our favor because of her youth, but sometimes I'm haunted by fears that our baby may be born ill or may die.

Still, our marital problems fade into the background as we anticipate our baby and my upcoming pediatric residency. Come March,
when I find where I've been "matched" for my pediatric residency,
we'll know much more about our future.

Match Day is an ordeal that all American medical students face
toward the end of their last year of medical school. We visit the residency programs that interest us, apply for our first three picks, and
then wait until we're notified whether we've been chosen or not. I
interview for the pediatric programs at the University of New Mexico
in Albuquerque, at the University of Washington in Seattle (where I
had cancelled my interview five years earlier when I decided that Irvine
was the only place I wanted to attend), and a program of the UC San
Francisco Medical School that's based at Valley Medical Center (VMC)
and Valley Children's Hospital (VCH) in Fresno. At VCH, I'll be working with children, which I want to do for the rest of my career.

That's where I want to go. Fresno is only an hour from Goshen
and, even though I feel so uncomfortable around my family, I still
want to be around for holidays and celebrations and when problems
come up so we can face them together. Fresno would also be great for
Debbie because her aunt and uncle are still in Sanger, and her parents
would be only three hours away. It would be nice for her to have family nearby once the baby arrives. On the other hand, moving would be
something of a wrench because she's started taking classes toward a
graduate degree in biology. It has an illustration component to it that
taps into her art background.

On Match Day, we all gather on the Irvine quad, where the letters notifying us of our fates are handed out to us. None of our spouses
are present, which strikes me as odd because these letters determine
where they'll also be living for the next three years. I pray that I haven't
been rejected, because there are always some students who don't get
a match. I slit open the envelope with trepidation. It's from Fresno!
My top pick has matched me to its program! I'm so surprised, excited,

and relieved that I hurry right home to tell Debbie. I'm feeling that this is the first time in five years that something has gone my way without a stumble. I've conquered all the obstacles I've faced so far. The next step is graduation.

I suspect that Fresno might have been easy for me to match with because their program isn't highly regarded by most of my classmates, and maybe even by residents in other parts of the country who are drawn to bigger, more exciting cities where their spouses can find jobs or activities to fill their free time (which, given how intense residents' schedules are, they'll have a lot of). Fresno is scarcely a cultural center, nor does it offer the excitement of a San Francisco, Chicago, or Los Angeles. But it works for me.

A few weeks before our graduation ceremony, I invite my whole family to come. For the past five years, Ama's been asking me whether I'm "done" yet, and I've had to keep explaining how long medical school takes. When I tell her I'm finally going to be a "real doctor," she asks, "Does that mean you'll have a job now?"

"Sort of. But I want to become a baby doctor, and that takes three more years."

"What do you mean, more training? I thought you were a doctor already." I have to explain to her and other family members that it isn't enough to finish medical school and that I need to do a pediatric residency for three years to become a baby doctor. I tell them that some medical specialties can take as long as seven years. "I'll be getting paid while I study more," I say, "I don't know how much, but they'll be paying me instead of me paying them." Then they ask me how much it cost to attend medical school. I say, "A couple of hundred thousand dollars, but I only owe fifty thousand because I got grants that covered the rest." They're shocked. They have no idea.

"I think it's about time you made some money," Ama says, "so maybe you can start helping me with my bills." She adds that she probably won't attend my graduation because Irvine's too far and she isn't feeling well, and that Apa, who's now eighty-one, isn't in good health either.

The same members of my family who came to my Santa Cruz graduation show up for me this time too—Bill and Kitty, Al and Kris, and Joe and Anita. Of course, Debbie's mom and dad fly down. Since they survived medical school as a young married couple themselves, they're the only ones who really understand what Debbie and I have been through.

The actual ceremony is anticlimactic. When I walk on stage and receive my diploma, I don't feel gratitude and a sense of accomplishment. Instead, I feel angry about the years of misery I've gone through, and relief that I managed to survive.

After the ceremony, we have dinner with Al and Kris, Joe and Anita, and Debbie's parents. Debbie's pregnancy is showing, and the reactions of our two sides of the family are quite different. My family's excited for us, while her parents make it clear that they don't think it's wise for us to be having a baby while I'm still in residency. They express concerns about how hard my internship is going to be on us, even though we tell them we'll manage just fine. They don't understand why this baby is so important to me. It's because I've always wanted to be a father and a better parent to my children than my parents were to me.

When Joe calls me by my new title, "Dr. Resa," I can see he's in awe.

"Dr. Resa"! Now that I have "Doctor" in front of my name and "MD" after it, how do I feel? I write my name, "Ramon Resa, MD," and stare at it in wonder. I've achieved something that few people who had faced the problems I've had to overcome would even have attempted. I think back to all the people I'm grateful to for their inspiration and support. I even have to thank people like Mr. Moss, who tried to stifle my ambitions so long ago, because he made me determined to prove myself and excel. My family has waited for generations for one of us to make it in this society and to live the American dream. I now know that it's

Debbie's dad, Dr. Charles Binger, and her mother, Barbara
at my medical school commencement, June 1981

possible—but not without a grueling baptism.

Since my residency doesn't start until July 1, I have two weeks to relax, for the first time in five years. No studying, no constant fear of failing. I have a job waiting for me that will pay me more than I've ever earned. All I want is to enjoy being with Debbie without my studies getting in the way. It's been a long, hard time since those early years in Santa Cruz. I miss the butterflies I used to feel in my stomach whenever I saw her. Now I rub her tummy with a surge of anticipation for our baby. I rest my head on her stomach and whisper to my little baby, "Do you know how much I'm looking forward to holding you in my arms?" Secretly, I'm wishing for a little girl. I don't know why, but I'm not like most men who want their first child to be a son. I want a son one day, but I want my first child to be a girl so I can spoil her rotten!

During my two-week break, we go to a family gathering near Visalia. Ama and Frances are both there. We're all having fun eating and drinking and watching all the kids and babies play when I happen to overhear my grandmother and Frances talking.

"Now my son is a doctor!" Ama boasts.

"He's my son!" Frances counters.

"I raised him since he was a baby!"

"Well, I gave birth to him!"

They start outshouting each other with their claims to be my "real" mother. And when Ama calls over to me, "Come, *mijo*! Come sit on my lap!," I can't stand it anymore.

"Neither of you is my mother!" I shout, and storm off. I've never exploded like that before, but with everything I've had to overcome without any parental support, their comments are too much for me. I've kept my resentment bottled up for years and dismissed my lack of a mother as just one of those things I had to deal with.

Debbie follows me. "What was that all about?"

"I couldn't take it," I fume. "They did nothing to raise me, and now they both want to claim they have a son who's a doctor so they can brag! They don't care about me! They only care about how important it makes them look." Debbie hugs me. She sees more clearly than I can that my rage is covering up my sorrow that I never had a real mother. She makes me feel better, especially when she presses against me and I feel a slight tap from inside her tummy. My baby wants to reassure me that everything will be okay, that I'll never again have to face the obstacles and the racism I had to overcome, that now I'll be treated as the equal of anyone I meet. I've made it. From now on everything's going to be smooth sailing.

I have no way of knowing that in just a few weeks, my family will suffer a terrible tragedy, and the most painful failure of my life so far will shatter me to the core.

PART SIX

Intern and Resident
(1981–1985)

Marina, about 2½, "helping" me study, Fresno, 1984

CHAPTER THIRTY-FOUR

Intern . . . for a Month

E'RE MOVING UP IN THE WORLD. Life is finally good. Joe helps us move by driving the U-Haul to Fresno, while we follow in the Toyota pickup we just bought. I'm very proud of it because it's the first vehicle I've ever owned, and it's brand-new, too. (Of course, we'll have to trade it in after the baby is born because we'll need a car we can put a car seat in.) We give the pickup to Debbie's parents so one of her brothers can use it.

Debbie's Aunt Beth has a friend who owns a small house for rent less than three blocks from VMC. I'll be able to walk to work much of the time and leave the VW bug at home so Debbie can shop or just get out.

The house is one-and-a-half times the size of Ama's and Apa's. It has three bedrooms, a living room, a kitchen with a dining area, and two bathrooms, for just the two of us. There's also a big yard and an area where we can plant a garden. The neighborhood is a bit seedy, but I consider it a step up compared to Goshen.

We store our bits of furniture in the garage. Joe and Bill promise to help move us in but then get busy with work, so that's where it stays. Debbie, now more than six months pregnant, has nothing to sit on except a big pillow. Once I start my orientation, she's left to clean up and sort out our stuff.

July is one of Fresno's hottest months, with daytime temperatures that average over ninety-six degrees and stretches of several days at a time of temperatures over a hundred and five. We have only one small air conditioner, in our bedroom. Debbie's not used to Valley weather in the first place, and at this stage in her pregnancy she's miserable. I come home one evening to find her in the backyard trying to cool off in a rubber raft filled with water. With her legs and head hanging over the sides and her tummy sticking up in the middle, she looks like a beached whale. I have to help her get out. I can't help laughing, but that doesn't go over too well with her.

The biggest change in our lives now is that I finally have a paying job. My salary is the most money I've ever made, so I'm perfectly happy. Now I can tell Ama that I'm making a living and can help her out. The problem is, I've forgotten about my student loans. When I receive my first payment notice, I realize that they're going to take a significant part of my salary each month. Still, looking at the overall picture, I can't be too upset. After all, where would I be if I hadn't borrowed that money in the first place? Debbie's too far along in her pregnancy to look for a job, but I know when I open my practice a few years from now, I'll be earning many times what I owe in loans.

VMC's pediatric program is comprised of six interns. We're required to be on call every third day except for our first two weeks, when we're on call every other day because one of the interns is out with chicken pox. During my med-school rotations, the students were on call for the interns (first-year residents), supposedly so we could gain experience. However, most of the time the interns treated us like "gofers," there to make their lives easier by doing all their scut work. At VMC, we don't have the luxury of medical students under us. We have to do everything ourselves.

The interns, residents, and doctors of my class
in the UC San Francisco program at Valley
Children's Hospital, Fresno, 1981

My first day as an intern gives me a foretaste of what my life will be like for the next three years. I'm run ragged from the get-go. Last year's interns are now second-year residents, and their patients are assigned to us. We have to rotate through three divisions: the ward for hospitalized patients, the neonatal intensive care unit (NICU), where the premature or extremely sick newborns and infants are treated, and the clinic. In the clinic, we're assigned to patients who will become ours for the three years that we're in training. The main emphasis of this training program is to develop doctors who are committed to staying and working in the underserved Central California region—which is exactly why UCSF created this residency program. The clinic is our introduction to the types of patients we're likely to meet once we go into private practice, and it also gives us a preview of private practice in the Valley towns. When we're on clinic rotation, we still have to be on call, but we don't have hospital patients of our own. We basically babysit at night and on weekends. When patients are admitted at night, we pass them on to the incoming on-call doctor, and they become our patients the next day.

My first days are a blur. Before long, I feel totally inadequate because I can't keep up with the basic work. As interns, we're constantly under the gun, and we get subjected to verbal abuse for our incompetence by everyone from the attending doctors to the nurses.

The worst part is twice-a-day rounds. These are especially frightening for me because I have to present to the third-year resident and the attending staff doctor, who of course is Anglo. Morning rounds start at seven A.M. and can sometimes take until noon. All I can think of is how much time we're wasting standing around discussing the patients when I have so much work to do. We six pediatric interns come in early, do rounds on our patients, and prepare ourselves. A while later, the resident in charge comes in, and we do quick rounds with him or her to bring them up to speed before the attending staff doctor arrives and the real rounds begin. The good residents give us hints on how we can impress the attending. Each of us interns has three patients, but sometimes, on a busy night, I'll end up with eight overnight admits, and I have to present every one of them.

The moment the attending doctor arrives at seven, my stress level skyrockets. Without even saying hello, he barks, "I don't have time to squander. Let's get going." The whole troupe of us—the attending, the interns, the residents, the nurses, and sometimes other doctors—stop at every patient. If the child is a new admission, the intern has to give a full H&P. Of course, we never give a perfect presentation. We always makes mistakes and leave things out. The attending knows this and takes every opportunity to drill us. "What's the patient's previous hospitalization history?" he asks me.

When I say I don't know, he snaps, "Well, don't you think this is a pertinent piece of information?" Yes, it's a crucial part of the history, and I forgot to ask that simple question. "What's the CBC (complete blood count)?" he barks. "You didn't relay it with your presentation. Did you forget?" He carps about my lack of preparation while I dig around in my notes until I find the CBC results and recite them to him. "What does the chest X-ray show?" he goes on. The chart doesn't have that report, and I didn't have time to go down to X-ray to get those results, so I have to admit that I don't know this either.

"What do you mean, you don't know the chest report? This kid's differential diagnosis is asthma or pneumonia, and you don't know?" I feel like an idiot, and everyone else is squirming and uncomfortable for me. The other interns know only too well that their time will come. Then I'll be the one feeling sorry for them, except that I'll also be glad not to be in the hot seat.

As soon as morning rounds are over, I run around trying to get all my information ready for the evening rounds, which start at six P.M. Fortunately, these don't take as long as morning rounds and we're done by seven or so. I then have to finish my daily progress notes and check my patients for last-minute complications before I check out to the intern on call and walk home. Even in mid-evening, the temperature is still in the nineties. When I get home, all I can think about is a cold shower.

Over dinner, Debbie and I talk about how our day went. She's frustrated that our furniture is still in the garage, but I haven't had the time or the energy to move it in. Each night after dinner, I have to get out my books and research my patients' medical conditions so I can prepare for tomorrow's rounds.

No matter how much I study, though, it's never enough. The next morning, when the attending doctor says, "Give me five possible causes of asthma and its treatment," I can't think of more than three, even though I looked it up last night. I also draw a blank on treatment. When I don't answer to the attending's satisfaction, he asks one of the other interns—who never pass up an opening to score points and make me (or anyone else) look dumb. However, if that intern's answer is also inadequate, the resident will be on the spot because the attending will assume that he or she isn't doing a good job of educating us. Obviously, the residents hate it when their "stupid" interns make them look bad, and we pay the price—biting criticism and more scut work—later.

If I thought medical school was hell, it was nothing compared to the torture of internship.

✸·✸

My first on-call, when I have to stay overnight in the hospital, is the most harrowing experience of my life. It starts at six-thirty in the morning. After two hours of rounds, I do my ward work. I then prepare for afternoon rounds. By the time they're over at six-thirty when my on-call begins, I still haven't finished my afternoon work. By eight or nine, only the interns and residents who are on call are still at the hospital. When I go to the cafeteria to grab something to eat, I learn immediately never to count on being able to finish a meal. My beeper goes off. The ward nurse needs an order for one of the other interns' patients. I don't remember what information that intern gave me in her summation or what her concerns were, so I have to go and review the patient's chart and then confirm what I found in the chart by looking at the patient.

After that, I go back to the cafeteria, grab another bite of my food—and my beeper goes off again. The ER has a possible admission and they need a pediatric consult now. I leave my food on the table and hurry down to the ER, where an intern meets me and fills me in. I find this a little funny because neither of us has any experience with sick patients, yet we've been thrown into a situation where it's assumed that we know what we're doing. We do have residents overseeing us, so technically we don't have the final word, but we're supposed to act as if we do, and the residents want us to become proficient as soon as possible.

The better we are and the more we can do on our own, the less work for them (as I later learn when I become a second- and third-year resident myself).

For the rest of the night, my second-year resident and I get a constant stream of calls from the ER and from the floor. By three in the morning, neither of us has gotten any sleep. Then our beepers go off again. A five-month-old boy has been admitted with severe dehydration. We struggle for more than forty minutes to insert an IV. The rule of thumb is for the intern to try first. If I fail, the resident gets the next shot. I'm sure this drives them crazy because they can do it much faster and more efficiently than I can. In this case, though, the resident can't locate a vein either because all the baby's veins are collapsed. His life is in our hands. If we don't get some fluids into him soon, he'll die. I'm shaking and so frustrated that I throw the IV kit to the floor.

In desperation, we try to place a small IV drip in his scalp. This takes another twenty minutes, but we finally succeed and get a dose of life-saving saline solution into him. The baby perks up immediately, and we know he's out of the woods. Although a scalp IV is only a stopgap measure because the veins in the scalp are so thin that the saline will soon start seeping into the surrounding tissues, we've bought ourselves time to find a better site so we can continue the baby's treatment.

Our beepers go off again. Another ER admission. I hope it isn't another kid who needs an IV because my confidence is shot. Even if the vein were big and visible, I don't think I could hit it. The resident and I get no sleep at all tonight. "If you can catch two hours of sleep, you're fortunate," he tells me. "Very fortunate." The nights when I do get some sleep, I brag about it the next morning when the new intern coming on call arrives. The response is always, "You lucky dog! I hope I get so lucky!" When I get home, I also tell Debbie my exciting news: "I got two hours' sleep! Can you believe that?"

I don't tell her about the little boy who almost died. I'm learning too much about all the illnesses that can befall infants, and it scares me. So many things can go wrong that we can't control or even explain sometimes, like SIDS (sudden infant death syndrome). The baby's due in about two months, I don't want her worrying. But when she sees how upset I am, I can't keep it from her. We're no longer worried that she might miscarry, but I'm still concerned about a premature birth. I know that survival for premature babies can be very uncertain.

After several weeks, I finally hire some workers to move our furniture into the house so Debbie has somewhere to sit and relax. I start to feel better about our home.

But work is another matter. Within the first week of starting my internship, I start getting headaches that keep getting worse each day. After a while, they last all day and don't go away even when I'm at home. Over-the-counter painkillers don't help. Morning rounds become even more of a burden because I find it so hard to concentrate.

One day when Dr. Bjorn Nilson, the head of the pediatrics department, is the attending on rounds, he asks me why I'm not prepared. I tell him about the headaches. He says, "You're in a hospital, so go and get yourself checked out! You're useless around here if you can't do your work right." All of our attendings are hard, but he's the one we fear most. He's very difficult and expects a lot of us. He never holds back in his criticism of our work, and he can make our lives miserable. None of us would dare to cross him. I don't know if he's telling me to get checked out for my good, or for the good of the program.

The neurologist who sees me diagnoses me with a sinus headache and puts me on antibiotics, but the headaches continue. I go back and this time I get a CT scan, which comes out negative. I'm told that the headaches are due to stress. I can certainly believe that because I'm about as stressed as I can be. I'm worried about Debbie, about the baby, about my work performance . . . and now I have to contend with constant, throbbing pain. I don't know how much more I can take.

Then, about a month into my internship, I get a call from home. I've been aware for some time that my half-sister Annette, one of Frances's daughters, has been having problems with her abusive common-law husband. The day before, she decided she'd had enough, so she took her two kids and drove over to her brother Danny's house. He took them in. A few hours later, while Danny and his family were sitting around their dinner table talking with an insurance agent about buying a policy, they heard a knock at the front door. It was Annette's "husband." He said he was there to take Annette and the kids home. When Danny tried to block him from coming in, the guy took out a gun. He shot Danny in the head, killing him instantly, then forced his way into the house, chased Annette down, and killed her as well before getting away and escaping to Mexico.

Before even telling Debbie the news, I go to my supervisors and ask for some time off so I can go and help my family deal with this crisis. They give me two days' leave but tell me I'll have to make up my on-call shifts. This means I'll be on call every other day for more than a week. Debbie and I pack some clothes and drive to Goshen. Everyone in the family is in shocked disbelief. We have many abusive husbands and fathers in our family, but there's never been anything like this.

I feel guilty about not having been around much for the last nine years and for having put my education before my family, even though I probably couldn't have done anything to prevent this tragedy. Still, I feel rotten because I never spent much time with Danny. He looked up to me. He understood what I was trying to accomplish with my life. Of all my half-brothers, he was the one who seemed to have his life in order. He and his wife seemed devoted to each other and to their two kids. He was learning the upholstery business from his father-in-law and seemed happy about how his life was going. Now he's dead, murdered while trying to protect his younger sister, and his kids are going to grow up without a father.

After the funeral, I return to the hospital with a heavy heart. I feel disheartened and guilty. I know I'm not mentally or emotionally ready to go back, but I have to be on call. My fellow interns take over some of my workload, but there's only so much they can do. We're a small residency program, and every person is extremely important.

In the weeks that follow, my headaches get worse and worse. One day after rounds, the chief resident calls me into his office. (Each year, the head of the department names the best third-year resident as chief resident.) "I know you're under a lot of pressure and that you've just been through a family tragedy," he says, "but I need to know if you're going to be able to continue this year."

"I just need some time to get over this and get back to normal," I tell him

"What about the headaches?"

"I've never had them before, and I think they'll go away eventually," I reply.

But he tells me that the attending staff is concerned about me and want me to meet with them. A couple of hours later, I arrive at Nilson's office. When Sandy, the pediatrics receptionist, ushers me in, she gives me a quick pat on the back and whispers, "Good luck."

Dr. John McCann, one of the senior pediatricians, is there with Nilson. As I sit down, I notice that he seems to be frowning. What is this meeting really about?

Nilson starts by expressing his sympathy for my family's loss. Then he blindsides me. "We don't feel that you're able to stay current with your fellow interns at this point," he tells me. "And we need to replace you before it's too late in this year's program to bring in another intern."

McCann adds, "Given your family tragedy and your headaches, we feel that for your sake it would be better for you to take a year off."

I'm in shock. "But what will I do for a year? Will I be able to return next year?"

"We can discuss that after the first of the year," McCann replies. I assume he means six months from now. "Yes," Nilson agrees. "We'll save a position for you. and we can give you some kind of stipend beginning in January." He obviously hasn't discussed this option with McCann, who looks surprised.

I don't know if Nilson actually has the authority to do this, but I feel somewhat reassured. All I can do is thank them for their time and walk out of the office. I get my equipment from the on-call lounge and leave the hospital without talking to anyone. How are Debbie and I going to make it through the rest of the year, especially with our baby coming? Worst of all, it's barely August, my internship started less than a month ago, and now I've lost it.

I thought that the worst was over. But now my life is turning into disaster on top of disaster. Our future has just gone up in smoke. It's too late for me to find another internship, not that I want to look anyway. I'm not up to it emotionally and, given the condition I'm in, if I can't make it here, I doubt that I could make it anywhere else. How am I going to break this news to Debbie, after she's finally accepted my ability to overcome all the obstacles that have come up for us and felt secure enough to start a family?

When I walk in the door, she's startled to see me home so early. I look at her, and all I say is, "They've cancelled my internship. I've let you down again. I'm sorry." I feel like a complete failure. After all the times when I felt like quitting but stubbornly fought my way out, now I've been done in by a family crisis and my own health. I've hit rock-bottom. And I don't know if I have it in me to bounce back.

What hurts most is the baby, because I wanted to give our child a solid foundation and all the opportunities life has to offer. Now there's nothing but uncertainty before us. I wanted this baby so much, but now I won't be able to provide for it. We won't have the money to buy even essentials, much less nice baby things. So I've let the baby down, too.

I'm too humiliated to face my family and tell Ama that I've lost my job after only a month. I'm ashamed to face Debbie's family, too. Her parents warned us against having a baby until my position was more secure. I guess we should have listened. I feel as if I've been living a dream that was never meant to be. How did I dare think I could overcome my own shortcomings? I'm getting exactly what I deserve. Nothing.

I don't want to get out of bed. I don't want to face Debbie. Neither of us knows what we're going to do. There's nothing I can say to reassure her. I don't want to think about it. I just want her and everyone else to leave me alone. Even enduring the verbal abuse of morning rounds would be better than lying around in this despair.

We're forced to do something I never wanted or expected. We have to ask her parents if we can stay with them for several months. We had always planned for Debbie to deliver at Kaiser in San Francisco, where we have our medical insurance. But we had never anticipated staying with her mom and dad for more than a few weeks before and after the baby was born. How were we to know that my internship would collapse?

It's the last thing Debbie wants to do, but it's our only option. We can't afford to stay in Fresno. We'll be going back with our tails between our legs because we need her parents' help. I'm sure they'll feel free to give us unwanted advice because they feel we've been rushing things the whole time, getting married too soon and starting a family too soon as well.

We leave Fresno toward the end of August with no idea of whether we'll ever be back, and we settle in with Debbie's parents for what we hope will be only a short time. There are a few bright spots about moving to Marin County. Debbie's pregnancy hasn't been easy. She's been retaining fluids and has been diagnosed with preeclampsia, a late-pregnancy condition that could jeopardize her health and the baby's if it gets worse. Moving out of the Valley heat will help, and she'll be able to deliver in San Francisco. Also, I need to pass part two of my boards, which I know will be grueling. I haven't had time to study since starting my internship, and now at least I'll be able to. The test is on September 23, which coincidentally is the same day that the baby's due.

I hide out in one of the back rooms and study as much as I can. Every time I take a break, Debbie's dad asks, "You think you're studying enough?" He's served on the state psychiatric examining board for years, so he drills me over and over on the psych material. Although I feel he's putting a lot of pressure on me, I appreciate his help and the insights he gives me into what kinds of questions I can expect.

CHAPTER THIRTY-FIVE

Marina

As September drags on, Debbie gets bigger and more uncomfortable. On September 23, the day of the test, I leave early so I'll be sure I get there in time, while Debbie and her parents go to Point Reyes for a day's outing. The exam is as hard as I imagined it would be, but I feel confident that I did okay, especially on the psych part. I get back to the house at about the same time that Debbie and her parents return. We're sitting in the living room. I'm finally relaxing a little from my weeks of late-night cramming, and am looking forward to my first good night's sleep in weeks when Debbie gets a funny look on her face and says, "I just wet my pants! I've been leaking all day, and I don't know why."

"Why didn't you tell us?" her mom says.

"Why should I? It's embarrassing!"

Her mom exclaims, "Your water's broken! You're in labor!"

Debbie is startled. She expected something more dramatic to happen. A short time later, she starts feeling the first contractions. The timing couldn't be better. If she had gone into labor a day or two earlier, I wouldn't have been able to concentrate on my boards. I forget about my exhaustion, and, like typical first-time parents always do, we panic. By now it's after nine at night. Debbie's mom and I bundle her into the car and head for the Golden Gate Bridge. After getting lost briefly, we find the hospital and go straight up to labor and delivery. Debbie's labor is advancing rapidly, and they put her right into a labor bed.

Midnight comes and goes. A female resident is handling the delivery because it's now almost two-thirty in the morning. Debbie's doing a great job of pushing and is holding up very well, while I'm as nervous as can be. "Here's the head," the resident says. "If you'll push now, I can get it out." All I can see is the baby's head and nose. I think its nose looks really big. Moments later, we see our little girl for the first time. It's September 24, 1981—a day I'll never forget. The resident hands her to the nurse to be weighed. I don't let her out of my sight. I can't wait for them to let me hold her.

My little eight-pound daughter looks right at me and my heart is hers forever. No words can express how I feel at this instant. I know immediately that my life has changed forever. I've never felt the emotions I feel at this moment. The person I was yesterday—a beaten-down twenty-nine-year-old who had lost almost all hope and was facing an uncertain destiny—has disappeared. In his place is a man who knows that from now on his life doesn't belong to him anymore. It belongs to his little girl.

When I hold her for the first time, all my troubles fade away. I'm in love with her from the first glance. There's nothing I won't do to protect her. I go back to Debbie's bed, and together we admire our beautiful little Marina, the name we had chosen if the baby was a girl. When she starts to fuss, I give her to Debbie so she can breast-feed her for the first time. I lay my head on the pillow right next to them, not wanting to miss a single moment. Twelve hours later, I bring them both back to Debbie's parents' house.

In the weeks that follow, Marina, who's obviously the most beautiful baby girl you ever saw, is very demanding of Debbie's time. She's constantly at the breast, and poor Debbie often weeps from the pain of nursing. But she's determined to breast-feed and she puts up with the pain until her nipples toughen. Whenever Marina isn't at Debbie's breast, I have her in my arms. I find it hard to put down the little girl I've dreamed about. She's my inspiration. I'm going to get back to Fresno no matter what. My determination and resolve return more strongly than ever before. When Marina looks at me and smiles, she melts my heart. She's carrying my whole future in her tiny hands.

I will not fail again.

We settle in with Debbie's parents while I study for part two of the boards and for the FLEX (the Federal Licensure Examination), an alternate credentialing exam of parts one and two, which will be held in December. I decide not to take part one again and to take the FLEX again. I could have elected not to attempt part two of the boards, but I wanted to prove I could pass the clinical part. If I don't pass, I won't be able to resume my residency. If I do, I'll be through with exams forever.

I tackle my studies with more purpose and resolve than ever before. Whenever I feel my energy flag, all I have to do is look over at Debbie with Marina nursing. They look so wholesome, so natural, so peaceful . . . looking at them fills me with pride and well-being. I take breaks just to hold Marina so I can feel her wiggle against my chest as she makes herself comfortable. She's growing fast, and is alert and smiling at everyone. I love how she looks at me with her big brown eyes and then breaks into a big, beautiful smile.

A few weeks later, I get the results of part two of the boards—I've passed easily. Now we wait for the FLEX results. At the end of the year, I'm notified that I've passed, but barely. If it wasn't for Debbie's dad's help, especially on the psych portion, I don't think I would have. We return to Fresno, where Nilson is true to his word. I start receiving a small stipend while I work at a level somewhere between a medical student and an intern. The money's just enough to cover our basic expenses, but we take it gladly because we want to be back on our own.

We move back into our house, which has been vacant since we left. I keep my hours at the hospital as regular as possible so everyone gets used to having me around again, but I'm also able to stay home and spend time with Marina during my study breaks in the evenings. I don't have to be on call or work on weekends, though I hope that will start again in time. Overall, I consider myself lucky. Not many pediatric residents can experience interacting with their baby hour by hour and observing every little nuance.

Money's tight. We have barely enough money for necessities, and our budget is stretched to the limit. I hate having to accept hand-me-downs for Marina and shopping for her clothes at the Salvation Army store. My family's really good about giving us baby clothes.

Debbie and I argue over whether I should look for a job, something that would at least bring in some money, in case the residency doesn't pan out. I tell her that even though I haven't been guaranteed a position, I feel I need to be there to show them how much I want to be there. I ask her if she doesn't think I'll be able to handle my residency once I start again, but she says she's just concerned about Marina's future. I feel a change in our relationship because of this, but I know it's the stress of the uncertainty we're facing. I can't blame her. She's being protective of our baby.

Although I stop by the pediatrics department office several times during the spring to try to find out what's been decided about my future, I keep getting the runaround. I need to reassure Debbie that I'm right about what I've been telling her and that I'll resume my residency in July. Finally, in late spring, I'm called into Nilson's office. Sandy, the same receptionist who was so kind to me nine months earlier, asks me to wait outside while she tells him I'm there. I hear voices and realize that he and some of the other attending physicians are discussing my situation. Some of the doctors express doubts about me, and one argues that I should be let go. My future is being determined as I sit here, and it seems that the arrangement I thought I had doesn't really exist! Debbie was right to doubt my attempts to set her mind at rest. But Nilson argues on my behalf. Eventually, the other doctors leave and he summons me into his office. I'm feeling frightened that they won't keep their word. Debbie hasn't been sure we can trust them, either.

"I'm glad to tell you that we'll have a place for you in July," he informs me. "I hope your new start will be different and more rewarding." I thank him and rush home to tell Debbie the good news. And to hold my little girl. I have a new lease on life, and I mean to make the most of it. I won't get another chance. Life works in mysterious ways. I have to think that I'm being protected by some force. I've been tested so many times. So far, I've managed to forge ahead through everything, but just barely. I hope that this is the last trial I'll have to endure.

CHAPTER THIRTY-SIX

Another Chance

AFEW WEEKS BEFORE MY NEW START, Debbie and I have our
long-delayed honeymoon, only five years late. We borrow
Debbie's parents' VW camper and take a week-long camp-
ing trip on our way to the Northwest, where we plan to visit one of
Debbie's aunts in Seattle. It's great having Marina with us and seeing
her enjoy the beach and all the other sights. When we arrive, the aunt
offers us a weekend at a hotel in Vancouver, British Columbia, and
says she'll babysit Marina for the weekend. But we can't bear to leave
her, and she's still breast-feeding, so we take her with us. She's barely
been out of my sight since she was born. How will I handle it when I
start on-call again and can't see her for thirty-six hours at a time?

On July 1, 1982, I kiss Debbie good-bye, look in on Marina asleep in
her crib—she looks so angelic, so unlike the voracious, squalling nine-
month-old who kept me awake late last night!—and head back to VMC
to continue my interrupted internship. She's crawling now, and I love
watching her scuttle around the house exploring. I know that her future's
in my hands, and this time I can't let anything get to me. I won't get
another chance, and if Marina isn't motivation enough, nothing will be.

When I met my fellow interns several days ago, I was surprised
to see Maria Valbuena, one of my classmates from Irvine, among the

new pediatric interns. She told me that her husband, Ben Padilla, had also come to Fresno to do an ob-gyn internship. They were among our few married friends at Irvine, and in fact they were the first people we told about Debbie's pregnancy. I remember that when we phoned them and asked them to come and see "Debbie's ring," they didn't realize we meant the pregnancy test. They thought I had finally bought Debbie a real ring to replace the twenty-dollar one I had given her at our wedding. Before coming to VMC, they both started residencies in family practice but decided it wasn't for them.

This time around, the internship routine is much easier than I expect. I'll be doing two six-week rotations in each of the departments though the course of the year. The days are long, as usual, and the thirty-six-hour on-call rotations are brutal. But I'm not as intimidated or tentative with my responses. I've learned to play the game a little better and more aggressively. Although I still have a hard time with rounds, my headaches don't return, no family crises erupt, and I find I can handle the work and the rounds just as well as the other interns do.

When I start on the wards again, I have a good idea of what to expect based on my previous experience. However, one of my first patients is a heartbreaker. Two-year-old Juan's parents found him face-down in a puddle of water, and he's admitted to the ICU under my care. Near-drownings of children are probably the most tragic cases you can see because the outcome is usually disastrous. All the organs are affected, from the brain to the kidneys. Nothing is spared. Day after day, I have to report on his condition—and each night when I get home, I take Marina in my arms, give her a big hug, and pray that such a tragedy will never befall her or us.

Little Juan never regained consciousness. His brain swelled with fluid, and he was eventually moved to a long-term care unit in Porterville where he lived in a comatose state for nine years. Soon after I opened my practice in Porterville in 1985, I saw in the paper that he had died the day before.

Coming home is so different now compared to last year. As soon as Marina hears me at the door, she crawls over to greet me and reaches for me to pick her up.

Actually, I feel terrible about how I almost ignore Debbie because I'm so eager to play with her. It isn't until years later, when Debbie and I are in crisis about our marriage, that I realize I'm feeling neglected, too, because Debbie's so involved in motherhood.

Before long, we settle into a routine. I get used to not being at home every third day and night. Some nights, I have only a few minutes to play with Marina before I need to start preparing my presentation for the next morning's rounds. She tries to get my attention by sticking her head between my arm and my books or by climbing up on my lap. I can't resist playing with her for a few minutes, but then I have to ask Debbie to take her.

When I was growing up, the family always kept a small vegetable garden. I'm so used to this that I plant one in our backyard. It's mostly tomatoes. I go out every night and take Marina with me. I love to watch her play in the dirt and mud and the water flowing down the row. I never leave her alone for even a minute because I'm still in charge of little Juan in ICU, and I never forget how quickly disaster can strike. While she's making a mess in the mud, I check the tomato plants to make sure no worms are eating the leaves. One evening I see that Marina's also examining the plants intently. She doesn't know why I'm inspecting the leaves, but she's copying me exactly. I love to see this. It reminds me of how I used to mimic Apa when I was a toddler.

The year drags on and the seasons change. We do six-week cycles in the wards, the NICU, and the clinics twice during the year. When I start my six weeks in the NICU, I have no real experience with neonatal intensive care because during my medical school student rotations we weren't allowed to even touch, much less care for, these extremely sick babies. All we could do was watch.

VMC's maternity floor is busy twenty-four hours a day. Babies are born every hour and C-sections are routine. We get beeped so constantly that I learn to call up to OB before trying to go to the bathroom or to the cafeteria. We have three neonatal specialists who come over from VCH to the NICU to oversee us. This is one unit where the on-call residents have a great responsibility because the neonatalogists come only for morning rounds, so the residents are in charge most of the time.

Before long, I realize how unique this residency program is. Most programs have an attending in-house, with neonatology fellows and residents all competing trying to get experience resuscitating infants that may weigh only one-and-a-half or two pounds. And here we are, right in the heat of it, during our intern year. I don't even realize how much hands-on experience I'm getting, but I'm glad to have a third-year resident by my side because I don't want to be the ultimate person accountable.

Sometimes when the NICU resident's tied up with a very sick infant, I go up to the delivery rooms by myself. One day when I arrive to help with a delivery, the OB resident, one of the most respected ones in the program, sees that I'm on my own. "Where's the NICU resident?" he asks.

"He's with a sick newborn and can't leave."

The resident turns to the nurse and yells, "Call the ward resident! I think we're going to have problems here!" I don't take this personally because I would do the same thing if I were in his shoes. Moments later, the nurse tells us that the ward resident's on an ER case and can't come either.

"Shit!" the OB resident exclaims. He's stuck with me, the nurse, and the respiratory tech. We have a hard time with the delivery and I'm thinking "Shit!" too because the baby, a little boy, isn't breathing. I grab him, and the nurse and tech and I start working on him. I remember everything I've learned. We manage to revive him. Minutes later, he's healthy and screaming. With a sigh of relief, I tell the resident that he's going to be fine. As we leave the delivery room, he tells me, "Good work."

I'm pumped! I actually did something without someone overseeing me, and one of the most respected OB guys told me I did a good job! That one comment makes my confidence skyrocket. I know only too well what would have happened if I had screwed up. I wouldn't have been allowed in the delivery room by myself for the rest of my rotation. What a difference one incident, good or bad, can make in our lives.

After I finish my first NICU rotation, I move on to the pediatric clinics, which include regular pediatric services and some specialty clinics as well. The clinic rotation is the only one we all look forward to because we get to go home right after we finish seeing all our patients if we're not on call. We see new admissions and do the H&Ps, and the next day we turn the new patients over to the on-call intern. Besides the clinics, we do call only for the ward and the pediatric ICU, so I won't be back in the NICU until I rotate through there again in the spring.

I discover that I have a knack for clinic care. After the first few weeks, I get irritated because I'm often left waiting for new patients to be placed in an exam room while they're trapped doing paperwork with the receptionist. I take it upon myself to start putting them into an exam room right off the waiting room where in many cases they can be seen, treated, and sent home instead of tying up an exam room for an hour. However, my attempt at a quick and easy triage solution upsets the receptionist. She tells me I'm bypassing normal procedure and complains to the attending.

When the attending questions me, I tell her that most of the children who come in are there for colds and coughs, but they're keeping me from seeing kids who have asthma or other more serious conditions. I figure that if I can clear the easy cases and send them home, I'll be able to see the more serious cases faster and spend more time with them.

The attending gives me permission to try this out. I end up seeing not only my own patients but also the other kids who aren't so sick. Before we know it, our side of the clinic is flowing smoothly and we all get to go home on time. I realize that I have an intuitive sense of how to run a clinic efficiently, and I know that my own practice will be run so my patients won't have to wait for hours to be seen.

The attending staff in the clinic treat me well, and my confidence and self-esteem grow. I even get a little cocky. But we all know what happens when we get too sure of ourselves. One day, we see a four-month-old girl who doesn't appear really sick. We have trouble doing the lumbar puncture, and by the time we get done and get an IV going, she starts going downhill rapidly. We transfer her to the ICU, but it's too late. Her organs have shut down. She dies of a massive infection. Everyone reassures me that she couldn't have survived because the infection was too serious, but I keep asking myself, what if I had started the IV more quickly or done the lumbar puncture faster?

When I go home, I have a hard time telling Debbie about my loss and my guilt, so I clam up. I look at Marina, who's now a year old and is walking and making all kinds of babbling noises. After all the tragedies I'm constantly exposed to, I'm more grateful than ever that she's so healthy.

Aside from an occasional cold, she's never sick, and she's always in a good mood. I only have to see her to raise my spirits on those awful days. This is one of those days. I can't help thinking about that little four-month-old girl who will never give her parents the joy my little girl gives me. But before long, Marina performs her magic and I start feeling better just from being with her.

When I have time to step back and think about it, I find the process we undergo to become fully trained doctors fascinating. We basically observe one procedure, do one, and teach one. And we repeat these three steps over and over and over until we can do a procedure in our sleep. Of course, we do a lot of things almost in our sleep because we're so drained by the end of on-call nights that we have to rely on caffeine and pure adrenaline to keep us functioning.

In the second half of the year, when the time comes for me to rotate back to the pediatric wards again, I'm amazed at the changes in myself and my fellow interns. I can care for more patients in less time. I'm more organized. I get my data all at once and check X-ray results before rounds. Rounds take less time because we're all more organized and efficient. I can finish all my scut work by two in the afternoon and actually have time to study in the library or even take a nap if I was on call the night before.

When I catch the chief resident checking our patients' lab values one day, I realize he always knows them before we do. He has learned through experience which results to memorize and which ones to discard. I learn this secret now. During my first disastrous rotation in the wards, I used to try to memorize everything and consequently couldn't remember anything.

On my on-call weekends, Debbie brings Marina to the hospital so we can all have lunch together. I still get beeper calls, but now the nurses trust me enough that I can handle most crises over the phone. It's nice to have my family see me in my hospital scrubs. It means a lot to me to have Debbie see that I'm confident, in control, and able to handle the situations that come up. I hope this reassures her that she doesn't need to have any more concerns about our future.

I feel myself swagger a little when I realize that during my first rotation, I would go into overload with three patients, but now I can handle three admits in an hour and it doesn't even faze me. I examine them, call for rooms for them, make all the arrangements, write the orders, and move on to the next patient.

My second rotations in the NICU and the newborn nursery are also like night and day, without any of the fear I experienced during my first go-round. After my first week and one on-call night, I get called up to the C-section unit for an emergency premature delivery. The baby's less than eight hundred grams—under two pounds—and this means trouble. The resident glances up, says, "Expect a bad infant," and goes on to give me a brief history. What he doesn't do is ask for a more experienced doctor! What a difference just a few months have made for me.

Despite the emergency, I feel calm and confident. We rush the listless, unresponsive infant, who's barely larger than my palm, over to the warmer, and insert an endotracheal tube down his throat to give him oxygen. Then we start chest compressions. Within minutes we get his heart beating. We take him down to the NICU, where we place an IV line through his umbilicus to check his blood status and oxygen level. He's going to survive.

But how normal will he be? Will he develop respiratory distress syndrome (RDS)? Almost every extremely low-weight preemie does, and RDS is the leading cause of death among infants born weighing less than two pounds. What about necrotizing enterocolitis (NEC), which attacks the intestines and colon and kills as many as fifty percent of the infants who develop it? Has this infant suffered brain damage? And if so, how serious is it?

These are concerns we'll look for and address in the next three months. But what's most upsetting is that this infant's mom is a drug addict, and that only about six months ago she gave birth to another premature infant who's been in our NICU ever since. She never comes to visit this older baby, and I'm sure we're not going to see her now, either. She'll probably continue doing drugs and will be back six months from now with yet another premature baby.

Toward the end of my intern year, I go through a rotation that I can't wait to finish—the sexual abuse clinic for children. The attending is Dr. McCann, who was at my meeting with Dr. Nilson more than a year ago when my internship was put on hold. Although he was tough on me at the time, in this clinic I see how good he is with the frightened, abused kids we see. I also learn a lot from him about how to be gentle and calming.

Even so, I almost lose it one night when I'm called down to the ER to see a four-year-old girl who may have been sexually abused. She looks at us blankly, without any facial expression. When we lay her down and turn her over to examine her, she rests her head on the table and lifts her bottom up in the air so automatically that it's clear she's used to being placed in this position. I see that her anus is gaping open. Obviously she's been abused frequently and over a long period of time. I'm enraged. I want to kill her father for what he's done to her. He has destroyed her childhood and possibly her entire life. We turn her over to children's protective services. but I'm never able to dismiss her from my mind.

Although these experiences haunt me, I sometimes find myself disassociating from the children I see in this clinic. I'm not even aware of it because I've blanked out the memory of what happened to me when I was about the same age as so many of them. I never tell any of the staff about my personal experiences because I've buried all those memories. All I know is that I want to get out of this clinic as soon as I can.

As this first year of training winds down, we're already being treated more like real residents than as interns. I know I'm no longer thought of as an intern when I'm summoned to the ER and no one asks where the resident is and why he or she isn't with me. Instead, the ER doctors simply give me a brief history, show me where the patient is, and tell me to take over. Then they walk away. They know that I know what I'm doing.

This isn't to say that I haven't become hardened in some ways. Even today, I look back and remember episodes I feel remorse about, especially one night that I spent with a very sick baby. We knew he was going to die. It was late at night. None of us had slept because we had been run ragged by the ER and the ward patients. And I remember thinking, "Please die so I can get some sleep . . . I'm so tired." We sometimes get to the point where we resent very sick babies like this one because of the anguish of enduring their deaths and the inquisition we'll face during rounds the next morning.

This year has been trying but satisfying. The trials and suffering have helped all of us grow in terms of our skills, our maturity, and our confidence. I feel a sense of accomplishment that I haven't known since sixth grade. I have no doubts about my abilities as a pediatrician in training. I finally feel I'm a real doctor. I can make a difference. I can save a life when called upon. And I no longer fear being the doctor in charge in the coming months.

CHAPTER THIRTY-SEVEN

The Path Clears

I END MY INTERNSHIP ON JUNE 30, 1983 and return the next morning as a resident, ready to oversee the new class of interns.
Meeting them really takes me back. They look as scared and
overwhelmed as I know I did, and I feel for them. My first rotation
with them is the ward.

As we move from room to room and I assign patients to them, I
sense their astonishment as I rattle off each patient's data, lab reports,
and H&Ps without any notes. The interns don't know that I studied
the charts last night and know how to look for relevant information.
I don't tell them this because I want them to think of me as being
superior, at least for a while. I like the feeling of being looked up to.
It's a feeling I've rarely had before.

My first night on call with Brad, the new intern assigned to me
for this rotation, is an eye-opener. He pages me constantly about
mundane things and can't complete even simple procedures, so I
end up doing them for him. He does nothing to alleviate my workload. He also reminds me of how inept I was during my first weeks,
so when I start feeling irritated and impatient, I also feel his distress.
I vow not to treat him, or any of the other interns, as badly as I was
treated—no matter how incompetent they are.

The next morning, Brad blows his whole presentation during rounds. He doesn't remember any labs or pertinent facts. When McCann, the attending, asks for X-ray results on one baby, Brad has no clue. I cover for him and tell McCann that the report was negative. Brad looks at me in shock. He doesn't know that while the baby was having his X-ray, I stopped by, caught the radiology resident, and asked him for a quick interpretation. It was just luck that everything fell in place, but Brad doesn't know this. I can see his respect and awe grow.

I feel bad for him because he's getting off on the wrong foot, just as I did. He knows he's going to face another grilling on evening rounds, so he'll run himself ragged in the meantime trying to gather all his reports. As we do a quick rehash of his patient before rounds begin, I see that he's failed to get the follow-up kidney function panel that McCann wanted to be run again. I dash down to the lab and ask the tech to run the panel for me "stat" as a favor. When I slip the results to Brad, he's both surprised and grateful.

Sure enough, the renal panel is the first thing McCann asks about during rounds. He obviously doesn't expect Brad to have them, but when Brad reads off the now-normal values, he comments, "Good job." Brad's stock goes up, and we move on to the next patient.

Being the resident on call or in charge of the floor is stressful, but as second-year residents we're cushioned by the third-year resident, who bears the ultimate responsibility or blame if something serious goes wrong. We always have one second-year and one third-year resident "in house" at all times. The third-year may be in the NICU dealing with critical cases, but if the second-year gets in over his or her head, the third-year is called in to take charge.

Toward the end of my first six months of official residency, I learn that Dave, our chief resident, has come up with a plan to handle our constant shortage of house staff. He's proposing to put one on-call resident in charge of both the ward and the NICU, instead of the present system, which calls for one resident for the ward and one for the NICU. This would mean more work for us while we're on call, but we'll be able to space out our call days over a longer time period and will only have to be on call every fourth or fifth day instead of every third day. We all have enough confidence in our interns that we feel this system will work.

I'm asked to attend a small meeting to hear about this plan, and when I arrive I realize that only a few of the residents are there. Some of the second-year residents and about half of the third-year residents are missing. Apparently Dave and Jeff, the other third-year resident who's been working with him on this idea, have only invited residents who they feel are competent and responsible enough to oversee both the NICU and the ward at once. Dave tells us that Nilson has already approved this "dual-call" plan as well as the list of candidates that he and Jeff have recommended.

And I've been invited to the meeting and included on the list. That means that even though I'm only in my second year, I'm seen as more valuable and more competent than some of my peers, and even some of the third-year residents. After having been made to drop out of my initial internship and almost not being allowed back in, now I've been invited to be part of this new program, which may affect many generations of residents to come. What a boost to my ego! I don't care if I won't get any sleep while I'm on call.

When I get home that day, I sit down, put Marina in my lap, and proudly tell Debbie about this new development. She's concerned at first because of all the added responsibility, but she sees what a huge validation it is for me. Of course I'm concerned that I could screw up, but I vow to work my butt off and show the attending doctors who wanted to get rid of me how wrong they were.

My initial call with the two interns and the whole pediatric department under my charge is full of trauma and intense activity. I run from the ER to the intensive care unit, up to the C-section wing, down to the neonatal floor, and onto the ward. Then I do it all again. The two interns do a good job, and I'm grateful for their abilities. I don't sleep the whole night, but I make it through without a disaster. The next morning, I have to do rounds twice and bring the resident in charge of the neonatal ward up to date. I head home extremely pleased with my performance—and with no more doubts about my abilities. When I walk into the house after thirty-six hours of being on call with a smile on my face, Debbie takes one look at me and knows that everything's going to be okay from now on.

Doing dual calls gives me enormous satisfaction. My second year goes by rapidly, and the new system even lets us enjoy several weeks of vacation. New confidence, a salary, no need to pass any more tests . . . no regrets, no doubts. What a change! And what a relief to be able to escape and really relax.

⟵·⟵
⤜

During our third year, we start doing call evenings and weekends at VCH, where we rotate through various pediatric subspecialties, including cardiology, radiology, and oncology. We move back and forth between VMC and VCH. At VCH, we're on call not just for newly admitted patients but also for the patients of the community doctors who are on staff there. It's a busy hospital, and it's not unusual to admit as many as ten new patients over a twelve-hour call period, but because we don't have interns to supervise and teach, we can do our job faster.

Unlike at VMC, at VCH we're really on our own, with no supervision. I'm the sole pediatric resident on call except for the ER doctors, who call constantly to admit patients to me. At night, I feel completely in charge of every patient except those in the ER and in the neonatal unit, where the neonatologist is in charge. The NICU is always very busy, with very sick kids at all times, but taking care of extremely sick babies and kids doesn't faze me much anymore.

This is also the first time I have to deal with pediatricians in private practice. Some of them are more than happy to have us take over, but others want to stay involved and give orders although I soon discover that some of them aren't actually up on the latest developments in the field. I bow to their experience until I realize that I know more than they do. At that point, I start going over their heads or ignoring their orders because they're actually risking doing harm to their own patients. We're not supposed to even be seeing the patients of the private doctors, but sometimes the nurses will bring up concerns and I'll take over—only to face hostility from those doctors for "interfering" with their patients. Are they even aware that I've kept their patients from harm and saved them from a possible malpractice lawsuit? No. They're more concerned about their reputations.

Although we see some really difficult cases at VMC, we see even worse at VCH because that's where the other hospitals in the Valley send their most challenging and highest-risk patients. I see them when they're transferred from the ER or come in as direct admissions to the floor or to the ICU. We get a lot of near-drowning cases, and we lose many of them. As soon as I learn that we're getting a near-drowning, I know that the weekend will be a hard one. It isn't that I don't want to take care of these children. It's that most of the time it's hopeless, and it's horrible to see the parents suffering as they watch their baby lying comatose.

One day a baby girl named Megan is brought in to the unit. "I was giving her a bath," the mom tells me. "The phone rang and I went to answer it. I was only gone for a minute." But during that minute she forgot about her little girl, and when she remembered and ran back into the bathroom, Megan was floating face down in the tub. "If only I hadn't gone to answer the phone," she keeps repeating.

I can't say anything because she's right. Because of that moment of forgetfulness, she's about to lose her little girl. To make matters worse, when the dad, who's been out of town, rushes into the hospital and sees Megan lying unconscious, he obviously blames his wife. He doesn't say so out loud, but he makes no attempt to console her. He just turns away from her and leaves her weeping with her arms wrapped around herself. I want to reach out and say something, anything, but I know what the final outcome will be.

When Megan's electroencephalogram (EEG) comes back flat, it's up to me to relay the sad news. I would give anything not to be the person who has to go in and tell the family. I walk into the waiting room. The whole family is there—mother, father, grandparents, aunt, and uncles. They look up hopefully. But then I sit down next to the mom and say, "Megan's brain test shows no activity. There's nothing more we can do for her. I'm so sorry."

I can't remain professional in this moment. As the mom and dad start to sob, I find tears rolling down my face, too. I've been Megan's doctor for only a few hours, but I've grown attached to her. I wipe my eyes and tell her parents, "We need your permission to disconnect Megan from the ventilator." I escort them to her bedside and leave them alone to say their final good-byes. We remove the breathing tube and shut down the other monitors. I then put her into her mother's arms one last time. Without the beeping of the monitors, I can't tell when her heart stops, so I have to stand by with my stethoscope and listen until I don't hear a heartbeat anymore. I bend over to listen once. Twice. The third time, there's only silence.

"She's gone," I tell the mom and dad. "I'm sorry." They break into sobs and walk out of the unit for the last time. I go up to the on-call room and try to get my emotions under control. My Marina is safe and sound at home, and they've just lost their child. I can't help but feel their loss, and I call Debbie just for a minute to see how my little girl's doing. I want so much to be at home and to hold her right now. But my beeper goes off. Time to deal with my other patients.

The worst deaths we see are the ones due to parental neglect. Like the case of four-year-old Emily, who's admitted with fatally high levels of iron after swallowing all of her mother's prenatal tablets. It's only a matter of time before we lose her, but we do all we can. When she goes into cardiac arrest, we manage to resuscitate her. I then call the mom to tell her that she has to come in right away because Emily's next episode may be her last. "I'm busy. Do I have to come in?" the mom complains.

"Your daughter's dying. She's not going to last much longer." I'm so furious I can hardly get the words out.

"Okay, I'll be right in."

She never shows up. Several hours later, Emily goes into cardiac arrest again. After twenty minutes of trying to bring her back, we call off our efforts. We call the mom's house. The person who answers the phone tells us she's out playing cards. When the mom finally arrives, I confront her and say, "While you were out gambling, Emily died." Then I turn my back and leave. I'm so angry I can't say anything more.

Another patient I can't forget is six-month-old Bobby, who's brought in with multiple skull traumas. To our amazement, after weeks in a coma he recovers enough to go home. His mother's boyfriend, who we think may have caused Bobby's injuries, hasn't been found or arrested, so Children's Protective Services tells the mom that if he shows up, she shouldn't allow him near the baby. The following week, Bobby's brought back into the ICU with severe head injuries. The boyfriend has beaten him again, this time fatally. We took care of him for five weeks, only to have him go home and get beaten to death by the abuser who had all but killed him once before.

So many tragedies . . . but sometimes we see miracles, too. I remember one young man at VMC who's there for months with valley fever, a life-threatening fungal infection of the brain. Even though we treat him by injecting a new antibiotic directly into his brain, we know that his chances of surviving are almost nil. The whole time he's there, I can't help wondering why we're bothering with such a hopeless case. One day, I happen to pass his bed. He's not there. I'm astonished when the nurse tells me he's been discharged. "He suddenly recovered and was sent home," she says. No one knows why. Sometime later, I learn that he's attending COS! He not only pulled off a fantastic recovery . . . he didn't even suffer any brain damage. This teaches me to never give up hope.

This year has been a time of tremendous learning, not so much in medical terms as in learning about myself. I've always been afraid to speak out or to call attention to myself. I've never wanted to be in the spotlight because I was afraid I'd be exposed as a fraud. Now I believe in myself.

At Santa Cruz, I struggled to pass my science classes. I was never confident in my knowledge or in myself. At Irvine, I knew I didn't belong. By some stroke of luck I got in, only to endure the worst time in my life.

Without Debbie's encouragement and determination to see me succeed, I would have quit a thousand times. Then I graduated from med school only to come up against even bigger horrors as an intern. At the time, I thought that being let go less than a month into my internship meant I was the world's biggest loser. I mean, how can someone go all the way through med school and then fail their internship? But that year off was the best thing that could have happened to me. I was able to get my boards out of the way, and I got to be with my precious Marina during the first months of her life. Looking back, I wouldn't have traded that experience for anything in the world.

I compare myself with another resident I heard about during the year I was off. He was Mexican, too, and his family expected a lot from him because he had made it and become a doctor. But he couldn't take the pressure of work and his family's demands and expectations. Instead of telling anyone about his pain, he committed suicide. Hearing about him really shook me up. I wondered how close I had come to the same fate. I was saved by my year off and by Marina's entry into my life. She gave me a reason to exist. I couldn't let her grow up without a father the way I had.

A few months before I finish my residency, Lindsay District Hospital recruits me to open an office in Porterville. This comes about through Kathy Hall, a family practice doctor in Lindsay. In our third year of residency, we were able to do "clerkships" with area doctors, working in their offices. She arranges for me to meet with Hugh Olsen, the hospital's CEO, and we reach an agreement that includes a guarantee of my first year's salary. This will let me relax and establish a practice without any concerns about money. Plus, they'll pay our moving expenses and even assign Shirley Rowell, their assistant administrator, as my liaison to help set up my office.

During my final days of call, I'm not that busy. The interns are almost residents, so I'm not needed as often. I can sleep if I want to, but I find I can't. I sit and talk with people, something I've rarely had a chance to do in the past. I realize that although I've endured a lot of suffering, these experiences have given me things I've always lacked—more self-esteem, and a sense of belonging. Both of those qualities have been missing from my life until now. I've grown as a man and as a person. During these three years, I've overcome adversity, racism, doubters (including myself), and shame.

Looking back at my achievement, I can't help but wonder how I actually arrived at this time and place. By all accounts, I shouldn't be what I am—a doctor. And starting next week, I'll be a pediatrician with all the knowledge, skills, and training to treat and care for my very own patients.

Little do I know that in just a few years, my past will rise up and overwhelm me. The bright new world I'm envisioning will come crashing down around me, and I'll come close to losing everything, including my family.

PART SEVEN

Doctor

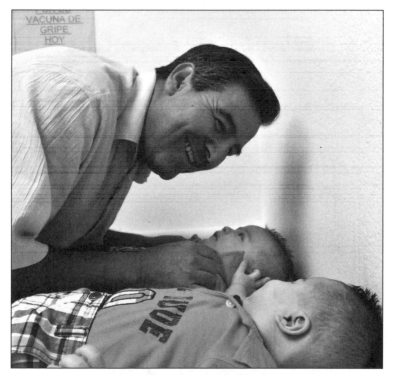

I can handle taking care of babies like
this for the rest of my life . . .

CHAPTER THIRTY-EIGHT

Porterville

Eᴀʀʟʏ Aᴜɢᴜsᴛ 1985, I ᴏᴘᴇɴ ᴜᴘ ᴍʏ ᴏғғɪᴄᴇ. The sign reads:

RAMON RESA, MD
PEDIATRICS

I'm on top of the world! What a great deal I have! Debbie and I take our first real vacation and go to Hawaii for ten days, leaving Marina with Debbie's parents. She's almost three now, and her grand-parents love having her with them. For the first time since we can remember, we have no worries. We feel reassured that everything will be up and running when we return and I open my practice on August 15, 1985.

Instead, we return to find a major upheaval at Lindsay District Hospital. Hugh Olsen's been fired, and the new CEO refuses to honor the contract I signed only a few weeks earlier. Did I have a lawyer review it before I signed it? No, I had never used a lawyer in my life and hadn't seen any need for one. Besides, I didn't know any.

We've already moved into a rented house in Porterville. Now, overnight, my brand-new office and salary have evaporated. I'm in despair. I should have known it was too good to be true. When I do consult a lawyer about suing for breach of contract, I'm told I have a case but that it could take months or even years to resolve. In the meantime, I'll be in limbo. Another option would be look for another opening in another city or town. I decide to stay and try to work something out on my own.

Hugh Olsen gives me an introduction to the manager of the Bank of the Sierra in Lindsay. He meets with me and assures me that he'll make every effort to help me. He asks me to return the next day to meet with the area manager—who informs me that he's been authorized to advance me fifty thousand dollars! This is enough to see me through the first six months and to repay the hospital for the costs they incurred in setting up my office.

To this day, I don't know why the bank took a chance on me. I had no collateral, no work experience except as a farmworker, and no letters of recommendation except from a recently fired CEO, yet they gave me a sizable loan overnight. I still marvel at all the important events in my life that have been influenced by outside forces. Without that loan, I never would have settled in Porterville.

Six months later, with Shirley's help and some aggressive marketing, my practice is solvent. To build it up, I put myself out into the community in every way I can. I attend birthing classes held by Ethyln Wheeler, who later comes to work for me as my nurse practitioner, and offer advice to the future parents. I attend every school function where I can meet people with kids. I even go so far as to speak to pregnant women in grocery stores. I hand them my card and let them know that they can come in for a free consult. (Once in a while, I approach a woman who appears to be pregnant, only to find out to my chagrin that she's just overweight.)

I also make it a point to pay frequent visits to a nice children's store not far from my office. The owners, Jimmy and Irene Howell, have lived in Porterville for generations and know everyone. After their granddaughter Elyse is born, her parents, Denise and Lou Marchant, start bringing her to see me.

During this period, I also do house calls, partly because I want to offer something unique in my practice, but mainly because I just enjoy seeing infants in their natural setting. One night, I stop by to see Elyse, who's a month old. I quickly realize that she isn't acting normal for an infant her age. Lou's filming us while I examine her, so I try to hide my concern because I don't want to alarm them. "I'm not sure what's going on," I tell him and Denise, "but you need to take her to the emergency room right away."

Within eight hours, Elyse is in a coma and on a respirator at VCH. After three days of examinations by several of the specialists who taught me, she's diagnosed with botulism poisoning. This is a rare condition, and she's one of only fifty cases in the United States that year. As near as her mom and dad can figure out, she must have contracted it by somehow consuming some honey from the bees that were infesting their yard that year.

(This is why parents are advised never to feed honey to children younger than a year old. Bees naturally ingest botulism spores when collecting nectar, and these find their way into the bees' honey. However, infants' digestive and immune systems are not developed enough to eliminate the botulism spores, so the toxin can grow in their intestines and cause paralysis and even death.)

Elyse is comatose for about four weeks, and I credit her Grandpa Jimmy for saving her life by singing to her all the time. After she recovers, her parents and grandparents tell everyone how I saved her life. They do more than anyone else in town to make my practice successful. I often wonder what would have happened with my practice if I hadn't picked up on Elyse's symptoms. (By the way, she has grown up to become a wonderful and talented singer, actress, musician, and student. In June 2009, she graduated from UCLA with honors and a degree in music with an emphasis in vocal music education.)

As word of mouth spreads, more and more patients start calling for appointments. Because I want to have a very active practice, I also place myself on the call schedule for both Lindsay Hospital and Sierra View in Porterville. I'm on call every other day and every other weekend, but it's still a less demanding schedule than I'm used to from being a resident.

It takes time for me to get established, but I know I'm making headway when I realize that the first couple of times I went to the annual Springville Apple Festival, I walked around unnoticed because no one knew who I was. I would see all the kids out having a good time and would hope that someday they would be my patients. Now I'm constantly stopping to talk or visit with families in my practice.

Less than a year after I open my practice, Debbie and I feel we're established enough to buy a house. She's pregnant again, and we want to have our very own place for our family. We find a house in the hills in Springville, less than twenty miles east of Porterville. It has four bedrooms, three bathrooms, a big swimming pool, a barn, and more than two acres of grounds dotted with boulders, oaks, and fruit trees.

When I was growing up, I would have been ecstatic to have a yard like that, with the pool, and lots of land to roam, and all the trees and rocks to climb. Maybe that's why I want to buy it the minute I see it. My first thought is that it'll be a great place for family gatherings. I feel I'm buying it for my whole family to come and enjoy. It's by far the most impressive and comfortable house anyone in the family has ever had.

Of course, I go straight to the Bank of the Sierras for the financing. With some financial help from Debbie's parents since my practice is so new and we don't have much of a credit history or financial track record, within weeks the house is ours. I realize that less than a year ago, we didn't even know if we'd be able to stay in Porterville.

Now we're going to be settling into one of the best neighborhoods in Springville.

In fact, we have our first family function even before we move in because we can't wait to invite my family to celebrate Easter with a picnic and egg hunt at our new house. Everyone comes. We have about two dozen cars lined up all along our driveway out to the street. (Of course, as always happens in my family, someone's car breaks down on the way, so I have to go pick them up and bring them to the house, and another family doesn't make it at all because they get lost on the way to Springville.)

We haven't yet met any of our neighbors, and I wonder if they're shocked by this crowd of Mexican folks showing up. That doesn't stop Breezy, the little girl whose family lives across the street from us. Breezy is just under five years old and not one bit shy. She comes right over. She and Marina are almost the same age, and they end up in kindergarten together the following September. It's funny to see this little blonde Anglo girl running around among all the dark-haired, brown-skinned kids.

Debbie's second pregnancy is much easier. The pool is a good place for her to cool off during the hottest months (instead of that small wading pool). Josh makes his appearance at Lindsay Hospital three weeks early, on December 9, 1986. I planned to take a week off to devote to him and Debbie, but not only is he born early, Kathy Hall is out sick, so I'm taking care of her patients as well as my own. I'm so busy at the office that I don't get to Lindsay to see Debbie and discharge my new baby or to see the other babies at the hospital until late in the day after Josh is born. I arrive and find all the moms, including Debbie, griping about my being so late. All they want is to be discharged and go home.

CHAPTER THIRTY-NINE

Rotary

A ROUND THE TIME JOSH IS BORN, Jimmy Howell, a long-time
Rotary member, invites me to a meeting. I really enjoy the
fellowship and the friendly banter, and I think it's a wonderful service organization. If they ask me to join, I'll be surprised but very
honored. Thanks to Jimmy, I end up attending many Rotary functions.
He's my biggest cheerleader and frequently tells the other members
about Elyse's illness, her remarkable recovery, and my part in it. When
I'm finally invited to join, about three or four months after I start attending, I'm more than glad to accept. I attend the meetings every Tuesday
at noon and enjoy getting to know people. Rotary does a lot for the community and is considered the best service club to belong to.

But I still don't make any real friends. There's no one I feel I can
share my troubles with. When I was in college and medical school, I
was too busy—and too frightened, insecure, and driven by fear of possible failure—to risk trying to connect with new people. My friends
from high school are the people I've always felt closest to, but they're
now scattered all over California. I haven't seen them for years. I'm
isolated but don't know what to do about it.

About three years after I join Rotary, Glade Roper, an attorney who's
been elected incoming president, invites me to join the board of direc-

tors. I'm honored that he would even consider me because I'm such a new member, and I enjoy working with him. Being on the board teaches me more about Rotary's inner workings, and I become more and more involved. In 1990, Glade's term ends and we learn a short time later that the president-elect is leaving the area. Board members are the only ones eligible to take over in this situation, so Glade asks for a volunteer. Somehow I end up being chosen. (Actually, I usually tell people that I was looking down at my feet when he asked someone to step forward. Everyone else took a step backward, so that left me to take up the reins.)

I hesitate to say yes, but everyone encourages me to take a week or two to think about it. During that time, Debbie and I attend a district Rotary conference in Lake Tahoe, where other members keep approaching me and offering support and encouragement. They know that the job will be difficult for me because I don't have any experience, but they also assure me that all I'll have to do is run the meetings.

My reluctance isn't due to not wanting to take on the responsibilities of being president. It's that I'm still nervous about being in front of crowds. I'm afraid my stutter will get worse. I've never been in a leadership role, and who am I to be the leader and spokesperson for all the prominent Porterville citizens—judges, bankers, doctors, lawyers, CEOs—who make up the membership? But both Glade and the departing president-elect assure me that I'll do a good job. So I step into this new adventure. It turns out to be one of the best—and worst—decisions of my life because I'm not prepared. I have no idea what's involved, and I haven't had the usual year of preparation. It's overwhelming, and the pressure and expectations I put on myself are probably higher than anyone else would expect of me. What's more, it kicks off all my old feelings of not belonging, of being a fake or an imposter. I don't feel I fit in anywhere—not really as a member of the community, and not with my family, either, anymore.

At my first meeting, my heart is pounding and I gabble so fast that one of my colleagues has to keep asking me to repeat myself, but over time I lose my nervousness. I also make two very good friends in Glade and Dave Stuck, who becomes president after my term ends. He and I develop a good relationship because the next president is always elected a year before taking office. I have no way of knowing at this point how much I'll need their friendship and patience in the future.

It's during my presidency that the Big Freeze of 1990 hits just a few days before Christmas. It ultimately wreaks almost eight hundred million dollars in agricultural damage and puts many of the farm-workers in our area out of work. Because of my background, I relate to their suffering, and I decide to tell my fellow Rotary members my story. I've never spoken of it before, but I feel that the timing's right. If I can generate compassion for the farmworkers' plight . . . well, it'll be worth whatever shame or embarrassment I feel.

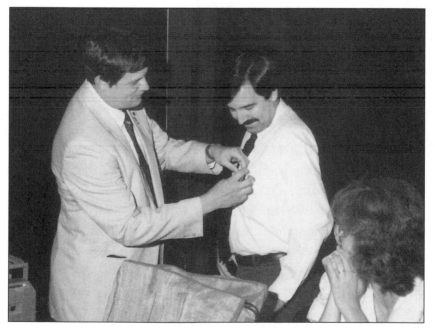

My friend Glade Roper pins me
as Porterville Rotary president, 1990

So at our next meeting, I tell them about the misery and the despair we felt when we couldn't work, and that the last thing we wanted was charity. I tell them that my family and others like ours were poor, but we were good at what we did and proud to put in a day's work. I also tell them what it was like to see our bare cupboards and what it felt like when I had to go to bed hungry, with only one tortilla to fill my empty stomach.

"It wasn't the fact that we didn't have food on the table that was so hard," I say. "It was more the feeling of hopelessness. I've never forgotten seeing my grandparents suffering because we kids were going hungry and they couldn't do anything to help us. I've also never forgotten the generosity of people we never met who left food baskets of rice and beans at our door. That's how we made it through."

I suggest that we help our farmworkers survive the freeze by buying and giving out rice, beans, and flour—staples that go a long way and last a long time. My fellow Rotarians overwhelm me with their generosity. We fill my truck several times over with donations that we deliver to a farmworkers' aid organization. When I also suggest that we use the money we would ordinarily spend on our lunches to buy more food, the fellow Rotarians agree without a moment's hesitation. From then on, we "fast" at meetings and donate the money.

To this day, I've never forgotten the food baskets of my childhood. Every year I still fill our church pantry with staples. I also donate money for clothes, especially jackets. I love nothing more than driving to one of the warehouse stores and loading up my truck with hundred-pound sacks of beans, rice, and flour like the ones our family lived on so many years ago.

CHAPTER FORTY

Who Am I?

S TILL . . . ALL THE SUCCESSES I've achieved—my thriving practice, my family, my standing in the community, and my great
experiences with Rotary—aren't enough to eradicate my old
insecurities. Deep down, I don't feel I deserve any of it. These old feelings return in force in the mid-1990s, when I'm named to the boards
of the Porterville Chamber of Commerce and the Porterville College
Foundation.

I question why the members of these organizations are inviting
me to join them. How long will it take them to discover their mistake
and ask me to resign? I'm convinced I'm a fraud and that it's only a
matter of time before I'm found out. I start questioning my right to
happiness and my very existence. I should be happy, but I'm not. Why?
What more could I ask for? What's wrong with me? I have everything
I've always wanted, but I don't have peace of mind. And gradually the
black mood I knew from high school envelops me again.

I can't face my fellow Rotary members. I make excuses to cancel our
noon meetings, or I call someone else to lead them. I have trouble speaking to people. I have trouble advising my patients. No matter where I am,
I don't want to be there. I just want to hide. I don't want to think anymore.
Why is this happening to me? How have I ended up in this situation?

Then I start taking out my fear and anger on Debbie and the kids. When Josh was a baby, I resented the attention she paid to him. I knew he was only a baby. I knew that she was a good mom. I knew that I shouldn't have been jealous. But when she would hold him and breast-feed him, I felt ignored, overlooked, and abandoned. Then I remembered that I felt the same way when Marina was a baby. I wanted Debbie to put her down and pay attention to me. But I blocked out all those feelings—after all, how could I be jealous of the little girl I loved so much? I did't think about the fact that when Marina was born, I was under the stress of starting my residency, and that when Josh came along I was in the middle of establishing my medical practice. I don't realize that Debbie's overwhelmed with motherhood and that we've both been involved in things that have pulled us away from each other.

All those old feelings rise up again. I work long hours and am rarely home, but when I am there, I make my family miserable. I'm angry all the time. I can't control my rage. I yell at the TV and throw the remote to vent my frustration. Debbie walks on eggshells around me, never sure what might set me off. When she tells me to calm down, I only get angrier. I storm out of the house. Debbie has no idea where I'm going, and frankly neither do I. I drive around at random wondering if they would be better off without me. I've shattered my own dream of being the perfect father and husband. I'm doing a lousy job of my whole life.

I start thinking about killing myself. How can I do it? I could drive off the road and into the lake, or drive head-on into a semi, but I would need to make it look like an accident so Debbie and my kids will get the insurance. Then I imagine Marina and Josh growing up without a father. What would their lives be like? I tell myself that they need me. I can't quit on them. Marina still loves me no matter what, but she's five years old and terrified. The teachers start telling us that she's hugging them and clinging to them all the time.

I tell myself, "Just live until tomorrow. For them." I keep going to work a day at a time. And Marina and Josh save my life just because they're my kids. They're all that keeps me from suicide. I manage to continue getting along with the Rotarians, but I keep everyone at arm's length. How can I let them know how I feel inside? When I go to our lunches, I feel like an outsider. I don't say no to anything they ask me to do. I contribute a hundred and twenty percent because I'm so close to losing it that I need all the positive gestures and kind words I can get just so I can keep on going for one more day.

At home I try to go through the motions of being a husband, but I snap at Debbie constantly. "You don't know me!" I tell her. "You have no idea what I'm feeling!" But what can she do if I don't open up to her? One day, she finally snaps. After one of my rages, she tells me, "Ramon, stop it! I can't take this anymore! If you don't get some help, I'm going to leave you. And I'll take the kids!" Looking at her, I know she means it. She's so shy and gentle, but underneath . . .

This stops me cold. I don't want to lose my kids. They're all I live for. Until now, I've resisted therapy because I'm afraid to admit I need help. Psychologists are only for the desperate, and I'm not one of "those people." I don't want to admit how messed up I am.

I finally agree to see a psychologist, but only to keep Debbie from walking out. Over time, we see "Mike" both individually and as a couple, but our first joint sessions are a waste of time because I refuse to open up or even engage in conversation. I told Debbie I would go, but I never promised that I would say anything.

One day, Mike asks me how I feel about my mother and father. I shrug. "I don't care one way or the other." He knows better, so he wears me down until I explode. "I hate them!" I shout. "I wish I'd never been born!" As soon as the words leave my mouth, something happens inside me. I feel myself drifting away. I go mute. Debbie and Mike are talking, but their voices seem to be coming from farther and farther away. After a few minutes, they realize I'm not participating. They try to engage me, but I'm not "there" anymore. I can barely hear them. I feel as if I have a choice I need to make—to stay, or to drift away and never come back. I half-realize I'm sliding into a catatonic state. It feels so peaceful . . . nothing to think about . . . nothing to be responsible for . . . I now understand why people in catatonia are the way they are.

"Ramon! Ramon!" I hear Debbie's voice pleading with me frantically from far, far away.

"Ramon! Ramon!" It's Mike. He sounds anxious too, but I don't want to come back. I'm so close to letting go and leaving reality behind for good because I'm realizing how much I always felt I had been abandoned.

After that episode of dissociation, I start opening up. I tell Debbie and Mike what happened to me when I was young, about how I never had parents or a childhood, and about how my stepbrother had robbed me of my innocence. I had never told Debbie about the sexual abuse before. Mike tries to give me permission to take things easy. "Try going home and doing kid stuff, like putting model cars together," he suggests. So I go out and buy model kits. I don't touch them.

A few weeks later, when we're talking about my mother, I suddenly fly into a rage, screaming, "I don't have a mother! And I don't care that I don't!" Then I storm out of the session and get into my car. But I can't drive away. An overwhelming sadness comes over me. For the first time in my life, I cry over the mother I never had. When Debbie comes out and sees me sobbing, she realizes I've had a breakthrough. I've never admitted until now how much I was affected by Frances's abandoning me.

After that session, I'm able to talk more. I start to understand how much my childhood and especially my immense anger toward my mother and grandparents are still affecting me. I'm so full of hatred toward them that I stop visiting or even talking to them. For the next couple of years, I go to family get-togethers with Debbie and the children, but I refuse to pay visits to Apa and Ama. Even as they grow older and feebler, I keep nursing my anger and hatred. It isn't that these emotions help me feel any better, though. Rather, I can channel my general anger about everything by making them and my mother the targets and scapegoats for everything that's wrong with my life—my problems with Debbie, the fact that I'm overworked and trying to do everything right but am frustrated and angry at the world . . . everything.

The problem is, I'm not becoming a better parent or husband. I'm too angry, and too busy making the best living I can. Neither Debbie nor I are at peace. Although we're living together, we don't feel any support from each other. Mike tells me I'm depressed and that my anger is my way of dealing with it. I keep on blaming Debbie because I don't feel she appreciates me. I still want to be part of a family, but even after several years of therapy, I'm still spiraling out of control. Counseling is helping me to identify the source of my anger, but what's the remedy? I need something else to bring me out of my depression.

As has happened so often in my life, the answer comes out of nowhere. For some time, Shirley, my office manager, has been trying to get me to go to the church that she and her husband, Joe, attend. I don't want to take her up on it. I don't need God. He didn't help me before, so why should I try to talk to Him now?

One night, I reach the end of the line. I'm in so much anguish that I call Shirley. "I need help now," I tell her. "I need to see your pastor." It's almost midnight, but they call him and he says I can come over right away. Later that night, after talking with him for hours, I get down on my knees and pray. And I feel peace for the first time in my life. I know that many people have been praying for me for years, but I've always brushed them off. Who needs prayers? I thought.

But now I pray for forgiveness, and I receive it. I feel the weight lifted off my shoulders. I forgive my mother. I forgive Apa and Ama. I'm able to see them in a new light. I realize that I know almost nothing about them or what their lives have been like. I also know now that they weren't prepared to raise me—that they couldn't help how they were raised or what happened to me.

Finally I'm able to go back to Goshen and be with them again. And it's very different for me. Ama's had several strokes that have left her with the mind of a two-year-old. Apa's now ninety-nine and can no longer go out and take care of his beloved garden and animals. One day while Debbie and I are visiting, he tries to say something to us. We finally figure out that he wants to go outside. He's always preferred to be outdoors, so we settle him in his wheelchair and take him and Ama out into the front yard. As Debbie and I are standing next to them chatting and laughing, she whispers, "Apa's not moving. I think he's dead." I listen for his heartbeat but hear nothing. I guess he wanted desperately to die outside. Not too long after that, Ama dies at home.

I feel blessed because I'm able to let them go without the guilt I so easily could have felt if I hadn't forgiven them. When I say good-bye to both of them, it's with a heart full of love. The bitterness is gone. Only forgiveness is left.

Ama and Apa in the Goshen house
toward the end of their lives

In the years since those dark days came to an end, my life has been so different. I get angry but I don't stay angry. Sometimes I throw down my clubs when I get frustrated playing golf, but I'm able to let go of my anger immediately. (Well, almost immediately.)

My life is good. I've reached goals I never could have imagined when I was a little Mexican kid picking cotton, oranges, and grapes and swimming in ditches and canals full of chemicals. I have a beautiful house with a big swimming pool. Josh and Marina grew up in a nice, quiet neighborhood and attended Springville's town school. They're both adults now, and living up to my dreams for them. My goal in life has been to have them surpass me. I'm confident that they will, and I'm looking forward to seeing what's in store for them.

Marina went to UC Santa Cruz and graduated with a major in theater. She's now an actress in Los Angeles. I have no doubt that she'll be successful because she's a determined, gutsy young woman. In June 2009, Josh graduated from Stanford University with a degree in biology. Stanford was a good setting for him because he was able to associate with other students who shared his interests and were as intelligent as he is. As I watched him receive his diploma, I couldn't help remembering that when I was thinking about college I never dared even consider Stanford, much less apply there. I felt it was out of my league. But my son not only attended this prestigious, top-ranked university, he also tutored other students and high-school kids in the sciences. Now, by extension, I'm associated with Stanford, too.

I've never had another recurrence of depression. I now know that I have too much to live for. Debbie stuck with me through all my problems and never stopped believing in me. I have Marina's career to follow (and I get to bug her about grandchildren, which to her annoyance I do constantly). And Josh is about to decide which top medical school he's going to attend. At this point, he seems to be heading to UC San Francisco, where Debbie's father taught. I know that I can't live through their lives, and that they may not choose to be as motivated or productive as I've been. So be it. I want them to feel happy and content. That's enough.

I now understand why I suffered for so many years from depressive moods and "imposter syndrome." Coming from a family in which it was a minor miracle to graduate from high school, who would ever have thought I could become a doctor? When I look back at my life and what I've accomplished, I marvel. Santa Cruz . . . my MD . . . my residencies . . . my practice . . . becoming a fixture in the Porterville community . . . serving on the boards of the Chamber of Commerce and the College Foundation . . . becoming president of our Rotary Club less than five years after joining . . . being treated like a peer by judges, CEOs, and political figures in my community. Even today, twenty years down the road, I sometimes still forget that I'm a doctor and a businessman, that I have the same qualifications my peers do—and that I'm entitled to belong in their world. I have to remind myself that I'm worthy of the position I've achieved.

This little farmworker boy, I remind myself, has earned his good fortune.

Debbie and me at home in Springville, late 1980s

Josh, 9, and me on our way to a
San Francisco '49ers game, mid-1990s

Marina, 11, Josh, 6, and me at
Yosemite, about 1992

Josh, 6, with his Easter basket,
and me at our house in Springville

Teenage Marina and me on our way to a
father-daughter event

Marina

Josh, Stanford graduation

Epilogue

T HROUGHOUT THIS BOOK, I've mentioned many of my family members, some at length and others only in passing. I want to say a little more about each of them now and communicate more of the flavor of my relationships with them.

As I say in an early chapter, when we were growing up, we drew no lines based on our actual blood or legal relationships. Although technically we might have been brothers, sisters, cousins, aunts, uncles, half-brothers, and half-sisters, in Ama's and Apa's house, we were all simply "brothers" and "sisters." There were sixteen of us in all, so you can see why. Also, extended family members were always in and out of the house, often visiting, but sometimes staying for weeks or months.

As I've mentioned, when my mother, Frances, married Cruz Martinez, she already had five children: Al, Domingo, and me, as well as Betty and Bobby, the two children who were raised in Los Angeles. I'm sorry that Betty and Bobby are referred to only in passing in the book, but they weren't part of our household—my mother's doing, not theirs. Frances had seven more children with Cruz—my half-brothers and half-sisters Candy, Joe, Velma, Annette, Danny, Angel, and Terry. Among the many unanswered questions in my family is why she let the five of us be raised by others, but over time I've come to realize that many factors, including her extreme youth, must have gone into her decision.

To me, my mother's sisters Elsie and Matilda were the adventurous ones because they moved away from Goshen. Without their example, I might never have seen the world outside our small town.

When I think about Anita, Lucinda, and Catalina, my mother's other sisters, I always see them in my mind's eye as married and with children tugging at their skirts. They were always present in my life enough to be influences on me. I admire Anita and Catalina for breaking away from their abusive husbands. This took enormous courage, especially given the fate of my half-sister Annette, whose common-law husband killed her when she tried to leave him.

My aunt Helen, of course, died much too early, but her death gave me the determination to follow my chosen career.

Among the girls in the family, Rosa had the biggest influence on my work ethic. She was a hard worker and she set an example I tried to follow.

Lily and Delma were the two I considered my "real" sisters because they always seemed to be there for me, whether at work or at home.

Elia was the fiery one. She had a temper, but she was also the one I knew I could depend on to fight my fights when I couldn't or didn't. From her, I learned not to back down, even when the going got rough.

Among the guys, Mercy was the oldest and therefore Apa's heir apparent. He was under a lot of pressure, and sometimes it proved too much, but his early refusal to turn to alcohol helped me decide that I would never allow it to control me.

Bill was an important presence for me. I saw him as wise and mature, and in fact he was my role model for good behavior. I always wanted to earn his respect.

Esmael (Mily) and my full brother, Al, were more in my day-to-day orbit than Bill was because we were closer in age. I don't know why, but for some reason, I gravitated more to Mily.

Domingo was the brother I was the closest to. His health problems gave me my first inkling of how important doctors were, although at that time I had no idea that I would end up a pediatrician.

Joe . . . well, he and I may have fought all the time, but he was the one member of the family who was always telling me I was smart. That made him probably the first person in my life, other than my teachers, to encourage me.

I hope I haven't left anyone out, because sometimes I forget how many brothers and sisters I have. (But I'm fairly certain that others exist because, if our father is truly unknown, he must have fathered other children along the way.)

When I look at my family today, I still see a microcosm of the problems facing our society. Many in my family are still struggling with survival on a daily basis and trying to keep their children away from drugs and gangs, often unsuccessfully. The family battle with alcoholism still goes on. Several of my sisters have lost husbands (in some cases, more than one husband) to drugs and alcohol. They have also lost children in the same battle. Some of the younger generation are in prison, others are fighting their addictions, and some are winning. Last year, I was there when one of my nephews graduated from drug court. He had a job and had been drug-free for a year. He was not the first in our family to go through this program, but I know he won't be the last.

Sadly, although I emphasize education in everything I do and say, we've only recently started to have college graduates in our family. After me, it took a whole generation before someone else went on to a four-year college. Some of my cousins attended community colleges but didn't make the leap to four-year institutions. Still, I'm seeing progress on this front. More and more of my family are beginning to see the importance of an education, and we now number a city government employee, several teachers, and others who are climbing the ladder to management positions.

Interestingly, some of the younger generation are exploring health-care-related fields, from medical transcription to nursing. And, in a strange coincidence, Josh and my nephew Jesus, Betty's son, both entered the UC San Francisco School of Medicine in the fall of 2010, when the two cousins met for the first time at their white coat ceremony. "A Tale of Two Cousins," a story about the boys and our family's history, appears on the school's website, and I've been permitted to include it in this book (see pp. 385-388).

My older siblings are nearing retirement age and enjoying their grandchildren and great-grandchildren. Their lives have been hard, and because many of them never had jobs with retirement benefits, all they have is Social Security (which isn't much this days). A few, like Bill, worked for the same employer for years, so they can look forward to a reasonably secure future.

Most of the girls in the family have been widowed or divorced. They've devoted their lives to earning a living and helping to care for grandchildren—sometimes by their own choice, and sometimes not, as my mother did after Annette was murdered.

⬱

I also need to say that, looking back, I have many regrets about how I failed my family. In my own mind, I went missing for twelve years. Whenever I was home from college, medical school, or my residency, I was so stressed that I was no help to anyone. Then, when I started to think about encouraging family members onward, my own family came along, and I concentrated on them.

This has cost us in terms of our ties with my family. We no longer get invited to family events as often as we used to, and I blame myself for this. Recently my sister Delma told me over the phone, "It seems as if you always looked down on us, that you felt yourself superior." That shocked me because, in all this time, I had never realized that they looked at me that way. It's unfortunate, and I must take responsibility for it.

I guess they didn't understand that I wasn't so different. I just happened to get lucky, and I took advantage of the situations that came my way. My family never knew how close I came to failing throughout those trying years. Maybe they thought I was sailing along because I was no longer out working in the fields.

Little do they know how I envied that they had their families and each other. In my haste to make a better life for myself, I left the family and wasn't around during the crucial period when the next generation was coming along. Sometimes I wonder if I would have done better to have just finished college and found a job, because then I might have been more of a role model. But by jumping into the uncharted and all-consuming territory of college and medical school, I failed to create a bridge or a road map to achievement for those coming along behind me in my family. Without any guidance, it was too difficult for others to follow my path. Not that they didn't have what it took—they just didn't have the self-determination or the encouragement I was fortunate enough to receive.

As I show in the book, growing up in Goshen was no easy feat for any of us. Much of what I write about my family was no different from what other families in this small farmworker community experienced. Alcoholism was rampant. Spousal, sexual, and child abuse were commonplace. Work was seasonal and hard to find. Frustration and despair were everyday companions. Education wasn't considered important because, in those days, a large family was the key to survival. The more hands to pick the crops, the more money at the end of the day. Racism, though not blatant (well, sometimes it was), also blocked any chance for upward mobility for Mexicans like us. We were limited to farmwork—and we were never promoted.

Sometimes the members of our younger generation ask me questions about our family history, but I don't have many answers. Still, I hope that this book will open a dialogue among the generations by helping the grandchildren to understand that their mothers' and fathers' lives were not easy. They had to overcome a lot just to survive, and even when they could have improved their own lot, they often chose to sacrifice to make life easier for their children.

Finally, everything I've written about here comes from my own point of view—what I saw and lived growing up. So my memories and insights will inevitably differ considerably from those of other family members. I know that this has already ruffled feathers, and for this I must say that I'm sorry.

I wish I could be totally candid about everything, because it all shaped my life, as it does for each of us. But that doesn't seem possible, so I've tried to resolve this dilemma by softening some language and changing names and identities, as well as the details of some events, to protect individuals' privacy and to soften the impact of my story on my family and on others. Also, with so many years having gone by, I've had to re-create conversations to the best of my recollection.

I think that to this day my family still knows little of what I had to overcome to accomplish what I have, but I know it isn't because they don't care. It's because I distanced myself and didn't let them in. I want them to know that I care deeply for all of them. Even when I didn't feel I belonged, I always tried to be with them.

I hope that my family will see this book not as a tell-all or exposé, but as what it is intended to be—inspiration for those who find themselves in a similar situation as mine, so they will continue striving to reach their goals, no matter what the obstacles.

A Tale of Two Cousins

By Susan Davis

T HE FACT THAT DR. RAMON RESA became a doctor is nothing short of amazing. His mother, who had five children before the age of twenty, gave him to his grandparents to raise in the late 1950s, in a small town near Visalia, California.

There he grew up picking cotton, grapes and oranges from the age of three, in an extended family filled with cousins, aunts, uncles, siblings and step-siblings. Despite poverty, neglect, a speech impediment, and almost no support from his family, Resa excelled in school and then supported himself—still by working as a farm laborer—through his undergraduate years at UC Santa Cruz and then medical school at UC Irvine. Once he finished his training, he moved to Porterville, where he now works as a pediatrician in a small clinic that serves patients who are much like he was: poor, Hispanic, and underserved.

That story alone is compelling. But what makes Dr. Resa's story even more interesting is that his son, Joshua, was admitted to UCSF's School of Medicine this fall, having just completed his bachelor's degree at Stanford University. And here's the twist: a first cousin whom Joshua never met before also entered UCSF's School of Medicine this year.

Jesus Granados (l) and Joshua Resa

Jesus Granados, Joshua's cousin, grew up in Rowland Heights, a suburb in Los Angeles County. He got his BA in psychology from Sonoma State University, then went through the pre-med program at SF State before applying to medical school. His mother, Betty Jo Zamora, is Ramon Resa's full sister, but Betty's mother gave her up for adoption when she was an infant, so Betty didn't meet her biological family (including Ramon) until she was about twenty-five. Even then, the siblings weren't all that close; the family was big, after all, and the distance ingrained. So neither sibling knew the other's child was on his way to UCSF until Betty posted the news on her Facebook page.

The UCSF School of Medicine is among the top five in the country, and the odds of getting in are tough for any individual. This year, the school accepted 149 out of 6,413 applicants. For two cousins to get in simultaneously is a rare event. But what makes this even more noteworthy, Joshua says, is that the two cousins are only one genera-tion removed from a culture that didn't value education highly at all. Ramon's grandmother—who raised him—had only a third-grade education.

"Between their own kids and their daughter's kids, my great-grandparents raised fifteen children," Joshua says. "Of those fifteen, my father was the first to go to college. The whole family worked in the fields. The other brothers and sisters did vocational education and got jobs as soon as they graduated from high school. Some never graduated from high school. Going to college—going beyond col-lege—was not considered a possibility. In fact, it was discouraged. It's incredible to think how much has changed."

For Jesus, knowing that he'll have a long-lost cousin with him during his first year, is "a really awesome feeling," he says. "It was so surprising and so shocking, because it's such a crazy coincidence." It also means that he, too, is getting a better sense of his extended bio-logical family. Jesus read his Uncle Ramon's memoir, *Out of the Fields: My Journey from Farmworker Boy to Pediatrician*, with considerable fascination. "He has photos in there of his biological parents and grandparents," Jesus says. "That was so interesting to me—to get that connection to personal history."

The two cousins met for the first time at this year's School of Medicine's White Coat Ceremony, which marks the beginning of first-year students' medical education at UCSF. Their families were there to celebrate with them. "Who would ever think this could hap-pen?" says Jesus' mother, Betty Jo. "Two cousins who weren't raised together—who didn't even know the other one existed—ending up in medical school together? I'm so proud of my brother and so proud of my son." Adds Ramon, "This is the first time all of us are together in thirty-seven years. Our lives have been so divergent and yet now they're coming back together again. This has made me discover that we truly are connected and always have been."

(from left to right): Al Resa, Betty Jo Zamora, Debbie Resa,
Dr. Ramon Resa, Joshua Resa, Jesus Granados, Lynette Zamora,
Bobby Hernandez

UCSF School of Medicine officials, of course, are delighted to have a role in this story. "UCSF is proud to be a part of this family's wonderful story of remarkable achievement and glorious reunion," says David Wofsy, MD, associate dean of admissions for the school. "This story is unique for the twists of fate that brought two cousins to the same place at the same time, but in most other ways it is representative of the strength of character and extraordinary backgrounds that amaze us in so many of our students and their families."

http://medschool2.ucsf.edu/spotlights/tale-two-cousins

Acknowledgments

EVERY TIME I TURN THE PAGES of this book, I'm reminded of how much I owe to everyone who has been in my life. Where do we stop when it comes to thanking and acknowledging the roles we've played in one another's lives? For years, it was a dream close to my heart to put my story into book form. But it was also a challenge that I would probably never have been able to meet without the support and help of more people than I can name. I am happy and grateful to be able to mention some of them here.

- First and most importantly, I thank Debbie, who has put up with me for more than thirty years although I've made her endure more than most people could handle. What's more, her art for the cover of this second printing truly captures the essence of the former farmworker boy she married.
- Thank you also to our daughter, Marina, who inspired me to never accept failure, and to Joshua, the son I always wanted and who turned out exactly as I had wished. He's smarter and wiser than I'll ever be (and even a better golfer!).

- Another thank you goes to Debbie's mom and dad, Barbara Binger and the late Charles Binger, who were always there for us and for our children.
- Of all my family, I must give Esmael a special acknowledgment. Mily was the only family member I contacted regarding some memories, such as our summers in migrant camps, that I didn't have in my memory bank. He helped them to come alive again.
- Because my life was literally transformed by my educational experiences, I want to express my gratitude to all of my teachers, but especially Mrs. Lambers and Mrs. Tobin. If they hadn't seen my potential, I would probably have spent my school years at the back of the classroom and ended up accepting life as it was.
- I'm also grateful to my high-school friends, Magda, Ernie, Eddy, Adolph, Amparo, and Pata, who insured my survival just by being there.
- Thank you to Linda Cuellar and Roberto Rubalcava for changing my life by paving my way into UC Santa Cruz.
- I still remember the kindness of Don Nagel, who was so generous with his help when the time came for me to leave home before starting college.
- I am also more grateful than I can adequately express to Rotary International, and especially the Porterville Rotary Club. It was there that I realized I was not an imposter and that I did deserve to be in the company of my peers. Special thanks go to Dave Stuck, Glade Roper, Judy Holloway (and her late husband, Al), Marty, Jim Howell, Randy, Glen, Milt—and actually to the whole club, then and now—for giving me that feeling of acceptance.

Acknowledgments

- I am especially grateful to Noe Lozano for inspiring me and so many others to get out of the San Joaquin Valley and follow him to Santa Cruz. Not only that, he helped me launch my speaking career, which led to my meeting author Jean Hollands. Without her encouragement and devotion, and the countless hours that she, her husband, Tom, and my first editor, Joy Thisted, spent on my work, this book would still be a first draft.
- Susan Drake, my family's next-door neighbor when I was growing up and the author of *Fields of Courage*, became my second editor and offered much support and many valuable suggestions.
- Thank you also to the many team members who have helped to bring my story to the world in its first two printings: interior and cover designers Bob Tinnon, Sam Kuo, and Kirk Thomas; proofreaders Rena Copperman, Cynthia Cuza, and Veronica Spencer; title consultant Nancy Friedman; website consultants Sam Kuo and Kathy Hernandez, and marketing consultant Jesse Gift.
- My final editorial thank you is to Monica Faulkner. I expected that she would make changes here and there, but instead she put her heart and soul into making this book much more than I expected. She checked facts and details for accuracy and made so many insightful suggestions that before long I realized I could trust and accept the changes she recommended without a second thought. In addition to shaping the book, she oversaw the process of bringing it into physical form with patience and expertise. I am so impressed with her dedication that I feel as if she almost cowrote it with me. Monica brought this book to life, and for that I owe her a great debt of gratitude.

About the Author

www.ramonresamd.com

Ramon Resa, MD

Recently, California-based pediatrician Ramon Resa, MD, was invited to speak at the first-ever TEDx in Monterey, California, with more than four hundred people attending in person and online as sixteen speakers addressed the theme of "Be the Solution."

Ramon was the only one to receive a standing ovation.

Lynn McDonald, the curator and organizer of the event, said afterward, "He's so genuine in his story, and it's so triumphant and amazing. People really connected with him. He just blew everyone away. When I was booking speakers, as soon as I looked at his website and saw his video clip, I said, 'He's in!' And afterward, when people were asked to rank their top three speakers, he got by far the most votes. His story connected with universal truths. His theme was perseverance, and it was perfect. I'll definitely be recommending him to anyone looking for a dynamic, powerful, and emotional speaker."

Author of *Out of the Fields: My Journey from Farmworker to Pediatrician*, Ramon never set out to be a speaker, but over time his community involvement (he became known as "The One-Man Tornado" after spearheading a campaign that raised over one hundred thousand dollars for new band uniforms for his town's high school) led to speaking invitations. After his first presentation to the Stanford Rotary club a

couple of years ago, he realized that his story could inspire others—
and so another career was born. He has been approached about a possible movie version of his memoir, which is now in its second printing.

Ramon says of his talks: "With tears and laughter, I tell my life
story in a way that makes the audience want to jump up and get involved.
Teachers are especially motivated by my talk because I credit them
with making my life possible. I let them know how important they are
to the children of our country. After hearing my story, they know that
they do make a difference. And students realize that if I was able to
make it in spite of all the hardships I had to overcome, they too can
make their dreams come true."

Ramon's video demo (5:00) can be viewed on his website
(www.ramonresamd.com) and at http://www.youtube.com/watch?v=
cmcfkT602kY&feature=channel_page

Growing up as a farmworker in a family of fifteen, Ramon never
imagined he could become a doctor. Abandoned by his single mother,
who had five kids before the age of twenty, he grew up in an environment of severe poverty, neglect, and a total disregard for education. At
the age of three, he was picking cotton in the fields of Central California. It was his elementary-school teachers who opened his eyes to the
idea of education and awakened in him the dream of going to college
and becoming a doctor.

It wasn't easy. He had to overcome low self-esteem, a speech impediment, recurring depression, prejudice, discouragement from school
counselors, and even opposition from his grandparents, who wanted
him to get a factory job and pay them back for having taken him in
when no one else wanted him.

But Ramon persisted and eventually fulfilled his dream. For the past twenty years, he's been in private practice in the same central California region where he grew up. "I see myself in many of my young patients who come from farmworker families as I did," he says, "and my mission is to be a role model who cares for their spirits as well as their bodies."

Ramon's heartfelt presentations inspire listeners, viewers, and audiences of all ages to achieve their full potential by:

- Finding ways to believe in themselves even when no one else does
- Overcoming every obstacle, including poverty, low self-esteem, and self-sabotage
- Making a difference in their community and in the lives of everyone they meet

His recent audiences have included business groups, schools/universities/colleges (students and teachers), and community groups such as:

- University of Indiana (Bloomington), Hudson and Holland freshman scholarship/training program
- Tulare County (CA) Gang Prevention Task Force Summit
- New Mexico Coalition for Charter Schools
- Albuquerque (NM) Kiwanis
- Northern Arizona Gerontology Institute
- Fresno (CA) First 5, Children and Families Commission of Fresno County
- Environmental Protection Agency, Hispanic Month
- Del Campo High School, Sacramento (CA)
- Chicago Systems Institute, Chicago (IL)
- Rotary International
- Partners for New Generations Mentoring Program (CA)
- Lindsay (CA) School District

- Celebrate the Child Within (nonprofit organization for adults recovering from sexual abuse)
- Redwood High School (CA) Diversity Week
- Porterville (CA) High School
- Palo Alto (CA) School District
- Kiwanis Club (NM)
- Stanford University (CA)
- Mar Vista Family Center (CA) Literacy Fair

He speaks on overcoming adversity, childhood depression, college challenges, diversity, dysfunctional families, education, combating gang involvement, goal attainment, issues affecting Latinos today, living out your dreams, parenting a Stanford or Ivy League child, students at risk, teacher burnout, and other topics.

Following a recent talk at the Salinas Northeast Rotary, club president Monika Fewtrell sent him this note: "Please know that you do make an incredible and needed difference in kids who rarely have the opportunity to hear about hope. The fact that you put yourself out there without really knowing the depth of your impact is your gift to kids in need. May you continue this journey, and may you hear more and more how you have saved, impacted, and changed children's lives by giving them new hope and the dream that life can get better, and that they do deserve to dream big. Thank you for your honesty, vulnerability and courage."

Schoolchildren Write to Ramon

AFTER HEARING RAMON'S STORY OF HIS JOURNEY from farm-worker boy to pediatrician, students at Watsonville (CA) High School wrote to him. Here are excerpts from some of their letters.

"I loved the way you made your presentation. I think it was really cool how you told us that you went from almost nothing to a great pediatrician. Before you started talking, I thought that you came from a wealthy family. I would have never imagined that you worked in the fields. I love the fact that you are really into children. I would like to become a pediatrician too. But I'm not sure yet. There are people that become doctors just because of the money. But not you and that's great! ♥—A.T."

"You're a great model for me because you never gave up on your goal. Now that you told us that you made it to your goal, I'm not giving up on mine. I've been through a hard life too, and I understand you. Sincerely, E.B."

"Most of the time when you see successful people, you think that they were just made like that. You never imagine all the struggles they went through. Thank you. K.S."

"I really want to thank you for telling us your story. I didn't really want to go to college. But after hearing your story I really want to go . . . because I want a good future for me and for my future kids. Thank you a lot, Dr. Resa. Sincerely, S.M."

"I liked everything you talked about. It's really nice to know that a Mexican who didn't have much to start with is now a doctor. I think you give HOPE to all the students who want to be someone in life by sharing your personal story. Thank you! Catalina M."

"You really made me think that I should keep going to college and get a good job. I shouldn't give up. I think you're great because you help kids out. Your kids are very lucky that you could pay for whatever school they want to go to. My parents can't afford it so it's kind of hard for me . . . I'm looking forward to reading your book and watching the movie. Sincerely, Patty M."